The Lords
of the Rings

Also by Vyv Simson & Andrew Jennings

Scotland Yard's Cocaine Connection
Revised version; Arrow Books 1991

The Lords of the Rings

*Power, Money and Drugs
in the Modern Olympics*

*Vyv Simson and
Andrew Jennings*

SIMON & SCHUSTER

LONDON·SYDNEY·NEW YORK·TOKYO·SINGAPORE·TORONTO

First published in Great Britain by
Simon & Schuster Ltd in 1992
A Paramount Communications Company

Copyright © Ceres Productions, 1992

Simon & Schuster Ltd
West Garden Place
Kendal Street
London W2 2AQ

Simon & Schuster of Australia Pty Ltd
Sydney

A CIP catalogue record for this book is
available from the British Library
ISBN 0–671–71122–9

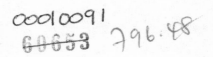

Photoset in Plantin 10½/13 by
Derek Doyle & Associates, Mold, Clwyd
Printed and bound in Great Britain by
Butler & Tanner Ltd, Frome

Contents

Illustrations   vii

Introduction & Acknowledgements   ix

1   Welcome to Barcelona   1

2   Horst's System   21

3   Dassler Takes Coke   36

4   From Montreal to Monte Carlo   48

5   With Arm Raised I Salute You   59

6   The Clever Chameleon   72

7   The Jewel in the Crown   85

8   ISL Rules the World   99

9   Flotsam and Jetsam   111

10 Olympia's Black Gold   119

11 The Bumps on the Logs   138

12 Twenty Million Dollars   155

13 The Cheats   164

14 Scandal   174

15   Before Your Very Eyes   184

16   A Lawyer from Des Moines   201

17   Alarm Bells   213

18   The Benevolent Dictator   222

19   The Shoe Size of the Second Daughter   238

20   Destroy the Olympics   260

Appendix A   Calendar of the Modern Olympics   275

          B   Members of the International Olympic Committee   276

          C   Abbreviations used in the text   280

Index   281

Illustrations

1 Juan Antonio Samaranch smiles after his election as IOC President in Moscow, July 1980. (Associated Press)
2 Primo Nebiolo: 'It is all for our great family of sport.' (Allsport)
3 Horst Dassler receives the highest Olympic honour from Samaranch in October 1984. (Colorsport)
4 João Havelange, President of FIFA, world sport's longest-surviving power broker. (Colorsport)
5 Dr Un Yong Kim and his wife with the Samaranchs. (Si-sa-yong-o-sa Inc.)
6 Kuwait's Mr Sport, Sheik Fahd Al-Ahmad Al-Jaber Al-Sabah. (ANOC)
7 Robert H. Helmick, who abruptly resigned from the IOC after his commercial dealings were revealed. (Associated Press)
8 Mario Vasquez Raña takes the oath of Olympic membership. Only thirteen members voted for him. (ANOC)
9 Out with the old, in with the new: retiring FIFA President Sir Stanley Rous congratulates his successor João Havelange in 1974. (Associated Press)
10 Lord Killanin, the last of the part-time presidents, hands over power to Samaranch in Moscow in July 1980. (Associated Press)
11 IOC President Samaranch honours Romanian President Nicolae Ceaucescu, the Butcher of Bucharest.

12 Former French premier Jacques Chirac with Havelange and Samaranch. His oratory threatened to overturn the Barcelona bid and win the Games of 1992 for Paris. (Colorsport)

13 Samaranch, in the fascist Blue Shirt and white jacket of the *Movimiento*, is watched by General Franco as he is sworn in as a national councillor in 1967. (Vanguardia)

14 A Blue-Shirted Samaranch greets his leader just a year before General Franco's death. Behind the dictator is Spain's future king Juan Carlos, also wearing his Blue Shirt. (Vanguardia)

INTRODUCTION

So This is Sport?

This book discloses what you are not allowed to see on your TV and what the newspapers do not tell you about the Olympics and world sport. For the last four years we have sought to discover who controls sport, where the money goes and why what a decade ago was seen as a source of beauty and purity is now tacky, anti-democratic, drug ridden and auctioned off as a marketing tool of the world's multi-national companies.

To our surprise it has turned out to be the most difficult investigation we have ever undertaken. In recent years we have written, or made TV documentaries, about the Mafia, the Iran-Contra affair, terrorism, corruption at Scotland Yard and other dark areas of public life.

The world of Olympic, amateur sport has proved the hardest to penetrate. Never before have we found it so difficult to obtain on-the-record interviews, documents and original sources. One venerated Olympian even set lawyers on us to prevent publication of criticisms of the Olympic leadership that had been made in a lengthy taped interview!

This is our discovery about the world of modern Olympic sport. It is a secretive, élite domain where the decisions about sport, our sport, are taken behind closed doors, where money is spent on creating a fabulous life style for a tiny circle of officials rather than providing facilities for athletes, where money destined for sport has been siphoned away to offshore bank accounts and where officials preside for ever, untroubled by elections.

This book is not about the competitors who chase the gold medals. It is about the hidden world of the men in suits, the men who manipulate sport for their own ends.

We are not sports journalists. We are not part of a circuit where too many reporters have preferred to keep their gaze fixed on the sporting action and ignore the way sport has been destroyed by greed and ambition. As a result one of our most enlightening moments was being chastised by the International Olympic Committee's Swiss-based Director of Information for trying to put plain questions to a senior Olympian. We were doing what any reporter does on any story. Such behaviour is not permissible in the clandestine, selfish world of the IOC. If sport is going to survive it will need the attention of many more journalists without ties or loyalties to the Lords of Lausanne.

Repeatedly, as we probed behind the pomposity and hypocrisy of the modern Olympics and their Leader, we were reminded of the small child's observation the day the Emperor paraded in his new suit: the Great Man was not wearing any clothes. It should have been obvious to anyone not blinded by propaganda.

As in all our work over the years we can never thank in public the sources who have been most helpful. Eventually the documents did reach us and kind people who do care about sport gave us guidance and pointed towards areas which needed investigation and exposure. We hope that this book will help them in their battles to claw sport back from the hands of the few.

We of course take final responsibility for what appears here. We would like to thank Pat Butcher, Mark Dowie, Jock Ferguson, Pierlunghi Ficoneri, Sir Arthur Gold, Nick Hayes, Fred Holder, Dennis Howell, The National Security Archive in Washington, Susan O'Keefe, the late Ron Pickering, Claire Powell, John Rodda, Clare Sambrook, Montse Trivino and Giovanni Ulleri for their help and involvement in different ways.

We owe much to our translators, Sebastian Balfour, Franco Bossari, Patrick Buckley, Lucy Davies and Nicki DiCiolla, who gave us splendid advice far and beyond the meaning of the words. We commend readers who want to know more about the Spanish background of Juan Antonio Samaranch to read *El Deporte del Poder* by Jaume Boix and Arcadio Espada, published in 1991 by Ediciones Temas De Hoy of Madrid.

We would also like to thank the officials of the British Olympic Association for allowing us lengthy access to their library.

Finally, and as before, we owe the greatest debt to those close to us who gave the essential support without which this project could not have been undertaken.

Vyv Simson
Andrew Jennings
January 1992

CHAPTER 1

Welcome to Barcelona

Welcome to Spain. Welcome to Barcelona. The old Roman town of Barcino. The medieval walled 'City of Counts'.

Welcome to Barcelona. The capital of proud and independent Catalonia, the second city of Spain and for centuries the deadly rival of the capital, Madrid.

Welcome to Barcelona. The city to which Christopher Columbus returned after his discovery of the New World in 1492.

Welcome to Barcelona. The city of Salvador Dali and Pablo Picasso, of José Carreras and Pablo Cassals and of Cobi the surrealist dog.

Cobi the surrealist dog? Certainly. For Barcelona is also the city of the 1992 Olympic Games and Cobi, a cartoon canine, is the city's Olympic mascot.

It is the week before the start of the Games. The capital of Catalonia is thronged. Four hundred thousand Olympic spectators are expected. They will push the city to its bursting point. The greatest show on earth is about to begin. Welcome to Barcelona.

For the Barcelona organising committee of the Olympic Games, the men responsible for devising and financing the two-week extravaganza, the moment of truth has arrived. The committee, like almost everything else in the world of international sport, has its own acronym – COOB'92. Its president is Barcelona's socialist mayor, Pasqual Maragall. He speaks with fervour of his city's 'love affair with the Olympics'. Barcelona's passion has cost Maragall and his executive board over £1 billion just to stage the two-week event.

A further £2 billion of public money has been thrown at the city to buy land for reclamation and development, build an Olympic Village, lay down twenty-seven miles of new ring road, refurbish or create from greenfield sites the forty-four venues required to stage the groaning Olympic sports programme, and finally to upgrade Barcelona's airport.

Six years ago, in October 1986, Barcelona defeated Brisbane, Paris, Amsterdam, Belgrade and Birmingham in the contest to stage the 1992 Games. The jackhammers, bulldozers and cranes moved into the city. They have been working flat out ever since. For the residents of Barcelona, it has been like living in a giant construction site. And it is still going on. But Mayor Maragall and his men can sleep sound this week in the knowledge that all is now ready for the Games.

On 2 October 1988, at the closing ceremony of the Games in Seoul the Olympic flag, designed by the founder of the modern Games Baron Pierre de Coubertin, was handed over to Mayor Maragall. On Saturday 25 July 1992 the white flag with its five interlocked rings, which represent the five continents and have become the best-known symbol in the world after the Christian cross, will be raised over Barcelona's Montjuic Stadium. All will be ready for the opening ceremony of the 25th Olympics.

The Montjuic Stadium is the centre piece of Barcelona's two-week orgy of sport and six-year orgy of spending. At Saturday's ceremony 70,000 spectators will surround the kings and queens, princes and princesses, sheiks and rajas, prime ministers and presidents in the prime positions in the grandstand. Tickets are changing hands at $500.

The stadium dominates what the organising committee calls 'The Olympic Ring', an area atop Montjuic which overlooks the city to the west and the Mediterranean to the east.

The stadium has a long Olympic history. The cornerstone was laid sixty-four years ago by the then Olympic President Comte Henri de Ballet-Latour. Montjuic had been built for an earlier attempt by Barcelona to host the Games. In 1931 the 30th session – or annual meeting – of the International Olympic Committee, who own the rights to the Olympic Games, was held in Barcelona's Ritz Hotel.

Ten days before the session was due to open the new left-wing government of Spain declared the country was now a republic. One marquis and five counts were among the gallant band who ventured to the Barcelona Ritz but most of their colleagues stayed away. They agreed to organise a postal ballot to decide which city would be awarded the Olympic Games in 1936. When the votes were returned Barcelona discovered she had lost to Adolf Hitler's Berlin.

Disgusted and disappointed, the radically minded citizens of Barcelona staged their own alternative in their new Montjuic Stadium. They defiantly named the event 'The Barcelona Popular Olympics'. In July 1936 5,000 athletes and 20,000 spectators were welcomed by Barcelona's mayor to the city and to the People's Games.

Barcelona's Games ended almost as soon as they had begun. The following day saw the beginning of the military uprising that launched the Spanish Civil War. The People's Games broke up and many athletes and spectators joined the republican forces massing in the Catalan capital. Barcelona became a bulwark of opposition to General Franco and his fascist supporters. It was an opposition which the dictator never forgave and for which the citizens of Barcelona were to pay a heavy price over the next forty years. Thousands of Franco's opponents died and many thousands more were jailed, but Catalans who were prepared to outstretch their arm in salute to the dictator's fascist *Movimiento* prospered.

The Generalissimo's revenge on Barcelona extended even to the city's Olympic ambitions. In December 1965 Barcelona competed against Madrid for the nomination as Spain's candidate for the Games of 1972. The meeting to decide between them was scheduled for Christmas Eve. A few days before, Barcelona's leader was telephoned and told not to bother to come to the meeting. 'It's not important,' said the caller 'it's just to settle the accounts.'

Barcelona had been tricked. Three days after Christmas the headquarters of the Olympic movement in Switzerland were told that Madrid had been preferred as Spain's candidate for 1972. 'In those days,' say Catalans who remember General Franco's absolute power 'the man from El Prado was still alive.' Now the leader is dead, Spain is again a democracy and Franco's fascist comrades have exchanged their uniforms for lounge suits. This week the Montjuic Stadium will at last fulfil her Olympic destiny.

Over the last six years the stadium has been gutted, re-designed and completely rebuilt. Its classic 1930s shell has been preserved 'as a tribute to the sporting and Olympic spirit of the generations of the people of the city who have fought since the beginning of the century to be awarded the Games.'

Four giant escalators will move 14,000 people an hour to the Olympic Ring to watch the stars of track and field make their assaults upon world records; the stars of gymnastics, volleyball, and basketball compete in the avant garde Palau Saint Jordi sports hall; the swimmers battle it out in the massive Picornell pools.

At Poblenou along the Barcelona waterfront stands Parc de Mar. A 160-acre development of six-storey blocks looking out over the sea, Parc de Mar is the Olympic Village and so is home this Olympic fortnight to 15,000 athletes from more than 160 countries. The whole area is surrounded by a high-wire security fence. The safety of the athletes has been a major worry since eleven Israeli competitors were murdered by terrorists at Munich in 1972.

Behind the wire, the compound is complete with restaurant, post office, bank, travel agency, car hire, supermarket, bookshop, chemist, pub, lounge and reading room. The restaurant will serve the athletes more than 900,000 meals during the Games.

Close by the Montjuic Stadium, on the edge of the Olympic Ring, stands the Main Press Centre. It is linked to satellite press centres at each competition venue, the Olympic Village and the two purpose built 'media villages' at Badalona and Val d'Hebron in the Barcelona suburbs. The MPC, for even the press centre has its own abbreviation, will handle the 10,000 accredited members of the world's newspapers, TV and radio who have descended on Barcelona.

Finally, on Barcelona's famous Diagonal, the longest street in the city, stands the luxury Princesa Sofia Hotel. In the last two years its Spanish owners have spent $10 million on renovations. The hotel has been lavishly restored to receive the most important guests at the Games. Forget the star athletes, the star swimmers or the gymnasts. The Princesa Sofia will, for the next two weeks, be the headquarters of The Club.

'The Club' is one of the most secretive, powerful and lucrative interlocking societies in the world. It is led by a handful of self-promoting 'Presidents'. Between them, the members of The Club run world sport.

In the presidential suite of the Princesa Sofia is The Club's most important member, the Olympic pontiff, the undisputed king of world sport, Spain's own Juan Antonio Samaranch. He is the president of the IOC, the International Olympic Committee, the group of disparate individuals who actually 'own' the Olympics. He has been at the top for the last decade. Samaranch claims that the Olympics are, 'The most important contemporary social movement and the most prestigious one in the world.' This might surprise millions of TV viewers who thought the Olympics were just a four-yearly festival of sport.

'He's just like royalty, my boss,' confides one IOC member. The world's political leaders appear to agree. They treat this diminutive, silver-haired, seventy-two-year-old who has fought only one election in his twelve years as president, as a *de facto* head of state. When he is not visiting the White House, the Vatican, the Kremlin or the Hall of the People in Beijing, Juan Antonio Samaranch grants his own private audiences to petitioning prime ministers and presidents at his Olympic residence in Lausanne. He is honoured everywhere. Universities and heads of state lavish orders and medals, awards and honorary doctorates upon him.

Samaranch says that his International Olympic Committee is 'the world's leading moral authority on competitive sport'. This is from the leader of an organisation which was humiliated in Seoul when it had to snatch back the 100-metres gold medal from a steroid-soaked Ben Johnson.

Samaranch describes the Olympic movement as a pyramid. Naturally, he and his ninety-odd fellow members of the International Olympic Committee, drawn randomly from just 75 countries, are at the summit. This week those IOC members, their families and their guests have flown in first class from around the globe to fill the hundreds of rooms of the Princesa Sofia. The hotel was block-booked years ago to serve as the headquarters for The Club.

This week Samaranch will be a president fulfilled as he holds court at the Princesa Sofia. Barcelona is Samaranch's home town. Bringing the Olympic Games home is the leader's crowning glory.

In a slightly less grand suite at the Hotel Princesa Sofia, as Olympic protocol dictates, sits another powerful Club member; the Brazilian Dr João Havelange. He has been an IOC member since 1963, two years longer than Samaranch. He is the king of the most popular sport in the world – soccer. In 1974 Havelange was elected president of the mostly professional International Federation of Football Associations, known by its acronym of FIFA. Like his Olympic president, Havelange has not had to face an election since he took over the presidency. For nearly twenty years President Havelange has been one of sport's most influential power brokers.

When Barcelona launched its fight for the Games, back in the early 1980s, Olympic President Samaranch, as a Spaniard and a Catalan, declared he would remain a neutral in the contest. He could afford to. Everyone knew where the President stood and there were others to take up the running for his home town. The most powerful was his friend from Brazil, João Havelange. He organised the Spanish-speaking members of the IOC behind the Barcelona campaign.

It was an unedifying sight, described as 'The unacceptable face of the Olympic Movement, lavish receptions, members being invited all over the world to visit the respective sites, gifts being offered and finally kings and prime ministers becoming involved in the final bidding process.'

In 1985 at the IOC session in Berlin Jacques Chirac, the former French premier who led a rival bid from Paris, attacked Havelange's political manoeuvring to win the Games for Barcelona. Chirac, no stranger to power politics, could see that Paris was losing. 'Chirac,' said one commentator, 'threatened to use his influence in Africa to ensure that Havelange is not re-elected President of FIFA. There is no doubt that Havelange, with his South and Central American power, can create majorities within the IOC.'

Further along Barcelona's Diagonal is the Hilton Hotel. This has been earmarked for one of the props of Samaranch's Olympic pyramid, the international sports federations, known as the IFs. The federations are the worldwide controlling authorities for the twenty-five sports that make up the Barcelona Games. They set the rules and regulations of their Olympic competitions.

Being chauffeured in from the airport to his suite is Club member President Primo Nebiolo. A number of scandals have temporarily reduced his power in world sport but when it comes to the Games, he holds the key cards. Nebiolo is the boss of athletics, the key Olympic sport, and the third most important member of The Club.

The Italian is vital to Samaranch. The Olympic president fears Nebiolo's power because without track and field, the Games could not be the world's number one sporting spectacle. Nebiolo's events are the jewel in the Olympic crown. They provide both sparkle and dollars. TV companies around the world lay down their money for the sight of stars setting records.

There is no profit to be had from athletes who believe that taking part is reward enough. Nebiolo's quaintly named International Amateur Athletics Federation, whose 'amateur' athletes now drive Ferraris and Porsches, controls the supply of Olympic stars.

Primo Nebiolo, pivotal as he is to the continued success of the Games, has been kept out of the International Olympic Committee. Many IOC members are wary of Nebiolo. His ambition is tangible, it oozes from every pore in his permanently sun-tanned face. He is not like the smooth and diplomatic IOC President Samaranch or FIFA's urbane and worldly Havelange. Nebiolo is a bruiser, a survivor, a street fighter and that offends the sensibilities of many of the self-selecting members of the International Olympic Committee.

Nebiolo has not given up hope. Last year an equally controversial sporting president became a member of the committee. Arriving in Barcelona in his own private jet to take up residence in yet another presidential suite is President Mario Vazquez Raña, Mexican media magnate and multi-millionaire. Raña is also a senior member of The Club. He is president of the Association of National Olympic Committees, known by its acronym ANOC.

The national Olympic committees are the third point of Samaranch's Olympic pyramid. Every country has one but they make few headlines except in Olympic year when they raise funds to send their teams to the Games.

The duties of NOCs are laid out in one of the world's great unread documents, the Olympic Charter. Once upon a time the Charter was simply a statement of ethics, aims and ideals. As the Games have grown so has the pomposity of the Charter. The function of the NOCs is to 'propagate the fundamental principles of Olympism at national level ... and otherwise contribute to the diffusion of Olympism in the teaching programmes in schools'. NOCs decide which of their major cities will bid to host the Games. Only one city from one country can bid but, because of the cost, few nations can contemplate applying.

There are now more than 160 national Olympic committees ranging from the Republic of China, with a population in excess of one billion, to Monaco with about 25,000. The Olympic Charter says they must 'resist all pressures of any kind, including those of a political or economic nature'. This is a rule which was ignored in the years when communist parties ruled the East Bloc and sports administrators were promoted only because of their devotion to Marx and Lenin.

Many Third World countries integrate their NOCs into state-run Sports Ministries. Several IOC members and presidents of NOCs are high-ranking soldiers. Their countries are run by military juntas. Political and economic independence is as foreign to most of these countries as the ballot box.

In the rest of Barcelona's 2,300 hotel rooms reserved exclusively for the Olympic Family are more Club members. There is President Un Yong Kim of South Korea. Dr Kim is head of the World Taekwondo Federation – a Korean martial art. Samaranch says, 'Kim is my most trusted adviser.'

Kim is an old Olympic hand. He was the most important member of the committee which organised the last Games in Seoul. Dr Kim, who rose to prominence in one of the world's more brutal military dictatorships, was rewarded with the job of special adviser to the Korean State President. Some IOC members tip Kim as successor to Samaranch.

Also tipped for the highest Olympic office is The Club member from Canada, the outspoken, but sometimes too outspoken, Montreal lawyer Dick Pound. In 1991 Pound stepped down as an IOC vice president when his four-year term of office came to an end. But he remains one of the most influential Olympic figures for Pound is the IOC's most experienced TV rights negotiator. It is this apparently easy-going Canadian who leads for the IOC when the Olympics go up for sale.

One Club member conspicuous by his absence from the Barcelona bean-feast is Pound's former North American colleague, Robert H. Helmick, a lawyer from Des Moines, Iowa. Until late 1991 Helmick was president of the powerful United States Olympic Committee – known as the USOC. He signed their multi-million dollar sponsorship contracts. At the same time he was also a member of the IOC's executive board. Helmick was positioning himself to succeed Samaranch but last year he was revealed to have taken money from sporting organisations, marketing and TV companies who wanted deals with the Olympic movement. He was forced to resign from the USOC and later from the IOC itself.

Enjoying a rare taste of luxury are The Club members from the once powerful East Bloc: Russia's Vitaly Smirnov and Marat Gramov; Romania's Alexandru Siperco; Czechoslovakia's Vladimir Cernusak; Shagdarjav Magvan, the trade union boss from Mongolia; Poland's Wlodzimierz Reczek; Ivan Slavkov of Bulgaria; and of course the veteran Gunther Heinze, formerly of East Berlin and now from the new, unified Germany.

With the unexpected onset of democracy in their own countries many of them have been ejected from sporting office and power – but they remain on the IOC for life, travelling the world and representing no one but themselves.

In the twenty-seven years since Juan Antonio Samaranch joined the IOC it has gone from rags to riches. In the early 1960s the financial position of the Olympic committee was catastrophic. The Rome Games in 1960 had lost 300 million lire. But there was a glimmer of hope. The world's TV companies were coming to the rescue. But it was still a hand-to-mouth existence. The then IOC member for Kenya, Reggie Alexander, offered to find an accountant who might be willing to do the IOC's books for nothing. Since then, things have looked up. Now the prestigious international firm of Price Waterhouse audits the accounts.

Those IOC accounts are kept secret. We can disclose that in December 1990 President Samaranch sat at the top of an organisation with a $20 million annual budget and assets of $118 million. There is nearly $60 million in cash – wisely split with seventy-five per cent in Swiss francs and the remainder in US dollars to take advantage of the highest interest rates.

Samaranch's Swiss-based IOC has grown from a staff of eleven squeezed into three second-floor rooms in a house called Mon Repos to a staff of sixty-one operating out of a luxurious complex of marble-lined buildings and well-manicured parkland around the Château de Vidy in Lausanne. The annual wage bill alone now stands at eight million Swiss francs. And soon there will be even more offices. A new extension and underground rooms will link the Château de Vidy with the nearby Olympic House.

And the empire keeps growing. When the IOC meets in Lausanne for its 100th session in June 1993, President Samaranch will inaugurate his most cherished project; the opening of a $40 million Olympic museum. It is being funded by grateful international conglomerates, happy to queue up to offer a minimum donation of $1 million a time to the president. So confident is Samaranch of the Olympics' midas touch that he thought nothing of snapping up August Rodin's bronze statue 'The American Athlete'. President Samaranch was sure that a sponsor would come forward to cover the cost. His confidence was not misplaced. Sponsors have donated more than $20 million towards the cost of the museum.

The Olympic Committee's self-styled commissions, which deal with finances, doping, sports medicine and the organisation of the winter and summer Games, have grown from seven when Samaranch first arrived in 1966 to seventeen today. These commissions alone eat up 4.5 million Swiss francs a year.

Flying IOC members around the world on first-class scheduled flights or in privately chartered aircraft and putting them up in luxury hotels costs another two million Swiss francs. A further three million Swiss francs goes on press releases, glossy publications, and public relations exercises.

Professionally manipulated media coverage is crucial to Samaranch. The IOC has hired one of the world's largest public relations agencies. Samaranch says, 'The world of sport has been changing rapidly and the complexity of the issues and the range of commercial interests are growing constantly. To address these circumstances, we have decided to increase the reach and professionalism of our communications.'

The Grey Advertising Agency, which Samaranch has commissioned 'to increase the reach and professionalism' of his communications, puts it more directly. 'In our view,' insists chairman Ed Meyer, 'the International Olympic movement is like a "brand" which needs a guardian to nurture and develop its potential for the future. Grey prides itself on its successful record of assisting clients in building major global brands and we look forward to helping the IOC in this way.'

The Olympics as a 'global brand': Samaranch's Olympic movement is a world removed from that of a former Olympic President who declared that the Olympics 'are not a business and those whose aim is to make money from sport are not wanted. It is as simple as that!' Today those who want to make money from sport are welcomed with open arms. The price Samaranch's International Olympic Committee now extracts for its Games from television companies and multinational commercial conglomerates is staggering.

For this week's Games in Barcelona the world's television companies alone have agreed to pay a total of $633 million. The American network NBC has signed away $416 million. The European Broadcasting Union has stumped up $90 million. NHK leads a Japanese TV consortium which has been relieved of $62.5 million. Australia's Channel 7 has paid nearly $34 million. Even cash-strapped Eastern Europe has kissed goodbye to $4 million. This money is on top of the $289 million the world's TV companies have already paid out this year for the rights to televise February's winter Olympics in Albertville. At the Rome Olympics of 1960 TV paid just $1 million.

And that's just the beginning of the avalanche of dollars; thanks to TV, a worldwide audience of some three-and-a-half billion consumers is on offer. A dozen multi-nationals – from Coca-Cola to Visa and Mars – have paid up to $30 million each to secure the worldwide rights for their products to be linked exclusively with the Olympic Games. A further ten companies, amongst them names like Seiko, Danone and Asics, whose products must not compete with those of the major sponsors, have paid a minimum of $6 million each for the right to incorporate the Games logos into their advertising.

Rank Xerox, Philips, IBM, Seat and four other companies whose contribution has been considered 'essential to the organisation of the Games' and who have been willing to pay a minimum of $23 million each have been accepted as joint partners of the Barcelona organisers. Eighteen other companies willing to give goods and services of at least $2 million, in everything from office automation to power cables and signals, have cornered the market as official suppliers to the Barcelona Olympics.

Docked in the port of Barcelona are sixteen luxury cruise liners. They have been hired to supply the hospitality needs of all these corporate sponsors, partners and suppliers. They have 2,500 floating hotel rooms for the use of the corporate bosses and their guests.

In the cabins and on the decks of the *Royal Viking Sun* will frolic the 740 TV magnates, guests and assorted celebrities of the American NBC network. Moored alongside the media men and their guests are the cruise liners *Danae* and *Seabourn Spirit*. They are the equally luxurious floating hotels for the directors, guests and clients of IBM Spain and the American 3M company – another of the twelve worldwide commercial sponsors of the Games.

The cruise liner lifestyle enjoyed by the Olympic sponsors in Barcelona port is a reflection of the life enjoyed by the members of The Club on shore. All Olympic gatherings are a constant and glittering round of first-class travel, five-star hotels, champagne receptions, extravagant banquets, mountains of gifts and lavish entertainments. And frequently, there's not even an athlete in sight.

*

The five-star Hyatt Regency stands across the road from the new £160 million International Convention Centre in the heart of Britain's second city. The Hyatt is Birmingham's newest and most expensive hotel. It's big, it's brash and it's coloured blue and, to the chagrin of its owners, was recently branded one of the ugliest new buildings in Britain. It is a concrete-and-glass tower designed in the modern architectural style of international 'bland'. It could be placed anywhere in the world, wherever corporate executives have money to burn.

Outside the hotel flutters the Olympic flag. In June 1991 the Birmingham Hyatt Regency was the temporary headquarters of The Club meeting for the last time before Olympic year. Their host, who were picking up the bulk of the tab, was Birmingham City Council.

'Sorry Sir, this is a restricted area,' says one of the phalanx of West Midlands police officers stationed at the Hyatt entrance. Well, he's not actually at the entrance, more like twenty feet in front of it. You can't get near the entrance. He's one of a team of officers manning a huge airport-style security scanning system which has been erected on the pavement. It's complete with baggage search X-ray equipment and a metal detector arch. Both the Hyatt and the International Convention Centre, where the IOC session will be held, have been turned into what security experts call an 'island site'. That means that mere mortals cannot get in.

'But we are accredited press,' we remonstrate. 'I'm sorry sir, but they don't want you in there,' is the reply. A fleet of white limousines, all conspicuously marked with the five Olympic rings and the title 'official car' ply to and from the Hyatt. They are driven by a team of identical blonde, long-legged young women. The limousines deposit a stream of well-dressed people, mostly men, outside the hotel entrance. These are the ninety-odd members of the International Olympic Committee who have jetted in first class to Birmingham's International Airport.

The police relieve these very important people of their luggage, and escort them through the security controls. One particularly big and very stretched limousine arrives with an escort of police motorcycle outriders. It is the sort of car that Birmingham City Council could put a homeless family in and still have space for their relatives. Engulfed in the back of this monster, a twenty-four valve Rover Regency in discreet metallic grey, is the most important member of The Club; the Olympic President Juan Antonio Samaranch.

As with the Princesa Sofia in Barcelona, the whole of the Hyatt is block-booked exclusively for the use of the Olympic movement. It was closed off to the public three days before the start of this 97th session – or annual meeting – of the IOC. The patronage of President Samaranch's sporting bureaucracy, and the publicity that comes with it, is so sought after that cities now compete vigorously for the privilege of hosting mere IOC meetings, let alone hosting the Games!

Birmingham's rivals for this privilege were Moscow, Belgrade, Nairobi, Riyadh, Monte Carlo and Budapest. As with the real Olympics contest there were separate rounds of voting with the bottom city dropping out until the winner had an overall majority. On the last round only Budapest and Birmingham remained. One of Budapest's supporters, the IOC member for Kuwait, decided to leave the room for a quick smoke. In his absence Birmingham won the nomination – with a majority of one. Asked by President Samaranch what she thought of the result, Mary Glen-Haig, one of Britain's two IOC members, declared that 'Allah decided'.

The Birmingham organisers agreed to pay the Hyatt for all 319 rooms for the week-long session – regardless of whether they were occupied. The accommodation bill at this one hotel comes to £34,689 per night or £277,512 per week. In the penthouse presidential suite, at £595 per night and £4,760 per week, is Juan Antonio Samaranch. Here the President can entertain private guests around the twelve-seater dining table; relax in one of the many deep settees by the fireplace in the lounge; luxuriate in the jets of the jacuzzi built into the huge sunken bath tub; tap out a tune on the keys of the baby grand piano or simply take a nap in the four-poster bed.

Its previous occupants have been showbusiness stars like Gloria Estefan, Paul Simon, Rod Stewart and Billy Idol. Tina Turner would have stayed there but Cher got in first.

'It is sometimes used by private companies,' says the Hyatt public relations manager Catriona McFadden, 'but that was mainly last year. This year there's been a lot of cancellations because of the recession. There just isn't the money around. That's why this booking has been great for us. It was a guaranteed week when we would have been in the doldrums.'

The Hyatt's slightly less plush executive suites, at a mere £295 a night and £7,080 for the week, are reserved for the next three most senior Olympic members. The rest of the Olympic entourage, their guests and families have to make do with the remaining eight junior suites, thirty-five regency club and 242 de luxe rooms.

'The IOC arranged all the room allocations,' says Ms McFadden. 'They're very protocol conscious. They first visited us about a year ago to see if the hotel was up to scratch. Then they took a blueprint of the hotel, all the rooms, their sizes and did the allocating. They then visited us about once a month to liaise and see that all was well.

'Lausanne faxed us with all the room allocations. They changed pretty regularly. At one stage they were faxing us so often that we didn't even bother to enter them into the computer! I've never seen anything quite like it and I doubt I will again. The nearest I've come to it is a Tory Party conference – but that didn't really match anything like this. These people act more like heads of state.

'But it's certainly a good deal for us,' she explained. 'The hotel business is not too good at the moment and it makes us very high profile. We've been on TV every night this week!'

Inside the Hyatt the full Olympic circus is at play. IOC members, corporate sponsors, marketing men, national Olympic committee chairmen and international federation presidents meet and greet each other in what appears to be a giant greenhouse. There are potted palms, trees in oversized terracotta plant pots and floodlights and fountains. Under the glass roof with its discreet lighting a violinist plays popular classics. A pianist takes her turn at the grand piano. A string ensemble appears. They play 'Take Good Care of Yourself.' There should be no worries on that score.

The hangers-on press the flesh in the lobby. They circle the pool like piranhas, waiting to nibble at any little morsel. Behind the neo-classic columns in the main reception area and at corner tables in the restaurants are huddled groups of marketing men and agents with ideas to sell and deals to be done. The hotel staff move discreetly around the public areas constantly spraying and polishing the glass-and-marble effect table tops.

In one corner Kuwait TV are filming the young Sheik Ahmad. Gold thread runs through his robes and he carries a gold-topped walking stick. The Sheik's father, the late IOC member for Kuwait, was shot dead by the Iraqis in the invasion of August 1990. The young Sheik has taken his father's place as head of Kuwait's national Olympic committee. He expects to replace his father on the IOC as well. Everything he does is filmed. The Sheik stands up. The camera starts running. The Sheik sits down. The camera starts running. The Sheik orders tea. The camera never seems to stop.

In the bedrooms at the Hyatt are complimentary flowers, wine and fruit. Another welcoming gesture for guests is boxes of chocolates from the local manufacturers, Cadburys. Suddenly there is turmoil along the corridors. The chocolates are snatched from the guests' hands! Mars have paid tens of millions of dollars to be the official worldwide snack food sponsors of the Olympic movement and they must not be upset by a rival. 'A special welcome to the IOC Marketing Department,' says a specially printed note in the Hotel Brasserie's menu. A special welcome indeed.

Senior Club member Primo Nebiolo, the Italian supremo of world athletics, descends the hotel stairs. He moves around the lobby as if on castors. He embraces Charles Mukora, once Coca-Cola's man in Kenya and now that country's IOC member. Mukora is also on Nebiolo's own athletics federation council. One pace behind the president is one of his press handlers. There is much exaggerated hugging and kissing.

Wives and children have been brought along too. There is a week-long schedule of activities arranged for them to fill the hours when the IOC members are meeting. This 'Social Programme' includes a connoisseurs' trip around the Worcester Royal Porcelain Works and a visit to Shakespeare's birthplace at Stratford-upon-Avon. There is also an antiques tour of Shropshire with lunch at Stanley Hall, home of one of the directors of Christies, the world-famous auctioneers. And there's a private peek at the antiques of Willey Park with the owners of the stately home, Lord and Lady Forester.

These outings come on top of the social activities already laid on for the members of the Olympic Family. Ballet dancers will perform Swan Lake. The City of Birmingham Symphony Orchestra is in concert on another evening. Then there are the banquets. There is the dinner hosted by President Samaranch himself; the luncheon hosted by Her Majesty the Queen and the dinner given by the British Olympic Association in honour of the International Olympic Committee.

This glittering occasion was hosted by the Princess Royal, Princess Anne at Warwick Castle, one of the finest medieval castles in England. Princess Anne is one of Britain's two IOC members and the president of the British Olympic Association. For good measure she is also president of the International Equestrian Federation, a post she inherited from her father, Prince Philip. For this event the BOA hired the castle for the evening and entertained some 300 guests to a champagne reception in the Great Hall. This was followed, in a marquee erected in the Castle grounds, by a feast of iced watercress soup, whole salmon trout and strawberrries with brandy snaps and cream.

The guests of honour that night were President Samaranch and his wife. The president's wife stepped gracefully from the rear of their chauffeured limousine and in a reflex action she smiled and waved her hand to the crowd – even though there wasn't one. This was a private function.

An armoured knight on horseback and a marching pipe band greeted the rest of The Club members when they arrived. A lone piper played from the floodlit battlements of Guys Tower as they left for home some three hours later. When thanked for his hospitality the following day, a senior BOA official replied 'You're welcome. We like to keep it simple.'

The opening of the session was itself a grand affair. The ceremony began at 3 o'clock on Wednesday 12 June 1991, in Hall One of the International Convention Centre. Accompanied by a fanfare from the trumpeters of the Life Guards, President and Mrs Samaranch entered the royal box with Her Majesty the Queen and The Duke of Edinburgh. Behind them were seated the IOC members. Also in the royal box – and breaking all the protocol regulations of the IOC – was Primo Nebiolo. He was there at the request of President Samaranch. Some IOC members were put out by the Italian's presence but as they later conceded to us, 'How can anyone tell the IOC President who he may or may not have in the royal box at the opening of his own IOC session?'

After the obligatory references to the foresight of Baron Pierre de Coubertin, the founder of the modern Olympics, Samaranch told his audience that 'Olympic sport must not become mere show business'. He suggested that the way to prevent this would be to 'convince the mass media to help us give more importance to the ethical values of sport'.

He devoted a paragraph to the ethical problem of doping and then spent rather more time bringing his audience up to date with the progress of his Olympic museum. His theme was that 'solutions can be found to everything'. Her Majesty the Queen then spoke. She told President Samaranch, 'The eyes of the world will be on the results of your deliberations. I am confident that the movement will continue to thrive under the direction of those who, like you, serve its cause with such devotion.' And with that the Queen declared the 97th session of the International Olympic Committee open.

The audience was then treated to an hour of Birmingham's very own Royal Variety Performance. In a spectacle billed as 'A Taste of Britain', members of the Northern School for Contemporary Dance, the Grenadier Guards, the pipes and drums of the Scots Guards and the Midlands Massed Male Voice Choirs presented a potted history of the ancient Olympics and then an explanation of the design of the Union Jack in music, song and dance.

The IOC members loved it. When the 2nd Battalion, Scots Guards, entered from the back of the auditorium and marched through the audience down onto the stage with pipes playing and kilts swirling, the IOC members clapped and stamped to the rhythm. After listening in rapt silence to 'Amazing Grace' they broke into tumultuous applause.

The stars of the show were a troupe of children dressed as Irish leprechauns. 'Weren't they just wonderful!' exclaimed one IOC member as he made his way back for a nap at the Hyatt Hotel after the show. 'One of the best opening ceremonies we've ever been to.' Some of the more elderly IOC members might well have needed to rest if they were going to cope with the remainder of the day's activities. In a couple of hours' time IOC members and their guests were due at a concert followed by a late evening buffet.

Distracted by the glitter, ceremony and merry-making it was difficult to recall that the IOC session is the annual parliament and supreme body of the Olympic movement. In theory, it is this annual meeting which debates and then votes on the policies to be carried out in the name of the Olympics. Despite massive media attention – there were 500 accredited reporters, photographers and TV crews at Birmingham – very little of what the IOC actually debates is ever revealed. They hold their meetings behind closed doors. The world's media are excluded. Most of the information about what is debated and what decisions are taken is tightly controlled through the IOC press office. This operation is headed by Madame Michèle Verdier. The IOC call her 'a well-advised person whom journalists love to question', but the British press called her 'the IOC's Bernard Ingham' – an unpleasant reference to Margaret Thatcher's notorious information controller.

Madame Verdier controls everything. A trim woman with a pale complexion framed by dark wavy hair, immaculately dressed in dark suits and sensible shoes, she protects her Olympic charges like a dobermann. She is the official IOC filter. Under Madame Verdier's regime the day's agenda is always the same. At exactly 8.45 in the morning at the start of each IOC meeting, she escorts photographers and TV crews into the hall for a 'photo opportunity'. Here they may take pictures of The Club as it prepares to discuss the great issues of the day. On the platform sit the members of Samaranch's inner cabinet – his executive board. There's Canada's Dick Pound and South Korea's Un Yong Kim, Australia's Kevan Gosper and China's Zhenliang He. This 'opportunity' lasts exactly fifteen minutes. At that stage Madame Verdier, who has been hovering anxiously, escorts the photographers and cameramen out and shuts the doors firmly behind them.

The world's press then sit around drinking complimentary coffee. Some ask for something stronger,

'Give me a beer please.'

'Certainly sir, but I'm afraid you'll have to pay for it.'

The media centre is alive with the logos and the products of the paymasters of the Olympics. It is awash with free Coca-Cola and Mars bars. Electronic typewriters have been supplied by Brother and the fax machines by Ricoh. All are worldwide sponsors of the Olympic Games. Each journalist eagerly accepts a free briefcase from Adidas. It is all part of the public relations process. The press become part of the Olympic family – part of the Olympic team.

At the end of the morning session there is a press conference. It is chaired by Madame Verdier. Behind her, two giant Olympic flags have been unfurled. The assembled journalists listen to her brief account of the morning's proceedings. If pressed on any awkward point she retreats behind 'That was not discussed at length' or 'I don't believe that was on the agenda.'

Some of the more robust journalists complain. They have been kept out of the Hyatt Hotel. They cannot get in to talk to individual IOC members to find out what really went on inside the closed session. But Madame Verdier sees the problem from a different point of view. Two Japanese journalists had the temerity to approach one senior IOC member at the end of a session before he could escape to the sanctuary of the Hyatt. As a result, the security outside the meeting hall has been extended to prevent a repetition.

After two days of haggling, Madame Verdier announces a compromise. We will be granted a special pass system. But only forty passes will be available for the five-hundred-strong media squad. The next day a notice appears in the media centre; 'Please do not abuse this system or the privilege will be withdrawn.' It's from Madame Verdier.

The system of photo calls and press conferences continues. It is not until the final day that President Samaranch himself appears to address the world's press. This final conference is held in the hall recently vacated by the IOC members. Even at this late stage in the proceedings, the security staff will not let the journalists into the conference room until Madame Verdier gives the all clear.

Samaranch arrives. He opens by reporting that 'We found here excellent working conditions.' He speaks in English which, along with

French, is one of the two official languages of the IOC. At the back of the hall the translators are at work in six languages. Samaranch asks for questions. He is asked about Catalonia and Gibraltar, both pushing for independent recognition by the IOC. Samaranch says he has just set up another commission to look at the question. It is headed by IOC vice president Judge Mbaye from Senegal. 'I will ask him to comment on this,' says Samaranch.

The judge, who is sitting at the president's side, looks perplexed. He tells the questioner 'I can't tell you anything – I just took up the job this morning.' The problem of a recent doping scandal is raised. Will Samaranch set up an inquiry? 'No,' says the president. 'This is a matter for the International Amateur Athletics Federation.' So much for that.

Getting specifics is difficult, generalities abound. But few of the journalists press him hard. After forty-five minutes Samaranch declares the press conference over. As he makes his departure a sizeable section of the press stand and applaud him.

Enthusiastic applause will doubtless ring out again in Barcelona for the leader of The Club. The motto of these Games is 'Friends for Life'. Club members are friends for life already. And what a life it is. A constant round of meetings, trades and deals in the now lucrative, powerful and high profile world of international sport. The irony is that in Barcelona the only people missing from this latest reunion of The Club are the two men who made it all possible.

CHAPTER 2

Horst's System

One April morning The Club met in very different surroundings to the normal carousel of five-star hotels, banquets and international sporting spectacles. It was 1987, a year before the Seoul Olympics. The Club was gathered in Switzerland for a memorial service in Lausanne's Notre-Dame church.

The world's sports leaders were there from all three branches of the Olympic family – the International Olympic Committee, the international sporting federations and the national Olympic committees. They sat in shocked silence as The Club's most senior member, Olympic President Juan Antonio Samaranch, reminded them why they were there. 'We are gathered here this morning in order to pay tribute to a great man and to pray for him.'

The great man for whom the normally jet-hopping presidents and general secretaries of the wide world of sport had gathered was neither a great Olympic athlete nor a distinguished IOC member. He was a businessman. The luminaries of world sport who sat listening in the pews of the Notre-Dame church that morning had come to honour the memory of Horst Dassler, the German boss of Adidas, the largest sporting goods manufacturing company in the world.

'Horst Dassler devoted his whole life to sport,' intoned Samaranch. 'There is really no need to recall here all that he achieved during his career, as all of us present today are fully aware of it.' Samaranch was not exaggerating. Horst Dassler was not just the man who sold the world's best-known running shoes with their famous three-stripe motif. Horst Dassler created The Club.

'He had many friends amongst us,' the Olympic leader went on, 'and will long be remembered and respected by us all, who will sincerely miss his knowledge, foresight and deep understanding of the complexities of the sports realities of the world.'

Under Dassler's guidance through those 'complexities' and 'sports realities' the world's sporting leaders have achieved undreamed of power and prestige.

'For myself, and I am sure for many others,' Samaranch continued, 'Horst Dassler's most outstanding quality was his own personal contribution to all those in need of sports assistance.'

By cleverly manipulating those 'needs of sports assistance' Dassler created the structure of today's world of business-dominated international sport. In the process he also turned his sports equipment company Adidas and his marketing company ISL into two of the most influential sporting institutions in the world.

Five years after Dassler's death the Adidas brand is no longer controlled by his family. But his ISL marketing company is. It holds the exclusive world rights to sell soccer's World Cup, the athletics World Championships, basketball's World Championships and finally the Olympic Games. What's more, ISL holds some of these exclusive contracts until the next century.

'We are proud to count ourselves as his friends and I am sure that each one of us holds very special memories of an extraordinary man to whom sport owes so much. Thank you, Horst, for all you have done. Goodbye, good friend. We will miss you!'

With Samaranch's eulogy ringing in their ears the world's most powerful sports dignitaries filed out of the Notre-Dame church into the Lausanne spring and got straight back down to business.

Horst Dassler died of cancer on 10 April 1987. He was just fifty-one and at the height of his power. At the time of his death his Adidas empire had a worldwide turnover of $2.2 billion. He employed over 12,000 people and manufactured 400 separate sporting items from balls to bags and jackets to racquets. His factories from Europe to the Far East churned out over a 250,000 pairs of sports shoes every week.

Most Adidas buyers are not athletes. As one obituary pointed out, 'Millions of people wear the company's shoes for nothing more strenuous than reaching for the TV remote control.' But to keep the armchair enthusiasts buying his products, Dassler made sure that winners also wore Adidas. At the Los Angeles Olympics, the last Games before Dassler died, he boasted that over eighty per cent of the athletes who took to the track, swimming pool, football field, basketball court or boxing ring were wearing his products, displaying the Adidas three-stripe and trefoil motif to a TV audience of billions.

One man absent from the throng of Club members at the Lausanne memorial service for this colossus of the business world was Patrick Nally, Horst Dassler's former business partner and right-hand man. Nally too holds some of those 'very special memories' of Horst Dassler to which Olympic President Samaranch referred. Until now Patrick Nally has kept those memories to himself.

'When President Samaranch awarded Horst the Olympic Order three years before his death,' says Nally, 'he announced that Horst was getting it for his faithfulness to the Olympic ideals of the founder of the modern Olympics, Pierre de Coubertin. I know that the assembled world's sports leaders all nodded in agreement but poor old de Coubertin would have turned in his grave.'

It was Patrick Nally who worked most closely with Horst Dassler to develop The Club. Together they laid the foundations for today's structure of dollar-swamped, TV-soaked international sports championships, fabulously wealthy sports federations and their high-profile presidents.

'Horst became the puppet-master of the sporting world,' says Nally, 'pulling the strings to create massive changes, the pinnacle of which is his legacy of control of the modern Olympic Games. Horst got a tremendous buzz from controlling and manipulating. He really excelled in his enthusiasm at being the puppet-master. Behind the scenes he would know that whatever had happened it had happened entirely to plan.'

When Nally first teamed up with Dassler he believed that what they were going to do would be for the benefit of sport. By the early 1980s he was beginning to have his doubts. 'I was getting to the point where I was finding it difficult to know which side I was on. Was I on the side of the corporate sponsors who were shovelling out their money to improve their image? Was I on the side of the international sports federations who were spending that money? Or was I on the side of Horst Dassler who was exploiting it all for Adidas's benefit?'

★

The story of the origins of Adidas *Sportschuhfabriken* is well known. It has assumed the status of a Hans Christian Andersen fairy story or a tale from the Brothers Grimm. Once upon a time there lived two brothers, Adolph and Rudolph Dassler. The boys were both cobblers in the small German town of Herzogenaurach. One day the two brothers had a dreadful argument. So dreadful was the dispute that Adolph and Rudolph decided never to speak to each other again. They parted company and ran rival shoe businesses in the town on either side of the Aurach river. Rudolph called his shoe business Puma. The company run by Adolph and his wife was called Adidas, a not particularly imaginative combination of Adolph, known to everyone as Adi, and Dassler. But unlike the fairy tale, everyone did not live happily ever after.

'Even after the famous split between Adidas and Puma there were constant arguments within the Dassler family,' recalls Nally. 'Horst had four sisters and he constantly lived in fear that these family fights would result in another complete split like the one between his father and his uncle Rudolph. That constant fear, which one day coincided with yet another of the interminable bust-ups in the family, finally made Horst leave Adidas in Germany. He went to France and set up his own Adidas operation in Landersheim. Setting up Adidas France was Horst's solution to getting away from the family problems.'

Although he and Adidas Germany were still linked through the family holding company, there was a very competitive edge between the two. 'All the fights were basically down to a clash of personalities,' says Nally, 'but funnily enough, in one way the constant battling was very good because what it did was make them very competitive. Horst and his family were all very aggressive and all very successful.'

Dassler used Adidas France to build his own empire within sport. Secretly, through the company, he built up a monopoly in the sports equipment market. He surreptitiously acquired other sports manufacturing companies and bought into other competitor shoe makers like Pony.

'It wasn't just the Adidas brand that was Horst's,' says Nally. 'What he was doing was building up a second sports equipment group separate from the Adidas name just in case another fundamental split ever came. Then of course he could forget about Adidas, strengthen his base in France and take whatever he could with him.'

Dassler genuinely liked sport. He was a keen sportsman himself. He played hockey as a youth and was a junior javelin champion. But his first love was athletics.

'He used to fancy himself as a bit of a sprinter,' says Nally. 'Every now and then he used to challenge me to a race. Even though he was ten years older, he would nearly kill me.

'He was also fascinated by sports personalities, top sportsmen; he was really in awe of them. There was always this little boy in him who would literally get starstruck. I found it absolutely extraordinary the way the man would get so excited about meeting top sports people. And when he finally met them he invariably pandered to them. It really was quite strange when you consider how powerful this man was to become.

'Horst always employed lots of athletes. People like Robbie Brightwell and John Boulter, the Olympic 800-metres runner, were on the payroll. Athletics was a sport that he knew a lot about. He was also very closely involved with the Olympics, in which athletics is king. Athletics is one of the keys to the Olympic world. It was also the sport on which Adidas built their name and reputation. Jesse Owens in the 1936 Berlin Olympics won his four gold medals wearing Adidas spikes. Look back over the years at the pictures of athletics champions. The most repetitive image is the three stripes on their shoes.

'Horst's father, old Adolph, had started to see the importance of branding and the importance of the Olympics, which people now forget was the only real international track and field event in those days. Adolph Dassler saw that it was becoming more and more important to get across the personalised imagery that only Adidas produced winners shoes. "Winners wear Adidas." In other words, if there was going to be a gold medal won, it was going to be won in Adidas shoes.'

The strategy that Horst Dassler inherited from his father was to get to the athletes and pay them. The aim was to make sure that all the top sportsmen and all the top teams were wearing Adidas equipment. Then they could associate the 'personalised imagery' of those top athletes with the Adidas brand. The problem was that the athletes were all supposed to be amateurs. Dassler's attempts to make sure that the top athletes all wore Adidas shoes caused ructions within both the International Olympic Committee, at that time headed by the austere American Avery Brundage, and the International Amateur Athletics Federation, then led by Britain's Lord Exeter.

As a result of the 'shoe wars' between the rival companies, which spilt over into the changing rooms and onto the track at the 1968 Olympic Games in Mexico, the athletics federation voted that at future international events only shoes without identifying marks would be allowed.

'We decided to introduce this regulation as a result of what happened in Mexico,' said Lord Exeter. 'At the next meeting of the council in England we shall discuss the scope of this prohibition. Should the rule only apply to international meetings or also to national, regional or local championships?' Dassler said he was sorry, promised to behave, and went on as before.

At an Olympic press conference President Brundage complained, 'This is the price we pay for the success of the Olympic Games. Everyone wants to benefit from them commercially and politically.' And no one wanted to benefit more than Horst Dassler.

'Horst was adept at manipulating people,' says Nally. 'Horst used to tell me about all the inducements and incentives he offered the athletes to make sure that they wore Adidas. One of the most vivid stories I remember him telling me was about beating his cousin Armin, who was working with his uncle Rudolph at Puma.

'Horst was sent by his father to Melbourne for the 1956 Olympics. He was only just out of his teens. Melbourne was probably Horst's first introduction to the Olympic world. The Olympics then were still pretty modest, Melbourne was supposedly paid the princely sum of £80 for the TV rights! Adidas was fighting tooth and nail with Puma. Horst managed to bribe various people at the docks in Australia to stop the Puma equipment being unloaded. He was really chuffed that he had managed to beat his cousin so easily.'

Horst Dassler's achievement was in sharp contrast to the result obtained by more open traders. At Melbourne the International Olympic Committee was approached by a manufacturer who wanted to donate wrist watches to the medal-winning athletes. They declined with thanks because 'the IOC neither wishes to jeopardise the amateur standing of the contestants nor to permit the commercialisation of the

Games.' The unlucky watch manufacturer should have taken his chances with Dassler down at the docks.

It was not just the stars of track and field who were the focus of Horst Dassler's attentions. Twenty-five years after the Melbourne Olympics Horst Dassler was still at it. In 1982 a 'boot money' scandal broke in British rugby, which was still supposed to be amateur. The villains of the piece? Adidas and Puma.

Officials of England's Rugby Football Union threatened to ban from the game anyone found guilty of taking money to wear kit from either of the German manufacturers. The England teams from the colts upward had been getting free kit for years. Then an Adidas manager was forced to give the British taxman the names of sportsmen paid to wear Adidas boots. 'The tax inspectors will not reveal any names to the Rugby Football Union,' ran one report, 'so they are hoping that Adidas boss Horst Dassler will "clear the air" in his meeting with officials.'

The Rugby Football Union was disappointed. Dassler refused to name anyone. Instead he claimed, 'We were the victims of a situation provoked by our rivals. We were not the first manufacturer to pay rugby players.' He went on to admit that Adidas had given some fifty 'amateur' players brown envelopes stuffed with cash over the last couple of years. The mitigating circumstances, he claimed, were that 'none received more than a four figure sum'.

Rugby players in Wales were less bashful. Former Welsh captain Mervyn Davies agreed that he had taken up to £50 a match from Adidas and pointed out quite reasonably, 'I wasn't the only one.' Arthur Young, who worked as an Adidas representative, told BBC TV that he had been the paymaster to Welsh Internationals since the early 1970s. According to Young, he paid players up to £75 a match. Former Welsh International Glyn Shaw backed up Young; 'Arthur was like Santa Claus to me when he paid me £50!'

Horst Dassler's reaction to Young's disclosures was that 'naming names was unethical'. His stance did him the world of good.

'The British advertising and promotions industry is full of admiration for the way Adidas boss Horst Dassler has handled his company's involvement in the great "boot money" scandal,' crowed one business journal. 'It has been a masterpiece of company promotion at virtually no expense,' said another London PR executive. 'Dassler has played it right all the way down the line. When it's all over we shall probably use the whole campaign as a classic example to our trainees of how to turn potentially disastrous publicity into free promotional profit.'

'He saw all this as being fun,' says his former partner Patrick Nally. 'It was just business, he didn't see it as in any way immoral. It was competition and he was very competitive. Whatever it took to beat the competition was the way that Horst would do it. I think it was the family battles that produced his paranoia to succeed. Horst always believed that there was someone waiting around the corner who was going to trip him up.

'His whole life was one of secrecy. He was always looking over his shoulder and spying on the opposition and paying to get one up on them. Everything with Horst was intrigue, everything was suspicion. He kept information files on people and details of what they were up to. He trained his staff like spies! All of his sports people whose job it was to look after the athletes were always told to spy on the opposition. They'd all be trained to go into other people's brief-cases. I know it seems ridiculous but he even trained them to bug the telephones. Horst was out to do whatever he could to the enemy. And he was very good at it.'

Across the English Channel Patrick Nally was developing the links between commerce and sport in a rather different way to Horst Dassler. Nally is a public relations and marketing man. As a teenager he worked for Littlewoods Pools, enticing people to bet on the outcome of England's football league games. He got involved in running promotions for a big brewery but all the time the germ of an idea was growing in Nally's mind.

'Masses of people watched sport, masses of people followed sport. Somehow if I could bridge their sporting interest to a commercial message, then I would be in business. I was looking for a way of using sport as a means of communication.'

In the late 1960s Nally met Peter West, a TV celebrity and well-known British sports broadcaster. West had worked for the BBC for many years commentating on everything from cricket to rugby. He had even compèred a classic BBC TV series called *Come Dancing* – a ballroom-dancing competition.

'When I first met Peter,' recalls Nally, 'he thought that his TV career was on the decline. But he still had a high-profile image. He wasn't a business man but he knew sport. We came together and formed Peter West and Associates which later became West Nally Ltd. The idea was to use sport to carry a commercial message and the way we were going to do that was to convince companies to hand over money to sponsor sports.

'One of our first attempts was with Green Shield – the stamps-for-free-gifts company. We got Green Shield to sponsor a programme to teach British kids to play tennis. Most people saw it as a rich kids' game and what we did, courtesy of Green Shield's money, was to go around the country giving children the opportunity to pick up a tennis racquet and of being taught how to play. That culminated in Green Shield sponsoring the Wimbledon youth championships.

'There was no such thing as a specialist sports sponsorship company at that time. Peter and I were the first. You had a Mark McCormack somewhere in America looking after sports personalities – but he didn't come into the sponsorship business until a lot later. But Peter and I showed that here was an opportunity to bring companies into sports sponsorship and that was something that nobody had managed to do before.

'If you go back to those early days of the late 1960s and early 1970s it's hard to remember just how new the idea of sports sponsorship was and what resistance there was from the sports establishment. Journalists, for example, were unwilling to use the sponsors' names. It stuck in their throats to call something the Benson and Hedges Cup or the Gillette Cup.

'Peter never thought in a million years that we would have commercial advertising on the hallowed turf of Twickenham – he thought he would be dead before that happened. But we proved that it could work. We brought in Ford and Kraft as well as Green Shield and we turned a small company into a fairly sizeable one.'

Into the West Nally office in Berkeley Square one day came John Boulter, the former British Olympic runner. In 1974 he was working for Horst Dassler. Boulter still works for Adidas today. He was at last year's International Olympic Committee session in Birmingham renewing his acquaintance with the most important Club members. He now heads the Adidas international relations division.

Boulter knew that Nally was running a successful sports sponsorship business in the UK and had watched as the company had opened up the cash coffers of big commercial companies and put them in the hands of sport. 'Nally was an ambitious young man who wanted to meet Horst Dassler,' says Boulter. 'Horst said he'd never heard of this Englishman. He asked me to check Nally out.'

The first time Patrick Nally met Horst Dassler was in the German shoe maker's retreat at Landersheim, Adidas' French headquarters. The big modern block is set in the Alsace hills looking out over the flat agricultural land of the region. In front of the building, reflecting Dassler's love of sport, stands a tennis court and an Astroturf football pitch.

During the opening discussions it soon became clear that Dassler was intrigued with what the young Englishman was doing and was excited by the idea of bringing money from big companies into sport.

'He talked about the sports trading wars that had been going on behind the scenes at the Olympics and of the cut-throat tactics being used by the rival shoe companies to get athletes to wear their products,' recalls Nally. 'He told me that bargaining went on right up to the start of the race. The athletes had all learned to haggle so well that they were switching shoes almost as they went out on to the track!

'He was having big battles with the IOC and with some of the sports federations about the payments to "amateur" athletes. Horst was under pressure to put a stop to it. Remember when the great Finn Lassie Viren, who won two gold medals at both Munich and Montreal held up his Tiger spikes in front of the cameras? It was too obvious that there was an enormous and unedifying war to get supposedly amateur athletes to wear certain products.

'I have to admit that at that first meeting with Horst I was a bit dazzled. There I was sitting with this very dynamic person – you could feel that immediately. Alongside his French headquarters is a private restaurant and hotel. You go there, you meet him, you are entertained with fantastic food and wine. Looking back, I realise how modest this all was in those early days. It got more and more extravagant as Horst's power and the Landersheim restaurant grew together.

'He was the sort of man who would always want to get you relaxed. He wasn't a let's go straight for the jugular, let's hit business, type of operator. His style was just chatty, discussions over a period of time, getting to know each other. And out of this first meeting emerged this very determined, very eager, person who had assessed the realities of his current situation and now wanted to talk with me about his vision of the future.'

Every Olympic sport is ultimately controlled by its own international sports federation. In the late 1960s and early 1970s most of them were still very amateur organisations. Few had any permanent staff, many were run by volunteers who loved their particular sports, had usually competed themselves when younger and were prepared to take on the burden of running a federation. Many federation presidents worked from home. Even today's most powerful sporting federations, like football and athletics, were then fairly small organisations. The IAAF had very modest offices in suburban Putney. FIFA headquarters was a house in Zurich. Only the International Olympic Committee was beginning to establish its importance as TV money started to flow.

'Horst was brought up in sport and the Olympics and was well aware of the sports federations,' says Nally 'The federations were at the root of his vision for the future. He was clever enough to see that the federations were going to go through a rapid change. They were going to have both their importance and their finances improved by the increasing amounts of TV money being paid for the Olympics.

'Horst wanted to be in a position where he could control those changes for his own benefit. He was well aware of the federations' structures and that people had to be elected to run them. His new strategy was to get away from paying individual athletes and towards working with the federations and the national teams. He saw that the future was with the federations, that they would be the ones to decide what the athletes would wear and that if he could control them, everybody out there would be wearing his product.

'It was the money that started these developments. It was the fact that suddenly TV became such an important and integral part of the picture. Live TV didn't exist much before that time. TV money forced the development of the federations and forced the interest of Horst and of others to start manipulating and becoming involved.'

Dassler was confident that he could turn his vision into a reality. He was a clever man and was already studying several languages. As well as his native German he spoke French, Italian, Spanish, English and he had a smattering of Japanese. He was also adept at moving around and getting to understand people. He knew how to trade, how to do deals with people.

'Even in the early days it wasn't always money that Adidas offered,' says Nally 'Horst always knew just who he could approach with money and who he should approach with some other inducement.'

When Nally first met Dassler in Landersheim in 1974 the German shoe maker had already started laying the ground work for his assault on the international federations. Dassler's operations had two bases: Landersheim and Paris 'There was a very smart Adidas shop on the Rue du Louvre that was really just a front,' says Nally. 'Upstairs was the Adidas promotions team. The real business went on downstairs.'

In the basement was a private restaurant. Here Dassler cultivated visiting federation officials and sports politicians. He also kept permanent rooms at the Terrasse Hotel in Montmartre. These too were made available to his targets. There was a barman whose job was to obtain the girls for Dassler's distinguished guests.

Dassler had also begun to establish his 'political team'. This group had responsibility for worldwide intelligence gathering, for getting close to the federations and the sports politicians and influencing events. Each member of Dassler's team looked after a different part of the world.

Dassler patrolled Central and South America himself. John Boulter looked after Europe.

Asia was Professor Anwar Chowdhry's patch. He has done well; Chowdhry is now the president of the International Amateur Boxing Association.

English-speaking Africa, and controlling the media, was the job of journalist Bobby Naidoo. He led the International Association of the Sporting Press which has close links with the International Olympic Committee.

French-speaking Africa was run by Colonel Hassine Hamouda of the former French colony of Tunisia. The Colonel had been a member of the French team at Hitler's Berlin Olympics in 1936. From an office in Paris, an important centre for French-speaking Africans, he ran a bilingual magazine called *Champion D'Afrique*. Hamouda was also a Tunisian athletics coach and vice president of the Tunisian Boxing Federation.

'Mr Hamouda wishes to help African athletes develop and improve through *Champion D'Afrique*,' ran a plug in the IOC *Review*. Horst Dassler also wanted to help African athletes develop, as long as they did it wearing Adidas. Dassler provided Hamouda's office and contributed to the funding of the magazine. He also created meaningless awards – like the *Champion D'Afrique* gold medals – and paid for the banquets at which they were presented.

'Very few companies were interested in Africa as a commercial market,' says Nally, 'But politically it was important to Horst because there were lots of federation votes to be had. It's not the sports administrators who decide the vote, its the politicians. Horst's idea was to use Colonel Hamouda and *Champion D'Afrique* to gain influence with those key African politicians and to help them become more important within the federations. Colonel Hamouda spent a lot of time and energy on Africa.

'The Africans were poor and that's where Horst could help. He could give sporting products to Africa. That was also important politically. Commercially it didn't matter because there wasn't going to be a rash of bulk buying and mass orders of Adidas shoes by the Africans. Horst could direct his help at the most popular African sports which won him support in the most important federations. Boxing was popular in Africa and of course football and athletics, the biggest single Olympic sport. Horst supplied a lot of equipment to Africa. If you look at those sports today they have strong African influence in their international federations.'

Russia and the East Bloc belonged to a Frenchman called Christian Jannette. He was just the sort of man Horst Dassler could use; Jannette had a long and influential association with the Olympic Games. He was the deputy head of Protocol at the Munich Olympics of 1972 and was awarded the French *Mérite National* for his 'kindness and competence during his four year stay in Munich'.

After the 1972 Olympics Jannette had two jobs; he worked as attaché to the French national Olympic committee and went on the Adidas payroll. He was in Montreal for the next Olympics and then moved to Moscow in the years leading up to the Games of 1980, where he was both the *Chef de Mission* of the French team and fixer for Dassler. 'Personal contact enables organisers to prepare a much more personal welcome,' was what Jannette learned in Munich. 'I would advise, get to know the dignitaries as well as possible.'

'I went to Russia sixty-two times between 1974 and 1980 for Adidas,' Jannette told us 'As far back as the mid-sixties Horst had a very good relationship with all the East Bloc countries. I can remember I signed a contract with Poland in 1974 for equipment for all their federations. And we already had some contracts with federations in the USSR.'

Nally recalls, 'Christian was Horst's constant liaison man with the Russians. He was forever flying in and out of Moscow with gifts. Potentially there was a big commercial market there for Adidas. In Olympic terms the East Bloc were the number one performers. The Russians and the East Germans were the top gold medal winners. The important thing for Horst was to be able to show the Eastern Europeans that he was the pipeline that could provide help from the West.

'Just like in Africa, supplying Adidas equipment was key. They didn't make any high-class shoes or clothing themselves and they couldn't afford to buy from the West. Horst could cultivate a position of importance by giving them Adidas kit. The other important thing was funding them to go on the attractive international trips that got them outside of a pretty grim Eastern Europe.

'Horst didn't throw cash at them. The way that Horst operated was first of all to get to know the administrators. He won their confidence and he supplied his product, his quality shoes, his quality textiles to the various federations.

'Dealing with most of the East Bloc federations was not like dealing with the Western ones. In the East you had to deal with a sports ministry which had an overseeing role in everything within sport and also the Olympics. That system of dealing centrally made it much easier for Horst to get into the infrastructure. Inside the system he would talk about which of their own sports administrators and officials should participate in the international federations and worked with them to make sure that there was one Russian or one Eastern European on the council of every important federation.

'So the Russians and the East Germans, like the Africans, thought that Horst was their friend. They were important because they were another group that had influence, had votes, not as big as the African group but still would be a group vote. So by making sure that their

prestige was always taken care of – that they were in key positions –
Horst could count on their support when he wanted it. It was one huge
trade. The East Europeans are all traders. You give them something
and they'll give you something.'

Nally would be the key to Horst's vision of billions of TV viewers
watching the world's greatest athletes standing on the winners' podium
wearing the Adidas three stripes.

'The fact that I was getting commercial companies to put money into
sport was like, Eureka! Horst said, "Let's put those two things
together and then we can really start moving." Horst wanted a way of
putting commercial sponsorship and sport together to benefit Adidas.
From his perspective it meant he would have power. Horst would get
the credit for what we did for the federations and that would put him
in a very strong position. He wanted me to get someone else to do the
paying.'

Dassler needed Nally to find that someone else pretty quickly.
When they first got together that day in Landersheim in 1974 Dassler
had already made a commitment to a man who over the next twenty
years would become one of the most important power brokers in the
world of sport.

CHAPTER 3

Dassler Takes Coke

When Diego Maradonna led his defending World Cup champions out into Rome's Olympic Stadium for the 1990 World Cup Final, the Argentine side had much in common with its West German opponents. Both teams were kitted out by Adidas. So was the referee. So were the linesmen. Fifteen of the twenty-four national teams in Italy displayed the Adidas trefoil and three-stripe motif on their shirts, shorts, socks and boots.

The game kicked off with a black-and-white Adidas ball. All the matches in the competition were played with Adidas footballs. It was the official ball. The company supplied the official boot.

Off the pitch, Horst Dassler had it all sewn up too. His marketing company ISL owned the exclusive rights to sell the World Cup. About the only thing that was not supplied or owned by Dassler at the 1990 World Cup Final was the referee's whistle.

Eight years earlier in the Madrid Stadium the picture had been the same. At the opening ceremony of that World Cup twelve-year-old Victor Puente released a dove of peace from a hollow football. The hollow football was supplied by Adidas. Young Victor was wearing Adidas kit. Even the draw for the finals of that year's World Cup was made with miniatures of that official black-and-white Adidas football.

'We're not closely tied to Adidas,' insisted FIFA vice president Harry Cavan. 'The Adidas company, as far as I'm aware, is a very generous company to sport generally and to football in particular. If they want to provide the equipment, I see nothing wrong with that.'

The 1974 World Cup Final in Munich between Germany and Holland was fought out by two European teams under the control of a European referee in a European venue. Off the pitch, that year marked the end of European domination in the world of international football.

The sparkling trophy which Franz Beckenbauer hoisted skywards to the roars of the faithful German supporters was a new one. The man presiding over the championship was also new to his post. Three weeks earlier Dr João Havelange had been elected president of the International Federation of Football Associations. He was the most powerful man in world football.

A new trophy was needed because the old one had been taken home by the Brazilians in 1970. Any team which won the final three times kept the cup outright. The original Jules Rimet trophy found a permanent home in Brazil after her dazzling footballers achieved the triple victory.

Jean Marie Faustin Godefroid Havelange, commonly known as João is also from Brazil. Today, at the age of seventy-six, Havelange is a kingmaker. He holds over fifty decorations and orders. He's a Cavalier of France's Legion of Honour; a Commander of the Portuguese Cavaliers of the Order of the Infant Dom Henrique; he holds the Grand Cross of Spain's Isabel the Catholic; he's a Cavalier of Sweden's *Vasa-Orden* and a Commander of Senegal's Order of the Lion.

It was Havelange who put together the block of votes that won Barcelona the 1992 Olympic Games. It was Havelange who traded with Horst Dassler to win Juan Antonio Samaranch the presidency of the International Olympic Committee.

Some will tell you that the man is now too old; that his power is on the wane; that Havelange is past his prime. Yet the Brazilian remains the only figure in world sport who can still dictate his own terms to the all-powerful president of the Olympics. That Havelange is able to do this results directly from his alliance with Horst Dassler.

João Havelange is a founding member of The Club. His election to the presidency of FIFA a few weeks before the start of the 1974 World Cup finals marked the beginning of a new Latin dominance in the running of world sport; of a dramatic shift away from its former Anglo Saxon control and its much proclaimed amateur values. This is only part of the story; what has never been told is that Havelange's election also marked the start of Horst Dassler's campaign to control the development of world sport.

'It was the election of Havelange that made Horst aware of the importance of the federations,' says Patrick Nally. 'Horst saw the election of Havelange as a watershed.'

Havelange faced one fundamental obstruction to his desire to become the boss of world football. FIFA already had one. The incumbent FIFA president was England's Sir Stanley Rous and he had no desire to go. Rous was FIFA's sixth president and, like all those before him, he was from Europe. He was passionately devoted to football; it was one of the most important things in his life. He was a school teacher who gave up his spare time to become a football referee. As far back as 1933 Rous could be found in the great football capitals of the world, in huge boots and baggy shorts, refereeing international matches. He was a big man, dedicated to the concept of fair play.

His knowledge of football's rules was encyclopaedic. He wrote *A History of the Laws of the Game*. He was knighted by King George VI for his work in the staging of the London Olympic Games of 1948. He became president of FIFA in 1961.

Under Sir Stanley Rous 'FIFA was rather conservative and reserved in its decisions,' says the official history book. 'Funds came strictly from the profits from the World Cup and this is how one had to live and work for four years. It seemed hardly possible to accomplish more without taking risks.'

'In those days,' says Nally, 'FIFA was working on limited resources. Its headquarters was an old private house, the Villa Derwald, in Zurich. There was the general secretary, dear old Dr Käser, and two dogs lying on the floor. You were greeted by a receptionist with a squeaky voice who Dr Käser eventually married. I think there was one other odd-job person. Otherwise it was just the two dogs and an old table with piles of books. It was quaint, it was antiquated, it was just like going back to a Dickensian novel.'

Havelange was a different character altogether. His sporting background had more to do with waterball than football. In the 1930s when Stanley Rous was refereeing internationals, Havelange was swimming for Brazil at Adolf Hitler's Berlin Olympics. He was in Brazil's water polo team at the Helsinki Olympics eighteen years later. He led the Brazilian delegation to the 1956 Olympics in Melbourne; while Havelange sat in a VIP box, the young Horst Dassler was bribing Australian dockhands to keep rival sports goods locked up at the quay side.

Havelange says 'I am a businessman, and I have too much money to need to make even more from soccer.' That may well be true, but what Havelange spotted, as one observer remarked, is that 'sport represents one of the modern world's most magnificent vehicles for the undisputed exercise of pure, unalloyed, blatant, stark-naked power.'

Havelange's early career was in business. He dabbled in the import and export of steel, in mining, in chemicals and in transport. He is today the president of the national Brazilian bus company. But he made his money from insurance. He was a director of one company in São Paulo and of another in Rio.

With his background in water polo he became the president of the São Paulo swimming federation and in 1955 managed to get onto the Brazilian Olympic committee. In 1963 he joined the élite society of the International Olympic Committee. Three years later he was joined by his future Olympic leader, Juan Antonio Samaranch.

His most important position was president of the all-embracing Brazilian Sports Association. Havelange's own promotional literature claims that while in charge of Brazilian sport he 'became Brazil's most successful football manager' and that he was 'the architect of Brazil's success at the World Cups in 1958, 1962 and 1970.'

While some may think that Brazil's footballing success had more to do with the skills of Pelé and Garincha than with Havelange, there is little argument over the fact that he used his position as the power base from which to launch his campaign to take control of FIFA.

'Havelange had seen the future,' says Nally. 'He knew that if he became the next president of the only federation already running its own high-profile world championship then he would enjoy huge economic and political power.'

Havelange launched his campaign for the presidency in 1970. Trading on Brazil's three world cup victories, Havelange toured the world to canvass football's potential voters.

'There had never been an election campaign like it for a sports presidency,' recalls Nally. 'Sir Stanley Rous hadn't travelled to all the countries throughout Asia and Africa and certainly not to all the little islands. It was such a radical change to suddenly have this dynamic, glamourous South American character, brimming with *bonhomie*, travelling the world with his wife, meeting people, pressing the flesh, bringing over the Brazilian team, travelling with the likes of Pelé. It was

Brazilian carnival time.'

Havelange attacked the old European domination of FIFA. It was a clever move. He had spotted that the new converts to soccer in Asia and Africa were kept out of top-class competition. In return for their votes Havelange promised to increase the number of World Cup finalists from sixteen to twenty-four. He promised to create a new Junior World Championship. He promised cash to the developing countries for football stadia, courses for referees, doctors, trainers and more club competitions in the Third World.

'Sir Stanley suddenly woke up to the fact that he was about to be ousted by this Brazilian,' says Nally. 'And it was his German friends who suggested, at the last minute, that he talk to Horst and see if he could help him out.'

Dassler obliged. He rallied round with his team and started a high pressure lobby of the delegates coming into Frankfurt for the 39th FIFA Congress. He almost turned the election round. Right up to the end, it looked as if Havelange would lose. The contest went to a second ballot and Havelange scraped in by just sixteen votes.

'Havelange had spent a fortune going around the world with the Brazilian team and had canvassed every single member of FIFA,' says Nally. 'It was unheard of. No sports president had ever gone round the world glad handing and campaigning.

'Horst stepping in for Sir Stanley at the last minute and almost getting him elected, put the frighteners on Havelange. And that brought the two of them together. Horst so impressed Havelange with his ability to almost knock him off his perch before he got up there that Havelange thought, "Jesus, if this guy can do this to me, almost scupper me before I've started, I've got to have him on my side."

'For his part, Horst saw a man who had come from nowhere to oust Sir Stanley, in spite of his attempts to stop him. And Horst was always one to go with a winner. If you weren't any use to him anymore he'd spit you out just like that. The bond was created by the two of them respecting what the other could do.'

Once elected, Havelange was faced with the fact that he did not have the money to put his manifesto into practice. He turned to Horst Dassler. A deal was struck. If the Adidas boss wanted the benefits of a relationship with FIFA, and the deals with the national federations so that the players would all appear in Adidas kit, then the price that

Dassler was going to have to pay was the funding of Havelange's manifesto.

'Horst didn't have the money either. That's why he turned to me,' says Nally. 'At Landersheim he talked to me about FIFA. He asked if I could help him raise the money to help Havelange live up to his election promises.

'I was a means to an end. I was a marketing person. I could raise money and he would get the benefit for himself.

'This was fundamental to his plan to get inside and control the sports federations. He wanted to control their development, which was good for them because they needed to develop. But what Horst wanted to do was develop them in such a way that he was the linchpin. It would be Horst who would work to elect a suitable president, work out what that president should promise, and do the deal on how they were going to fulfil their promises.

'Once you've got into the federations you've got a toehold in the International Olympic Committee and that means controlling the Olympics, the biggest event in the world. Horst wanted to be the key to the whole thing. He wanted to make himself indispensable. When the decisions were made, when somebody wanted something, either money or elections, he wanted to be the only person who at the end of the day the calls were coming to.'

Even after Dassler's death the Adidas involvement with world football remains total. Pop stars receive Grammies, film stars get Oscars. Soccer players get Adidas Trophies. They get Adidas shoes, Adidas balls and the Adidas trefoil and three-stripe logo in gold, silver and bronze.

At the World Soccer Gala to mark the end of the 1990 World Cup, all the stars were out. Lothar Matthaus, West Germany's victorious captain who shares his home town of Herzogenaurach with the Adidas German headquarters, was presented with 'soccer's highest award'. That's what the Adidas publicity machine called the 'Golden Adidas Trefoil' for the 1990 World Soccer Player of the Year.

Picking up the Adidas Franz Beckenbauer Prize from the man who held up the world cup to the roars of the faithful in Munich twenty years ago, was Cameroon's thirty-nine-year-old, lambada-dancing forward, Roger Milla.

Grateful recipient of the Adidas Golden Shoe for the World Cup's top goalscorer was Italy's Salvatore Schillaci. 'He came to the World Cup as a reserve, and left as a superstar,' trills the Adidas publicity magazine *Adidas News*. 'As an added bonus,' it continues, ' "Toto" picked up the Adidas Golden Ball award for the best player of the tournament.' Lucky old Toto.

Adidas Golden shoes also went to Hugo Sanchez and Christo Stoichkov, Europe's top goalscorers. At the same Gala where Adidas distributed its largesse to the world's soccer superstars, FIFA handed England's captain Gary Lineker its Fair Play Prize, awarded to the England team for their performance in Italy. Lineker was also awarded FIFA's personal Fair Play Award of 50,000 Swiss francs.

Despite these blatant ties between Adidas and FIFA, president João Havelange has stoutly maintained that 'Mr Dassler had no influence on the politics of FIFA.' He then expresses bewilderment at the thought that anyone would even want to suggest such a thing. 'Why is this hatred directed against me when I have worked so hard for the development of football?' he asks. 'Football sells products all over the world. All this is due to my work.' Indeed it does and many of those products are manufactured by Adidas.

Even the FIFA president himself, when turning out for an exhibition match to mark the opening celebrations of his new FIFA House in Zurich, was pictured in a pair of boots marked with the ubiquitous three-stripe motif.

A glossy FIFA history celebrating the international federation's eightieth birthday relates how Havelange's 'first concern' after his election in 1974 was a comprehensive, worldwide football development programme. 'As FIFA did not have the necessary financial means the FIFA president implemented his vast experience and fantasy as a businessman, in order to materialise these ambitious plans.' What the official history neglects to divulge is that Havelange's 'vast experience and fantasy as a businessman' was in reality Horst Dassler and Patrick Nally.

'Politically it was important for Havelange to fulfil his promises to the Africans and the Asians,' says Nally. 'He'd promised the Third World that he would get more African nations, more Asian nations into World Cup soccer; he'd promised the creation of a world youth championship; he'd promised a development programme to take the best of European and South American soccer skills to Africa and Asia; he'd been elected on that manifesto. If Horst was going to help Havelange implement this he needed lots of money to develop lots of events.

'Horst had committed himself to help Havelange get the money. The question I asked myself was, "How the hell am I going to get it?" I was left with the job of creating a marketing programme which would justify bringing big money into soccer to help Horst fulfil his obligations and if I was going to do that I was going to need one hell of a big company to sponsor it.'

Time magazine once ran a cover picture showing the earth as a man with a bottle of Coke at his lips. The caption read 'The World Drinks from this Bottle.' The world of international sport also sustains itself with Coke.

Coca-Cola is the biggest and the best-known Olympic sponsor in the world. The product sells itself on purity, youthfulness, energy and zest. The world's best-loved syrup and the brave new world of international sport were made for each other.

Coca-Cola has a long involvement with the Olympic Games. They were there in Rome in 1960 and at Mexico City in '68 where 'astronauts' in red-and-white space suits pumped the magic elixir from canisters strapped to their backs.

They were at Munich in '72 , at Montreal in '76, at Moscow in '80. American athletes may have had to boycott the Russian Games but the Coca-Cola company was there, selling its orange drink Fanta.

At Los Angeles in '84 Coke became 'the official soft drink of the Olympics'. It was the same at Seoul in '88 and it is the same in Barcelona.

Over the last sixty-five years the Atlanta-based company has ploughed more than a billion dollars into world sport. The sport that Coke first gave its money to on a truly worldwide basis was soccer.

'Coca-Cola is one of the top companies in the world,' says Nally. 'Anything that Coca-Cola does has to be a success. And everybody follows Coke. If you can convince Coke to do something, then you are on your way. If you're into Coke, you're into the biggest blue chip company on a global basis.

'Horst always maintained that what we were doing was bringing money in to help people achieve their ambitions, which in a way we were, and they all thanked him profusely and showered him with their awards. But really, it put him in an incredibly powerful position to manipulate and organise the federations and the sponsors.

'There wasn't a single company in the world at that time that had an international marketing budget. Ours was a totally new approach. You couldn't just go out and say "We want you to make a decision internationally". Most companies, however big they were, always had local promotional budgets.

'That's why Japanese companies became so important in expanding this business later on. The Japanese had two things. First, they normally used a standard worldwide brand name. Toyota was Toyota worldwide, whereas many of the European and American companies had different brand names in different parts of the world. The second thing was that they often had a central decision making process. Where they had local managers, they tended to be Japanese, and they always referred back to Tokyo for their decisions.

'I knew that trying to get a deal with Coca-Cola was going to be a lot of work but I hadn't realised what a monster of an exercise it would turn out to be. It took something like eighteen months, I travelled all over the world, and went through countless series of negotiations that I often felt would collapse.'

Coca-Cola, which everybody thinks of as a huge international conglomerate, was structured as a whole series of fiefdoms. The Germans controlled Germany, the British controlled Britain. It was a multi-national in name but it was national in operation. The management was structured to have their own power in their own country and the budgeting responsibility was held by the local management.

'When I said I wanted to marry the interests of the company with one sport worldwide, there was mayhem' says Nally. 'Everybody said "No fear, I've got my own sports. I'm more interested in tiddlywinks than I am in soccer." It was warfare. There was blood on the carpets. Nobody wanted to give up their ability to control their own decisions.

'Eventually, at an incredibly stormy board meeting in Atlanta, the decision was taken,' remembers Nally. 'Coca-Cola would enter into a worldwide sponsorship programme and all of the various national markets would contribute. They weren't asked to contribute, they were told to contribute, and they were forced to cough up a percentage of their promotional money to a central pot in Atlanta which would be spent on soccer.'

The decision by Coke gave Havelange a multi-million dollar war chest. Now he could keep the promises which had got him elected.

There was no organisation to carry out Havelange's big ideas. It was left to Nally to turn the new president's promises into practice. What was a development programme? How do you start up a world youth cup? FIFA had no answers to such questions. The federation had no full-time personnel. Dassler and Nally not only found the money, they then had to set up the new events and the development programmes. They were taking over world soccer. It was all done outside the federation and Dassler and Nally were writing all the rules.

'Horst turned to Klaus Willing who had been working for the German swimming federation. Klaus was a lovely man. He spoke fluent English, was eloquent and a good writer. He put together the plan that eventually became the FIFA development programme. Klaus was responsible for writing the whole strategy of taking the knowledge of the strong soccer nations in Europe and South America to one hundred countries, of taking top coaches, administrators, sports medicine people to Africa, to Asia, to all those places where the votes were important to Havelange. Sadly, Klaus was killed in a car crash leaving Landersheim one day after one of those Adidas political dinners.'

Nally and Dassler next created the world youth tournament. With Coke, they started to build a multi-million dollar sponsorship deal. They decided that the new youth competition would be restricted to players under the age of twenty, it would be held every two years and it would be called the FIFA/Coca-Cola Cup. The first tournament kicked off in Tunis in 1977.

By the time the third Coca-Cola Cup was held in Australia in 1981, money was no object to FIFA. The men from Atlanta who had said 'Yes' to Patrick Nally were handing over $600,000 for the privilege of seeing their name on the trophy. They were also footing the bill for the fifteen teams travelling to Australia, as well as the expenses of the referees. Forty FIFA officials from around the world also joined in the jamboree. Coca-Cola also guaranteed up to a quarter of a million dollars in case the tournament lost money.

'On top of this, we created a worldwide soccer skills programme,' says Nally. 'That was for the local Coke bottling plants. It gave them good promotional opportunities. Then slowly, we brought Coca-Cola into the World Cup in Argentina in 1978.' Coke guaranteed a previously unheard of $8 million to underwrite the event.

Nally and Dassler also created new commercial rules for FIFA's competitions. There was a lot more to it than drowning the event in Coca-Cola logos. 'You would have to get control of the franchise for the bars in every stadium so that Coke was the only soft drink,' explains Nally. 'In 1982 in Spain we had a huge fight at the Madrid stadium. Pepsi already had the franchise but Coke was coming in as the sponsor. Pepsi had to go.

'It also had to be a "clean" stadium, one where we could put in our own sponsors' advertising boards around the arena,' says Nally. 'We had to write that into the regulations. Before a FIFA event went to any given stadium it had to be guaranteed clean. These were all new ideas. We were writing the marketing rules, the event rules, how to stage the events, how to construct the development programmes, our relationship with the federation was total.'

It was indeed a 'total' relationship. Dassler took over the management of FIFA, even selecting their new general secretary. 'Horst recognised that FIFA, with Dr Käser and the secretary with the squeaky voice and the two dogs, wasn't going to have the capability to run the new-look federation,' says Nally. 'So Horst brought in Joseph Blatter who was working for Swiss Timing in those days. Blatter was trained at the Adidas headquarters at Landersheim before he went off to FIFA. He spent his time there working alongside Horst, getting to know the Adidas operation. Horst and Blatter became very close during the months he lived in Landersheim.'

The way that Nally and Dassler brought the Coca-Cola company into sponsoring soccer became a blueprint for the development of other sports federations. Havelange was a new breed of sports president. He had a high profile and the world of business had given him a bulging bank account.

By 1979 Havelange's expenses were running at £100,000 a year. By 1986 the cost of running his private office in Rio reached £250,000. By

the time the FIFA officials flew into Spain for the World Cup in 1982
their expenses were nearly £2 million – almost as much as it cost to
transport and accommodate the twenty-four teams. Their new-found
wealth was dazzling. In the next two years FIFA splashed out
£650,000 on international travel and gifts. Since the Coke money tap
was turned on, Havelange has remained the unchallenged president of
FIFA.

'But it was Horst who got the ultimate political and commercial
benefit of Coke's investment,' says Nally. 'He worked hand in glove
with the new federation we had created and kept very close to
Havelange. The contracts flowed back to Adidas.

'Horst needed that clean Coke image and that name. Other
companies would be dazzled into following Coke's plunge and other
federations dazzled into following FIFA. Just think about that clean
Coke image and the fact that at the same time Coke's money was being
used by Horst for his own benefit. Coca-Cola legitimised the industry
but they never realised the importance of their association and how it
was abused to enable The Club, this whole mafia within sport, to get
going. Coke started it all.'

CHAPTER 4

From Montreal to Monte Carlo

When Britain's former Sports Minister Denis Howell asked Horst Dassler 'Why does a shoe manufacturer need to be involved in sports administration?' he got a very blunt answer. 'We exist to sell boots and shirts and wherever the action is we need to be there.' Howell is a down-to-earth Birmingham politician and he appreciates a straightforward reply.

'But what still disturbs me,' says Howell, some ten years after his encounter with the Adidas boss, 'is that he went on to tell me that he had a better overall view of the total situation in sport than any other individual. He had "a department" which collected and filed information on national Olympic committees and the international federations.'

Dassler insisted that his files contained information from 'official publications' only and claimed that he was more than happy to make his data bank available to anyone who wanted it. 'The point is,' says Howell, 'that no one in his position as a commercial manufacturer should be involved in trying to seek control of world sporting bodies. It is a concentration of power which I regard as unhealthy.'

The former Sports Minister would have been even more disturbed had the German shoe maker revealed the true extent of his power, of his dealings with the world's top sports administrators, of his dedicated team of political intelligence gatherers and of their worldwide operations.

By the middle of the 1970s Dassler's political campaign was beginning to hum. The political team were building up comprehensive intelligence files on the world's existing and up-and-coming sporting administrators. They were reporting back from around the world on the international federations, the various national Olympic committees and the International Olympic Committee.

'Wherever the action is we need to be there,' Dassler had told Denis Howell and Dassler was as good as his word. There was nowhere in the world that a representative of those famous three stripes would not go to court, cajole and cultivate the men who ran world sport.

'If there was an international sports federation gathering, a meeting of regional national Olympic committees or of the IOC itself there was always the compulsory Adidas dinner,' says Nally. 'Whenever you attended an annual congress or anything else, the only company that was always there was Adidas.'

Dassler played the role of fairy godmother; Adidas turned up and everyone went to the ball. 'Horst was the only man who ever paid them so much attention. He'd even offer them his own facilities for their meetings, then he would turn up and invite them all to a jolly dinner. Here was Adidas, friendly, affable, pleasant and supportive. There was no hard sell. Horst was their friend. It became an almost natural thing and Horst started to build a great allegiance.'

Dassler and his political team did not always have to go out looking for information; it often came to them. Their data bank was swollen with intelligence from a procession of visitors from the sporting world, happy to enjoy the hospitality at Dassler's hotel and restaurant which stood alongside the Adidas headquarters in Landersheim. 'There were constant meetings and discussions with Horst, with sports officials and with the political team around that great dining table in Landersheim,' recalls Nally.

There were wild celebrations when the Canadian city of Montreal was awarded the Games of 1976. Montreal Mayor Jean Drapeau's grand dream to bring the Olympics to his city became a reality. Six years later, the dream had turned into a nightmare. The 1976 Olympics ended up $1 billion in the red and the tax-payers of Montreal will still be paying off the deficit when The Club jets into Atlanta for the centennial celebrations of the Olympic Games in 1996.

Mayor Drapeau claimed that the Games could no more produce a deficit than a man could have a baby. After a savaging in the pages of a four-volume report produced by Albert Malouf, then Quebec's leading judge, Drapeau himself experienced something like the excruciating pains of childbirth. The Judge said that Drapeau had 'appointed himself foreman and project manager' for Montreal's new Olympic facilities without the 'aptitudes and knowledge' for the job. The Mayor had commissioned 'unnecessarily luxurious and impressive install-ations' dictated by 'considerations of aesthetics and grandeur' without serious study of the costs.

To make matters worse, when the Games were opened by Her Majesty the Queen, twenty-two African countries were missing from the opening ceremony. Two days earlier they had walked out of the Games protesting about the New Zealand rugby team's tour of South Africa.

Two great stars towered over the Montreal Games, Finland's Lassie Viren and Cuba's Alberto Juantorena. Viren, the village policeman with the wispy beard, successfully defended his Olympic titles at both 5,000 and 10,000 metres. The nine-foot striding Juantorena became the first man to win the gold medal at 400 and 800 metres at the same Olympics.

The Montreal Games are probably best remembered for the achievements of these two great athletes. Even Judge Malouf's critical investigation accepted that for most Canadians the Games were 'a source of joy and national pride.' Patrick Nally remembers the Montreal Olympics for different reasons.

'Montreal was a catalyst. Horst's political team was in place. He was building files on who's who; which individuals were candidates to be groomed; who is going to succeed. He was having discussions with the Samaranches of this world, finessing future elections.

'1976 saw the birth of stage three of Horst's development. Stage one was paying the competitors to wear Adidas kit. Stage two was the period when he realised that he had to get control of the federations. Stage three was the implementation of the complete strategy. We went to Montreal with a structured plan for the first time. At Montreal we started sowing the seeds of our work with all the federations and the IOC. It became the launch pad of the Dassler and Nally era.'

The headquarters for the launching of the 'Dassler and Nally era' was a select mansion in an up-market quarter of Montreal. The two partners imported their own English chef to turn out a succession of

culinary delights for an unending round of dinners and lunches at which Dassler and Nally worked their contacts and built up their files.

'We were set up in Montreal well before the Games started,' says Nally. 'We'd chosen this lovely house where we knew we could create a good atmosphere and entertain people who would be only too happy to get away from the hotels. There should have been a lot more excitement at the Olympic Games and Montreal seemed to lack that – probably because the Canadians were so fed up by this stage. It was very difficult to find a heart to the Montreal Games.'

The mansion rented by the two businessmen soon filled that void. It became the heart of sporting politics at the Montreal Olympics, pumping out ideas and strategies for the up-coming rounds of meetings and discussions.

At those meetings the partners had a particularly juicy carrot to dangle in front of the sports federations: the multi-million dollar deal which Nally had secured with Coca-Cola for Havelange of FIFA. The man who ran world football was soon to announce to his fellow federation presidents that he had secured millions of dollars from Coke.

'We'd got commercial companies to bring money into the international federations,' says Nally. 'We could also show how we could help aspiring federation presidents with their campaign objectives.

'At Montreal we were able to use the development of FIFA and the establishment of Havelange as a powerful sporting president to show what an international federation could do. The money we'd brought into FIFA through Coke was clearly changing the face of the federation. Havelange was building a new international headquarters in Zurich, appointing professional full-time staff and PR and finance people. FIFA was showing the way. Other big federations like athletics were watching closely. Many others were eager to follow and were quick to fall into the hands of Horst and myself.'

As Havelange became richer and more powerful, everyone wanted to get to the top. It meant trips, it meant travel, it meant image, it meant awards and it meant status.

'It certainly beats sweeping out the back garden at the weekend if you're flying first class everywhere to major international events,' says Nally. 'As soon as people wanted to become presidents of sports federations Horst started trading to make sure that the right people were elected.'

Dassler paid special attention to building up valuable contacts within the Olympic organisations themselves. Many of the key people who organised the Montreal Games were either employed by Adidas or acted as unpaid Adidas consultants. 'They were all on the team,' says Nally. 'Their future career path was going to be linked with Horst and therefore during the period of time that they were on the Games, they would keep Horst supplied with all the up-to-date information, contacts, accreditation passes to get into the athletes' areas, or anything else he might need.

'In Montreal, we were totally integrated with all the key players, like Artur Takac who was and still is a technical adviser to the Olympics. Artur was just about the first person I ever met in Landersheim. He frequently played tennis with Horst on the Adidas tennis courts there. Takac was from Yugoslavia and needed support from the West. Horst provided that and Takac was helpful as a conduit into Eastern Europe and into the IOC.'

Dassler also cultivated more difficult contacts during his time in Montreal. 'I remember going round with Horst,' recalls Nally, 'and of course everywhere Horst went, gifts went with him. Some expensive Omega watches always went with us. We'd have a little chat with the person about life in general and how wonderful things were and how we were looking for new commercial openings in sport. And then Horst would say "Oh, by the way, here's a little token of Adidas' esteem," or something like that and these expensive watches would be handed over.

'As you went round you realised that this was taken for granted. The amount of gifts and goodies that one now gets through in the sports world is quite extraordinary. Some critics call it bribery but that's too harsh a word. It was done simply to make people feel good about you. It's just become an absolute hotbed for gifts to try and make people feel warm and friendly towards you. Travelling round Montreal with Horst was an education because he had a way of treating every individual as his friend. Everyone was treated in a different way and you could see that he'd actually assessed the person's character and personality perfectly because he got to every one of them.'

Tommy Keller was the head of Swiss Timing, the president of the

International Rowing Federation and a man who spoke his mind. Over the years he unleashed a barrage of scathing attacks on other leaders of world sport whom he consistently characterised as second rate.

'Careers in sports administration are often substitutes for ambitions not reached in other fields, for example, business, military life, politics,' wrote Keller in a typical early broadside. 'The functions of sporting officials, however, are too often a means of fulfilling their own personal pride before anything else.'

In the years before his death in 1989 Keller became even more outspoken, castigating The Club which Dassler built. He complained bitterly that the new world of sport was 'dominated by a Latin American and Latino-European Mafia,' and he tried to remind his colleagues what he felt international sport was really about. 'Now the dominant factors are the pursuit of money and the satisfaction of personal ambitions,' said Keller. 'For me, the function of sport is to teach young people through competition to submit themselves to the rules of human society, not to serve the interests of sports officials who were not very successful in professional or political life. They have found a niche. Personal interests have become more important than the interests of sport.'

The Club's supporters belittled Keller, likening him to Don Quixote, tilting at windmills. His official Olympic obituary notes archly that he 'crusaded against the pressures of commercialism and big business, demanding that his own federation members retain their amateur status and that his officials work for nothing.'

But back in Montreal at the Games of '76, Keller's relationship with Dassler was good. Keller had long been a powerful figure in international sport. Keller fought hard for the interests of the federations against what he saw as an increasingly powerful IOC. As early as 1967 Keller had been one of the prime movers in an attempt to get the federations to form a united front in their dealings with the Olympic committee. Along with the swimming and wrestling federations he set up the General Assembly of International Sports Federations, known by its abbreviation of GAISF.

From the very start, this move caused trouble in the International Olympic Committee. Avery Brundage, then IOC president, refused to recognise GAISF because it did not include some of the most important sports. One of the Italian IOC members said GAISF would be a threat to both the IOC and the Olympic movement, claiming 'competence and money' which belonged to the IOC.

What lay at the root of these unusually heated disputes in the normally placid world of the IOC was money. Television payments for the rights to screen the Olympic Games were going to become an increasingly valuable source of revenue. TV companies paid nearly $10 million to broadcast the 1968 Olympic Games from Mexico; and that was just the beginning.

The TV pot stands at $633 million for the Barcelona Games but at the time, the size of the Mexico money was unheard of. In the years which followed the Mexico Games the TV companies just kept offering more. Four years later at Munich they paid $17.8 million. By the time that Dassler and Nally were launching 'stage three' at Montreal, the TV money stood at $34.8 million. The American Broadcasting Company alone paid $25 million.

'Tommy Keller was what I would call "one of the few," the honourable old school of sports administrators,' claims Nally. 'Tommy saw that the Games were suddenly becoming valuable. In the past the Olympics were jolly good fun, jolly good show chaps, let's all turn up and play the game. You didn't have to think about money because there wasn't any. Suddenly there's TV money.

'The US networks had decided that the Olympics were good business; they drove the ratings up and the advertisers followed. For the first time there were big profits to be made from the Games. Now what does that do? How do the international federations get their share of the money? Who gets what? Is it going to be an equal split? How does an international federation liaise with this body, the IOC, that's now becoming very rich?'

Keller was one of the first to see that a new forum would be needed to provide answers to these questions. He also wanted the federations to become a counterweight to the increasing clout of the IOC and that is why he started GAISF. Dassler and Nally also saw the advantages of an umbrella organisation but for rather different reasons.

'At that stage,' says Nally, 'GAISF was a loose body that met once a year. It didn't have any central administration, it didn't even have an HQ. Horst and I thought, if we can actually capture GAISF and give it an HQ and make it a centre of information and data, this will give us the ability of talking with lots of federations at once.'

*

It was a Prince and an American film star who provided the solution. Monaco's Rainier rules a miniature state whose few square miles of land cling to the Mediterranean coast between the jaws of France and Italy. The House of Grimaldi has faced a perpetual problem; how to sustain the economy of their little principality. The climate of the Côte d'Azur and the fame of Prince Rainier's wife, the late American film star Grace Kelly, helped. Plane loads of American tourists enchanted by the story of the 'Hollywood Goddess who fell in love with a Prince' were only too happy to fly into Nice, 'do Europe', and then slip over the border into Monte Carlo where English was once again spoken.

Gambling also helped. The legend of the 'man who broke the bank at Monte Carlo' had been carefully cultivated for years. But more than just the fading lustre of the Casino and Grace Kelly would be needed to sustain Monaco's leisure-based attractions in the 1980s. Prince Rainier was constantly engaged in the search for new business which would bring hard cash into Monte Carlo.

'Horst had a child-like enthusiasm about some things,' says Nally. 'He always fell over himself to meet his sporting heroes for example. It was the same with Monte Carlo, just the name of the place had a real attraction for him. Horst was terribly impressed and flattered when he was told that Prince Rainier would like to meet him.

'He was unbelievably excited. Rainier told him that he was trying to build up the image of the principality by associating it with prestige international events. They already had the successful motor racing Grand Prix, they also had Grand Prix tennis and he wanted to talk about how Horst could develop the principality as a centre for international sport.

'As part of developing this relationship with the Rainiers, Horst and I set up an office in Monte Carlo. We decided that the marketing element of our work with the federations, like the work we were doing with Havelange and FIFA, would be done through a joint company that Horst and I set up called SMPI – *Société Monégasque de Promotion International*.

'I was given a wonderful shoreline apartment with a great view out over the Mediterranean and a residence permit. Other people from the sports world were also becoming residents about that time and we used to get together regularly in what we called "Toy Town". It was great when everybody was there but when everybody left and we were on our own, it was a pretty depressing place with a just a load of wealthy geriatrics.

'At the time that we set up shop in Monte Carlo, Horst was talking regularly with Madame Monique Berlioux. She was the executive director and grande dame of the IOC. One of Monique's problems was that the Swiss government was reluctant to give permits to allow foreigners to come and work at the IOC headquarters in Lausanne. For a while there was a discussion about the possibility of resolving her problems by moving the IOC to Monte Carlo. Horst encouraged this bit of thinking as he wanted to please the Rainiers.

'Over lunch with Monique in Montreal it became clear that the plan wouldn't work. So Horst chatted with me about what else we could do for Monte Carlo. There was a lot of discussion about taking top sports stars in there to set up residence and run businesses, like Franz Beckenbauer and Bjorn Borg.

'But the big thing that we came up with was GAISF. We talked to Tommy Keller and it was eventually agreed that we would set up a permanent home for GAISF in Monte Carlo.' Prince Rainier provided Keller with the base for his organisation and in May 1977 the charming Villa Henri, complete with lemon tree in the back garden, was inaugurated as the new GAISF headquarters with Keller as its president.

'The meetings of the international federation people were great fun,' recalls Nally. 'They would roll up their sleeves and really enjoy themselves and have a good laugh, unlike the IOC meetings which are very stuffy and formal.'

The US TV networks were there in force. ABC, NBC and CBS were competing for the Olympics and the money they were prepared to spend was escalating. The American broadcasting giants were also trying to buy their way into many individual sports. ABC's *Wide World of Sports*, NBC's *Sports World* and their CBS rival, *Sports Spectacular*, were becoming high ratings shows. In Monte Carlo, money was no object. Whatever it cost, the US networks would pay and the federations were falling over themselves to get onto the gravy train.

'Each one of the networks would throw a party,' recalls Nally. 'It was great, it was like a flattery competition. We ate so well, drank so well, had great entertainment as they tried to outdo each other. Here were all these sports officials who once upon a time struggled to get around. Suddenly a world of riches opened out in front of them. I suppose that's what partly set the scene. If this was what the new world was like, then let's make sure we a get a piece of the action.'

Monte Carlo was a honeypot for Dassler and Nally. Here they were free to buzz around the federations rebuilding them in their own interests. They stressed the importance of keeping control over all the rights to the selling of their individual sports. Nally gave formal presentations on how to put together development programmes like soccer's, the need to go out in the market place to get the money. He talked to them about structuring their sporting calendars, highlighting the inevitable loss of TV revenues if they all held competitions on the same dates at the same time.

'GAISF became a very positive forum not only for federations but for us to develop very solid relationships with them,' says Nally. 'The basics of their commercial education were laid at Monte Carlo. The impetus to start world championships and world cup competitions in swimming, athletics, and gymnastics came from there. We changed the federations' attitudes.'

Each sport followed the example of football and developed new events. Nally introduced them to the concept of 'the package', where he would get a group of companies to fund a particular event.

'It couldn't be single sponsors like Coca-Cola anymore,' says Nally, 'because no one sponsor could be like a Coca-Cola with that sort of money. We organised the rowing championships with Tommy Keller and brought in half a dozen companies like Canon and Metaxa to support the event. We got involved with the Gymnastics World Cup. We got involved with the World Cycling Championships in Holland. That was an utter mess. The stadium held the rights to sell the advertising boards around the track. When we moved in with Heineken as our major sponsor, there was no room left to put their boards up in the arena. I had to show the federations how to get clean stadia for all their events. Absolutely none of them had any commercial understanding. None of them knew anything about TV. They were just a very innocent, hard-working group of amateurs.

'But as that money came in, as the importance of the Olympics grew, my God didn't it change. Suddenly you had the political people who could seize the opportunity. Some very clever, astute manipulators started seeing the potential. These were commercial entrepreneurs and political operators who were going to wheel and deal, get votes, get themselves elected. A whole new breed of sports administrator suddenly appeared the moment it started to become a lucrative area.'

CHAPTER 5

With Arm Raised I Salute You

Welcome to Barcelona – again. The opening ceremony of the Olympic Games is nearing its climax. The teams of athletes have circled the track and soon a lone runner will enter the Montjuic stadium with the Olympic torch. Juan Antonio Samaranch, the IOC President, steps forward to address the 70,000 spectators and the billions of TV viewers around the world.

'I have the honour of inviting King Juan Carlos to proclaim open the Games of the 25th Olympiad.' Watch the President's right arm, is it stirring, is it twitching, is it taking on a life of its own, compelled by some visceral force to rise to an angle of forty-five degrees from his shoulder?

No? Well, it always did. For nearly forty glorious years Juan Antonio Samaranch was an active supporter of the longest-lived dictatorial regime in Europe. Looking at modern Spain it's easy to forget that until seventeen years ago the country was a totalitarian police state run by General Francisco Franco. Many Spaniards emigrated or turned their backs on politics and hoped that one day, democracy might return to their country.

Not Samaranch; he put on the fascist Blue Shirt and paraded through the streets giving the fascist salute. He rose to become a fascist parliamentarian, a fascist member of the Barcelona City Council, fascist President of the Catalan Regional Council and, for a while, fascist Sports Minister. In his own words, Samaranch was 'one hundred per cent Francoist'. He bowed and scraped to the leader of a political system that was shunned and isolated by the Western democracies.

Samaranch does not see his life story this way. He presents himself as a lover of sport who became involved on the periphery of politics. I consider it right to practise politics for the betterment of sport,' he says, 'but I think it is wrong to use sport in the service of politics.' The record shows the opposite. Only four of the twenty-one years of his career in totalitarian politics in Spain were devoted full time to sports administration. The rest of the time sport was a vehicle for working his way towards the pinnacle of the Dictator's hierarchy. When Franco's repressive regime ended abruptly in Spain, Samaranch had no future in real politics. The only career left was in the politics of sport.

How has Samaranch been able to embrace two apparently contradictory philosophies? How did his fascist world view, which he proclaimed until his mid-fifties, gell with the Olympic Charter which pledges to fight discrimination and keep politics out of sport? Samaranch's answer has been to be all things to all men.

Even after he had risen to become an IOC vice president, touring the world as a guardian of the Olympic ideal, Samaranch continued to lift his right arm in the fascist salute at political gatherings in Spain.

Now, in the 1990s and centre stage on the Olympic rostrum, his achievement is unique. Every other old fascist from that era of Europe's twentieth-century history has long since disappeared in disgrace. Samaranch is the last reminder of that Europe of the dictators still strutting the world stage.

For the next two weeks, the centre of that world stage will be the Olympic arena. The Games are the first great Spanish public spectacle in which Samaranch has been prominent since the death of the tyrant Franco in 1975. Shortly afterwards, he packed his bags and departed from Spain with the condemnation of his fellow countrymen ringing in his ears. He has lived abroad ever since.

The fact sheets issued by the IOC about their beloved President omit such information. The true story of Juan Antonio Samaranch, who leads world sport, is the story of a man who has re-invented himself.

Samaranch has meticulously reconstructed his public image. 'He has devoted his entire life to Olympism and is a man of culture,' claims one handout from Lausanne. 'No Olympic leader since Pierre de Coubertin has possessed such a variety of talents as the current IOC president,' gushes former Swiss IOC member Raymond Gafner. 'Juan Antonio Samaranch has been both highly successful and unique in his stewardship of the Olympic Movement,' says Canada's Dick Pound. The word 'fascist' is conspicuously absent from all the tributes

Samaranch is projected as a benign, slightly imperial, older man, selflessly devoting his latter years to the youth of the world and preserving the Olympic ideal from rape by commerce and politics. It all sounds terribly impressive and is accepted unquestioningly in the profiles that pour out in every Olympic year. The problem is, little or none of it is true.

Samaranch has become more handsome in his maturity. Photographs of the young businessman forty years ago in the company of the generals who wielded power in Spain reveal the sharp face of a hungry opportunist.

Today his physical features have mellowed. He has the appearance of a kindly old gentleman. As he prepares to make his short speech opening the Games, Samaranch can look back on his own wealthy and successful life in Spain with pride. But his experience was unusual. Tens of thousands of his fellow Spaniards were shot, tortured or jailed by military tribunals. Why? Initially because they had fought on the losing side in the civil war and later because they objected to living in poverty under the yoke of a one-party state. There were no civil liberties in Spain and no free elections until 1977. Until then, opposition parties were illegal.

Samaranch joined the fascist movement in his teens. He stayed loyal until it was disbanded on the eve of Spain's first democratic elections some forty years later. Samaranch never voluntarily tore up his party card. He remained loyal until fascism died under him.

The *Movimiento*, the Spanish fascist movement, controlled every aspect of life from justice to politics, from wages to sports administration. The dictatorship of General Franco mirrored the Stalinist despotisms of the East and nowhere more so than in sport. Healthy recreational activity was not for the benefit of young people, the enjoyment of their elders and a source of decency and harmony. It was a muscular advertisement for the credibility of the dictator's regime. With right arm raised upwards and wearing his *Movimiento* uniform of Blue Shirt and white military jacket, Samaranch set out to use sport to bring himself and the movement success.

He has done the same with the Olympics. Over the last decade Samaranch has turned the traditionally part-time, honorary position of Olympic leader into a full-time chief executive officer's post. He has fired the former paid director and created an imperial, presidential retinue and bureaucracy. For all the pronouncements about 'sport for all' Samaranch has managed to elevate the Olympic presidency to an aloof and Olympian status. Like a monarch – or a dictator – he occasionally descends for photocalls with selected athletes and other supplicants. But like the astute politician he was for twenty-five years, Samaranch has not only re-invented himself, he has re-fashioned the Olympic movement in his own style of politics: the leader grants and accepts audiences with heads of state; the leader issues orders; the leader selects new IOC members and imposes them on the movement; the leader knows best; the leader's will is carried out; the leader appears at press conferences flanked by the banners of the movement.

One of the most significant days in the life of young Juan Antonio Samaranch was 17 July 1936. It was his sixteenth birthday and it was the day that General Franco hoisted the standard of revolt. Earlier that year the Spanish people had elected a left-of-centre Popular Front government. The rich, the conservatives and the military refused to accept the verdict of the ballot box. Franco's rebellion was greeted with relief in the Samaranch household.

Franco was supported by Hitler and Mussolini who had already established the other great European dictatorships. Military garrisons all over Spain rebelled in support of Franco. The proud Catalans resisted Franco's armies for three years and Barcelona was one of the last major cities to fall to the Dictator. Resistance collapsed after the city was bombed by the Germans and Italians, practising for the world war that would begin within a year.

Samaranch came from a family of rich Barcelona textile manufacturers. His natural inclination was to rush to the fascist standard but this was impossible. Catalonia remained loyal to the elected government and Franco's 'nationalist' armies were hundreds of miles to the south.

Instead Samaranch joined the youth fascist organisation. His activities came to the attention of the police. He was summoned for an interview and his mother dressed him in tennis shorts to make him look younger than his years. The police let him go. Just before his eighteenth birthday Samaranch was conscripted into the republican army.

'Right from the beginning he was quite distant from all the other soldiers,' remembered Juan Llarch, who joined up the same day. 'His tactic was always to stick very closely to the captain, to the other officers and, a curious thing, he always had tobacco and chocolate – in those days there were very little going around – and when the captain ran out of cigars or cigarettes, he always had some to offer him.'

Juan Llarch had identified Samaranch's style of operating. 'This is what he's done all his life, offering something else to obtain something much greater.'

Samaranch had no intention of staying with the republican army a day longer than he had to. Llarch recalled how Samaranch's brief stay in the army of democracy ended. 'His objective was to get permission to leave and when he did leave he said that he wasn't coming back and was going to stay in Barcelona in the Red Cross. Afterwards I learned that once he was in Barcelona he deserted and went into hiding.'

Llarch became a prominent writer after the war. He did not see his turncoat colleague again until many years later, by which time Samaranch was an important public figure. Llarch said that Samaranch's manner was chilly and he didn't want to be seen with him.

'Samaranch now cries "Long live Catalonia" and tries to appear more democratic than anyone else,' said Llarch in the late 1970s, 'but we know that he has been Francoist all his life.'

Franco took few prisoners after his victory in 1939. He executed an estimated 200,000 opponents and more than a million refugees fled the country. His revenge on Catalonia and Barcelona, which opposed him most bitterly, was proportionately severe. In the month that Samaranch celebrated his nineteenth birthday the fascists were executing upwards of 500 people a week in the city. Visitors to the Olympic Games in the Montjuic stadium will be but a few minutes' walk from the old garrison of the same name where the enemies of the man who became IOC president were taken to be put down like dogs.

What Samaranch's political movement did to Catalonia after the Civil War is in bleak contrast to the Olympic ideals he now proclaims.

Every city granted the Games must agree to sponsor a cultural festival; it must 'symbolise the universality and diversity of human culture'. Barcelona's will feature the diversity of Catalan culture.

Fifty years ago Franco and his *Movimiento* set out to murder that culture. In scenes reminiscent of the Nazi book burning in Germany, the Catalan language was banned and private book collections and museums vandalised. Even stocks of bus tickets printed in Catalan were burned in the streets.

The ban on the Catalan language ran long after the execution squads were disbanded. In the 1960s, when Samaranch was a rising fascist politician, a Catalan singer, performing in Spanish, won the first prize in the Mediterranean Song Festival. The song was duly entered for the Eurovision Song Contest whereupon the courageous artist announced that it would be delivered in Catalan. The government immediately refused the singer permission to take part.

The language of the conqueror, Castilian Spanish, was imposed on the region of Samaranch's birth. Samaranch, a Catalan speaker all his life, was content to deny his own heritage. After Franco died there suddenly appeared a new entry in his IOC biography. As well as Spanish, French, English and Russian, Samaranch now admitted that he also spoke Catalan.

After the Civil War Samaranch joined his family's textile business. He became a manager and, with a non-union workforce producing considerable profits, was free to devote time to his real priority; manipulating sport to further his political ambitions. He used his family wealth to buy favours and lived the lifestyle of a young man about town.

In his early twenties Samaranch was a fixture in the Barcelona nightclubs that catered to the rich élite. Attractive young women could escape the poverty of the times by selling themselves as hostesses in these clubs. They were known as *cortesanos* and were hired by the male customers and Samaranch, according to his associates, rented more women than anyone else. It seems that few were for his own use. He would rent tables complete with girls in half a dozen clubs each night and then make gifts of them to his friends. With his unending largesse Samaranch soon became one of the leaders of the rich young set in Barcelona.

He became the subject of much gossip. His friends claimed that he kept the particulars of each girl in a pocket notebook and that over the years he built a collection of forty such books. Those who knew Samaranch say that he would list the girls' birthdays and the presents he had bought them. From early manhood he was documenting a lifelong habit; making gifts – and waiting to call in the favour.

In the early 1940s he took up boxing and competed as a featherweight in the Catalonia championships. Entering the ring in a silk dressing gown with the emblem 'Kid Samaranch' on the back he stormed to victory in the second round. There was sly comment that, without his knowledge, his rich friends had paid his opponent to fall down!

His own time in the ring was brief. Samaranch soon gave up serious competition to begin his life's work as an administrator. He cast around for an opening, for an opportunity that no one else had seized. He saw the potential in the sport of roller hockey, then popular in Spain and a handful of other countries. It was underfunded and there could be long-term benefits for a rich patron.

In 1943 he approached the Español sports club and formed a roller hockey section. Two years later he persuaded the Spanish Sports Minister, General Moscardó, to let him apply to join the international roller hockey federation and in 1946 he attended their congress in Montreux. It was Samaranch's first step on to the world sporting scene.

Samaranch was successful, at home and away. He built up the Spanish national team, funding them from his own pocket. Instinctively he had set out on the same path that has produced many of today's leaders of The Club; he used his own money to buy sporting – and so sports politics – success.

Another tranche of Samaranch's profits from the textile business went into funding the world roller hockey championships in June 1951. They were held in Barcelona. It was not just altruism; it was a carefully calculated investment paying off. Spain had been ostracised by the international community since 1945. Most Western governments refused to recognise a regime that had sent troops to fight with the Nazis. The UN had slammed the door in Franco's face. Samaranch's initiative, staging an international event in Barcelona, was the beginning of his country's slow trek back to international acceptance. There was a bonus; the Spanish team skated away with the championship.

For the mass of the people of Barcelona life was small crusts of bread and roller hockey circuses. While Samaranch enjoyed his rented girls, his cars and his success with the roller hockey team the bulk of the population teetered on the edge of starvation. 'The forties and early fifties were years of intense suffering for the majority of the Spanish people,' wrote Oxford historian Raymond Carr. 'Fountain pens were bought on the instalment system, toothbrushes were re-conditioned. Poverty bred prostitution and there were so many beggars that the police fined those who gave alms.'

Samaranch could be confident that his textile factories would make profits. In Franco's Spain strikes were forbidden and wages held down at gunpoint. Desperation bred rage. The roller hockey championships were staged against an horrific background. The illegal trade unions had called a general strike. Three hundred thousand workers responded. Police reinforcements arrived by rail and destroyers disembarked troops in the port. The police opened fire, two workers were killed and twenty-five wounded. The workers were forced back into the factories and thousands arrested. For many of them, the strike had been a disaster. For Samaranch it was a great success.

Stage-managing Spain's victory in the roller hockey championships had raised Samaranch's importance with Spain's only political party, the *Movimiento*, which incorporated the fascist party, the Falange. A decade earlier he had joined its youth wing, the *Frente de Juventudes*. Off the back of his sporting success he attempted to launch his real ambition, a career in politics.

On 22 October 1951 Samaranch wrote to the regional party boss asking to be selected as a candidate for the Barcelona city council elections. These were not elections of the kind that a citizen of any democratic country would recognise. The people of Barcelona had no say in the outcome. The Party alone 'elected' the council at one of its private meetings and the people were told by the state-controlled media who their new rulers were to be.

In the archives of the former Falangist Civil Governor of Barcelona are two fascinating documents from 1951. The first – number 994 – is full of praise for Samaranch. It seems that during the general strike the party had been woefully short of activists and it says, 'Samaranch has been one of the few Falangists present during the days of the strike.' Strike breakers had been in short supply and Samaranch had put in commendable hard work at the City Hall. But his private life posed a problem.

The Falange's secret police, who spied on everyone, were disturbed by Samaranch's playboy image. They thought it unacceptable in a civic leader. The second report – document 884 – criticised him for making gifts of cars to 'his many and changing girlfriends'. It concluded, 'We do not believe that he has the maturity to hold a public position.'

Undeterred by this rejection, Samaranch set out to win more sporting prestige for Spain. He became vice president of the committee organising the second Mediterranean Games which to his great good fortune were due to be held in Barcelona in 1955. This was another major event which would divert international attention from the continuing repression. It would also bring Samaranch the break through into politics that he craved. One of the factors of his success in the 1950s was a theme which followed him into his Olympic career; an unquestioning media.

His Mediterranean Games committee sought massive, favourable press coverage. To achieve it, they simply bribed the journalists. Like the good Falangist bureaucrats that they were, they wrote the scheme down. It is still stored today in the archive of the Civil Governor.

'In every publication there is a key man that by putting himself on the side of the Organisation – or turns a blind eye – and without writing a single line can motivate the treatment of the Organisation,' it runs. 'We need to talk to these men personally, before the propaganda campaign starts in the Press, and offer them money for their collaboration.'

This kind of routine bribery was the lubricant of Franco's Spain. Corrupt politics bred a corrupt society. The very businessmen who spoke most highly of the Generalissimo would often pay no taxes, steal from the state and practise blatant frauds. To Franco, it was an acceptable way of rewarding some supporters and buying off others who might make trouble.

Samaranch achieved a better press than many of his *Movimiento* colleagues. There was a corps of journalists in Barcelona who pumped out endless praise of him. He was a noted giver of presents to journalists, just as he was to the 'rent girls' of the nightclubs. There were even stories of journalists who had never met him receiving silver salvers as wedding presents.

According to a report in the IOC *Review*, the Mediterranean Games of 1955 were a huge success. 'They illustrated the Olympic ideal triumphing among the countries surrounding the "Mare Nostrum" from where our civilisation originated,' enthused the report. 'The prestige of these memorable days in Barcelona was enhanced by the presence of eight IOC members.'

The Games were 'an educational manifestation, filled with history, art, philosophy and beauty. The important thing was not to win but to have the honour to participate in them.' The author forgot to point out that the honour of participating had been denied one of the countries bordering on the Mediterranean – Israel. The author was Juan Antonio Samaranch.

With his idolatrous press coverage in full swing Samaranch sought once more to be 'elected' to the Barcelona city council. He applied again to the *Movimiento*. Again the rubber heels were sent to investigate his private life. The subsequent report, dated 6 November 1954, revealed that Samaranch's personal life had not improved. It was written cautiously with a coded sting in the tail.

'This man enjoys great prestige in sport. He is a perfect gentleman. Politically he identifies himself with the regime. With respect to his moral conduct, and bearing in mind his wealth, his age, and his circle of friends he shows neither ostentation nor scandal in his female friendships or affairs of the heart. He has many, and there has been a rumour that he owns a bachelor apartment for such needs. He is single.'

Despite this, the nomination went through. Samaranch was now too powerful to be ignored politically. At last, he had made it into big-time fascist politics, running Spain's second city. He was placed in charge of a wealthy suburb and given political responsibility for sport in the city. There was only one condition. Up to that point he had been a Party sympathiser, but not a Party member. Now he had to take out a *Movimiento* Party card if he wanted promotion. Samaranch signed up.

There was one more delicate adjustment required to guarantee his rise. The Civil Governor had a private word. 'Samaranch,' he told him, 'I believe that all councillors should be married.'

The signal was clear; if Samaranch wanted political advancement in the Party he would have to find a bride. Soon, his engagement to María Teresa Salisachs was announced. Universally known as 'Bibis' she was from another wealthy family. They were married within the year. Salvador Dali designed the wedding invitations.

Samaranch now had his eyes set on national power. He had lost four years since he first sought a political post on the city council and he wanted to make up for lost time. He also wanted to be a politician on the regional council, governing all of Catalonia.

The electoral process, as usual, had nothing to do with the ballot box. He approached a Barcelona doctor who was an influential figure in the *Movimiento* and, coincidentally, was funded by Samaranch's father. The doctor made a phone call. The next day the press announced that Juan Antonio Samaranch was now a regional councillor and also responsible for all sport in Catalonia.

The success of the Israeli-free Mediterranean Games was appreciated by the government. More phone calls were made and in 1956 Samaranch was nominated by the regional council to sit on the national committee for sport in Madrid. There was a price to be paid but to a man of Samaranch's opinions, it was far from odious. He had to continually demonstrate his unwavering loyalty to the *Movimiento*. Accordingly, his letters to senior sports officials were concluded with the ringing phrase 'Always at your command, I salute you with my arm raised.'

As for Samaranch himself, it removes any doubt that to him, sport was *the* route to political success. In Franco's Spain there was no differentiation between sport and politics. Sport was simply another tool of government in the all-embracing totalitarian state. It was a tool Samaranch could use to great effect. The generation of generals who had won the Civil War and become the government were rooted in an earlier century. They had little understanding of modern sport. Samaranch was clever, energetic, loyal and politically ambitious. He sought political advancement and at the same time would improve Spain's sporting image and keep sport under fascist control. They were pleased and progressively opened the door to their club.

Samaranch had made it from the political backwater of Catalonia to the centre of power in Madrid. But there followed a decade of frustration. He was not received well in all quarters of the Madrid political establishment. Samaranch's wealth and obvious ambition made him unpopular and he was nicknamed the 'señorito' – the spoiled brat.

But Samaranch, the Catalan textile magnate, used the time to make the contacts that would build a second fortune. In Madrid he met the financier Jaime Castell who became a business partner and a close friend. They embarked on a number of speculative property developments to cater for the influx of tourists on the Catalan coast. Samaranch also went on the board of more companies: banks, manufacturing and construction companies. Castell was well connected in Madrid. Through him Samaranch met the Franco family. He and Bibis became particularly close to the dictator's daughter Carmen.

A decade of patience and the astute distribution of gifts was finally rewarded in December 1966 when the Sports Minister stood down. Samaranch was chosen by General Franco to follow him.

The newspapers and the newsreels played a key role in Samaranch's rise. He had learned early that a combination of censorship, bribes and favours to journalists was essential to promote his political career. Now he ventured into newspaper ownership. He joined the board of Barcelona's *Tele-Exprés*. One journalist who worked there described his role as that of a 'political inspector'. When a report appeared about workers being sacked by a textile company Samaranch cut the report out and sent it to the editor with a note which read, 'As always, writing for the ones who don't read newspapers. We are going nowhere this way.'

But Samaranch was going places. He had joined the fascist-controlled Spanish Olympic committee in 1956. One of the key factors in his political rise in Spain was the influence he built – for himself and for Spain – in the Olympic movement. As early as 1961, five years before joining the IOC, Samaranch invited the wife of IOC President Avery Brundage to stay at his summer villa on the Costa Brava. The favour paid off. In 1965 the IOC held its annual session in Madrid. It was opened by the Head of State. General Franco could portray himself as a patron of the Olympic ideal of decency and fair play.

When a vacancy occurred for a new Spanish member of the IOC the following year, there was little doubt that Samaranch would be the nominee. At the next IOC meeting, Samaranch joined the Olympic élite.

CHAPTER 6

The Clever Chameleon

The Olympic flame bursts into life. Barcelona's Games have begun. At last the Montjuic stadium fulfils its Olympic destiny. Mayor Pasqual Maragall is the man who made it all possible. He has spent the last six years driving the team which has organised the Games of the 25th Olympiad. Maragall may be forgiven if he does not welcome the IOC president effusively. He is Barcelona's *socialist* Mayor and his family suffered not so many years ago at the hands of Samaranch's *Movimiento*. His brothers were arrested and his sister Monica was jailed for printing anti-Franco literature.

These two men represent contrasting strands of Spain's politics. The socialist was elected in a fair democratic process. The fascist won power firstly through influential contacts and then through a sham electoral system. This is another true story that cannot be found in Samaranch's IOC biographies.

By the mid-1960s the Spanish economy was in a mess. The Western democracies had slammed the door in Franco's face. They refused to let his dictatorship trade with the European Community. To survive, Spain needed to sell to France, Germany, Italy and its other neighbours across the Pyrenees. Franco was looking for a way to soften the hard image of his repressive regime. In 1967 he came up with a novel idea: elections.

The Spanish people were at last offered democracy but only on the *Movimiento*'s terms. They would be allowed to vote for members of Spain's parliament, the Cortes. Franco's idea of a democratic 'election' allowed him to appoint eighty-three per cent of the deputies; the people could vote for the remaining seventeen per cent of the seats.

Two types of candidates were permitted; right-wingers and ultra right-wingers. Before candidates could put their names forward they had first to declare their allegiance to the General. That ruled out any centre, liberal or left candidates. Just to be on the safe side all political parties remained banned – except for the official *Movimiento*.

One of the two official *Movimiento* candidates for Barcelona in 1967 was Juan Antonio Samaranch. He was elected with more than half a million votes. Second, close behind, came an independent right-winger called Eduardo Tarragona. Disillusioned by the lack of choice, only fifty-three per cent of the electorate had bothered to go to the polls.

Tarragona frightened the *Movimiento*. He gave Barcelona a chance to register a vote against Francoism. His campaign had to be shackled. 'They used every time-honoured device to obstruct him,' wrote one historian. 'They prevented him holding meetings in Barcelona until five days before the election; for one public meeting he was allocated a school classroom seating thirty, while for another he was given a hall without chairs. In contrast Samaranch had all the resources of the *Movimiento* at his disposal.'

Many Catalans preferred to vote with their feet. As Samaranch was 'elected' to the Cortes, the workers struck, demanding decent wages. A State of Emergency was declared, protesters were jailed. This was the framework of Samaranch's 'democratic' triumph.

Samaranch could be satisfied with his political achievements. By 1967 he was an MP, a Government Minister and a close friend of the Franco family. He was also a multi-millionaire and the darling of the media. He travelled Spain promoting himself and sport. He and Bibis saw the new year in at a country palace in the company of the dictator. But Samaranch was flying too high.

In 1970 he fell to earth. He was sacked. He lost his job as Minister of Sport. He was brought down by his own uncontrolled ambition. Samaranch's style jarred with the grey old men of the regime in Madrid. These reactionary veterans of the Civil War found the '*señorito*' Samaranch too pushy.

His fatal mistake was to annoy the protocol-conscious bureaucrats of the *Movimiento*. Firstly, he side-stepped them and directly invited Prince Juan Carlos to travel to Tunisia for the Mediterranean Games.

His second gaffe was to invite Franco to inaugurate a new sports centre.

The General Secretary of the *Movimiento* fumed. He had read about it in the press! Samaranch had over-stepped the mark. The old men gave the pushy youngster his come-uppance and a new Sports Minister was appointed. Samaranch was not fired because he had fallen out with fascism; it was just a clash of personalities. He was neither expelled nor did he resign from the *Movimiento*. He kept all his other positions in the Party and in Spanish politics. He suffered no more than a slap on the wrist.

'Elections' for the rubber stamp Cortes were called again in 1971. Yet again they were held against a background of rising civil discontent. The workers and the students, and by then the middle classes, had had enough of dictatorship and poverty whilst the friends of Franco lived in luxury. To protect their privileges, the *Movimiento* gave the police *carte blanche* to open fire.

Three workers were shot dead in Granada. In Barcelona 300 intellectuals gathered to protest at the Montserrat Monastery, the spiritual home of Catalanism. This was illegal. The police surrounded the monastery for two days and threatened to storm the building. When the protesters came out, many were arrested and punished.

At the 'elections' Samaranch was once again the official *Movimiento* candidate and once again his greatest rival was the independent right-winger Eduardo Tarragona. After his 1967 election Tarragona had started weekly surgeries for his constituents. This was a dangerous precedent; it suggested politicians should be responsive to the voters. Tarragona created residents' associations to protest the lack of schools, lighting and sewerage. He denounced middle-class tax evasion and urged slum clearance, cheap housing and more schools. He campaigned for social security benefits for subnormal children. In the Cortes he voted against the budgets because 'they were unacceptable to any competent accountant'.

Despite the advantages of being an 'official' candidate the 1971 'election' was nearly a disaster for Samaranch. He had two political slogans: 'No one ever did so much for sport' and 'We shall achieve the forty-hour week.' The electorate turned their backs on the polls. Turnout fell to an abysmal thirty-five per cent. Worse still, Tarragona soared past Samaranch, whose own vote slumped. Samaranch just managed to scrape back into the Cortes. Shortly after the 'election' a worker was shot dead during a strike at the Barcelona SEAT car plant. He never did see the forty-hour week.

The fact that Samaranch played a prominent role in a totalitarian system has never been disclosed by the IOC. In 1974 when he became an IOC vice president the Olympic *Review* reported that Samaranch held 'the record for the number of votes in the Spanish Parliament'. That had been in 1967. The *Review* published this claim long after his vote had collapsed in the second Cortes elections.

The Olympic movement was vital to Samaranch the politician; if fascism collapsed in Spain then Olympic sport could be used to launch an alternative career abroad. The IOC, the guardian of the lofty and Corinthian ideals of the Olympic Games, would provide the perfect cover for Samaranch to re-invent himself.

The IOC was still a gentlemen's club. A hard-working opportunist could – and did – go far. At the Mexico Games in 1968, just two years after he joined the IOC, Samaranch was put in charge of Olympic protocol. It was an ideal position for a man with a passion for rules, for regulations and for order. And it was a key post for a man with ambition. Now the junior member had the opportunity to raise his profile with the worldwide IOC membership.

The new head of protocol addressed the *chefs de mission* at the Sapporo winter Games in 1972. It was their duty, Samaranch told them, to impress on their athletes the importance of the opening ceremony. Any athlete who missed the parade would be guilty of 'gross impoliteness, cheating and damaging the moral value of the Games'.

Samaranch was also a stickler for the closing ceremony. He ruled that 'Strict but voluntary discipline must be observed by everyone. Athletes are not permitted to wave handkerchiefs, no cameras should be carried, and it is forbidden to break ranks.' It all smacked of Samaranch's authoritarian life at home in Spain with the emphasis on militaristic display, order and discipline.

The less ambitious members of the IOC seldom sit on the key Olympic committees. Samaranch rose fast. Soon he joined the press commission and then became a member of the executive board – the IOC's inner cabinet. Samaranch appeared to be on the fast track to the top. But this alone was not enough to secure the ultimate post in world sport, the presidency of the IOC. How could Samaranch get that extra edge? What could he do to guarantee a majority of the IOC votes? There could be only one answer: he had to make an alliance with the puppet-master from Landersheim.

How could Samaranch build the bridge to Horst Dassler? Since the late 1960s he had known Christian Jannette, the Frenchman who had been deputy head of protocol at the Munich Games. Jannette had been headhunted by Dassler and taken off to work on the Adidas political team.

'At Munich Samaranch was chief of protocol of the IOC and I had to work a lot with him and we became very good friends,' Jannette told us. 'In 1974 Samaranch knew that I was working with Horst and he told me that he would be interested to meet him. He invited us to Barcelona to his home and we spent two or three days there.

'Horst wanted to meet anybody who was involved in sports organisation and of course Samaranch was one of the most important men even at that time. He was chief of protocol of the IOC and people often say that the chief of protocol is the next president. I knew that Samaranch would like to be president. I told Horst that he was a good man, that he was ambitious and he worked very hard. Horst liked him. Later they became very good friends.'

Patrick Nally soon came across Dassler and Samaranch together on the Adidas entertainment circuit. 'Horst was talking to him in a way that made it clear that this was part of the build up to win the IOC,' recalls Nally. 'He knew he wanted to be the president of the IOC long before he went for it openly. Havelange got to the top on his own and then relied on Horst. I think that Samaranch was the first major player who campaigned full time but with Horst ever at his elbow.

'Samaranch was the beginning of the new breed of people who could see the big opportunity. They were going out there to campaign politically to get themselves elected. At that stage anybody who was going to do that went first of all to Landersheim, saw Horst and did a deal with him. You did a deal with Horst first and then he helped you to get elected.'

In one of the VIP stands at the Barcelona opening ceremony is Jordi

Pujol, the democratically elected president of the region of Catalonia. Like Samaranch he is a conservative and also a banker. The similarities end there. Samaranch tied himself to Franco, the *Movimiento* and the murder of Catalanism. Pujol fought for his language, his culture and for political freedom.

Franco paid an official visit to Barcelona in 1960. At a special concert many in the audience courageously began to sing Catalonia's banned national anthem. The authorities were furious. The doors were locked and the police called. The protesters were arrested and beaten up. Franco's secret police got to work and identified Jordi Pujol as the organiser of the protest. He was given a seven-year jail sentence. His reward from the people of Catalonia, when democracy finally came, was the high office he now holds. His predecessor in the post, Juan Antonio Samaranch, was not elected but appointed by the *Movimiento* in Madrid.

The presidency of Franco's rubber-stamp regional council in Catalonia in the early 1970s was an important political position. It had nothing to do with sport. By 1973, as Franco's life moved to its close, a mood of change swept the country. The dying General responded by appointing Admiral Carrero Blanco as Prime Minister. He was one of the most reactionary and hardline of Franco's colleagues from the civil war. A month later Carrero Blanco chose the best man, in the view of the regime, to keep rebellious Catalonia under control. That man was Juan Antonio Samaranch.

Samaranch made clear once again his opposition to democracy. At his inauguration he declared, 'I proclaim in an unequivocal way the loyalty and fidelity that ties my heart to the regime, fidelity to the principles of the *Movimiento*, my submission to the Prince of Spain and absolute loyalty to Franco.'

Five days before Christmas 1973 a bomb blew Carrero Blanco to pieces. The Basque terrorist group ETA had taken their revenge in a Madrid street. 'He was one of the greatest Spanish men of this century,' declared the leader of Catalonia. 'He represents everything that a good Spaniard should be.' Samaranch conferred the gold medal of the regional council posthumously on Carrero Blanco.

The assassination triggered a new reign of terror. Samaranch's job was to oversee the clampdown in Catalonia. 'Throughout 1974 and 1975 repression in the form of widespread arrests, torture and execution as well as the ready resort to firearms by the police and the civil guard increased to a level not seen since the late 1940s,' wrote one historian.

Samaranch seemed incapable of separating himself from the *Movimiento*. One incident that typified his endless loyalty, even as the undertakers' men prepared themselves for Spain's greatest state funeral in forty years, came early in 1974. Opponents of the regime had attempted to desecrate the monument in Barcelona to the *Franquistas* who died in the civil war. Tens of thousands of fascist supporters were bussed into Barcelona for a protest march through the city. Samaranch, dressed in his Blue Shirt and giving the fascist salute, took part in the parade.

Right until the bitter end Samaranch stayed loyal to the dictator. Franco's health was failing through 1975 but Samaranch did not desert the sinking ship of state. On 26 January and by now an IOC vice president, Samaranch put on his Blue Shirt and led the annual celebrations to commemorate the fascist 'liberation' of Barcelona. As always, he was seen to raise his right arm in the fascist salute.

At Easter, when the *Movimiento* celebrated mass, he again dressed up in his uniform. Later that year, again in his Blue Shirt he attended a mass for the fascist fallen of the civil war.

By the late autumn of 1975 Franco was near death. His family and old guard generals from the Civil War watched helplessly as the old man drifted away. He lay on his deathbed clutching the mummified arm of St Teresa, attached to every life support machine known to modern medicine. The rumour from the hospital was that he had been dead for several days. His inner circle refused to let the doctors pull the plugs.

On 20 November the Blue-Shirted Samaranch joined the annual ceremony in Barcelona to commemorate the founder of the Falange. Thirty years after the defeat of the Nazis a vice president of the IOC was strutting the streets with his uniformed comrades defiantly giving the salute that was the very antithesis of the Olympic ideal.

Late that same night he received the phone call he had been dreading. Franco was dead. Samaranch went to the Catalan regional headquarters and summoned troops to defend the building. Samaranch then sent telegrams of condolences to the Franco family, of loyalty to the king and of support for the government.

The next day Samaranch addressed the regional council. 'Spain and Catalonia are experiencing a bitter feeling of being orphaned,' he said, 'but there is no reason to be disheartened because we are a nation with a faith and a king. This is Franco's legacy.'

He ended his speech with the following phrase; 'The example of Franco will be with us always in the fight for a better Spain.' It was not just the sentiment that was odious; it was that Samaranch had switched to Catalan, the language he had denied for forty years, the language that his Leader had gone to any length to crush.

Six weeks later Samaranch attended the 1976 annual ceremony commemorating the 'liberation' of Barcelona. It was the first one since Franco's death. For the first time Samaranch left his Blue Shirt in his wardrobe. He wore a white one instead.

Samaranch was desperately looking for a new niche for his brand of old politics. A Catalan language magazine called *Arreu* published a long and damning summary of his years serving the old regime. It was the first time in forty years that anybody had dared to criticise Samaranch publicly.

The headline on the article was 'Samaranch, we're not part of your set-up.' A team of three journalists had researched his political career. Their conclusion was that they did not believe Samaranch's frequent claim, 'I consider it right to practise politics for the betterment of sport, but I think it is wrong to use sport in the service of politics.' They had no doubt that Samaranch had used sport to further his political career.

'Here we are dealing with a very clever chameleon,' they wrote, 'because he cleverly graduated the changes – but he has not been able to deceive public opinion.'

Fortunately for Samaranch the spirit of the new Spain was one of reconciliation. There would be no war crimes tribunals. But Samaranch's political career was dead. His record of complicity with the dictatorship destroyed any future for him in his own country.

The end for Samaranch in Spain came on 23 April 1977; 100,000 people demonstrated outside the Catalan regional council building in Barcelona. While the president stayed behind locked doors they shouted abuse which we can only translate as 'Samaranch, Get Out!'

★

'One of the most important decisions of my life,' admitted Samaranch some years later, 'came when I realised my public life in Spain was finished. Not only politically but socially.' But Samaranch was not finished. He decided to re-invent himself. This was not difficult for a 'clever chameleon'.

The dilemma for Spain and for Samaranch was that he had to be got rid of but both sides needed a face-saving formula. He was still in place as president of the regional council and Spain's interim government did not seek confrontation as it planned the return of democracy. The solution Madrid came up with was the diplomatic service. With his international experience at the IOC and his deftness at surviving the twists and turns of *Movimiento* politics for three decades Samaranch could be an asset to Spain – if he was abroad.

The legend in the foreign ministry in Madrid is that he was offered a comfortable but lightweight posting to Vienna but declined it. Instead, Samaranch was keen to be sent to the austere capital of the Soviet Union. The civil service was mystified but Samaranch had his reasons. There was a new political campaign for the chameleon to wage.

Spain's loss was the IOC's gain. With great relief the country of his birth parted company with one of its leading fascists. On 18 July 1977 Samaranch departed for Moscow to re-open diplomatic relations that had been broken forty years earlier. In Moscow his priority would be representing himself.

The Russians had just three years left to complete their organisation of the 1980 Olympics. The Games were to be a showcase for their political system. But the Soviet bureaucracy creaked and the officials had great difficulties in meeting the needs of both the international sports federations and the IOC. Now, to their great relief, they had Samaranch on their doorstep. He was the first vice president of the IOC: the number two in the Olympic hierarchy.

Everybody in sports politics could see the deal on the table. In 1980 Lord Killanin would retire from the leadership of the IOC; Samaranch was hungry to step into his shoes. He was actively canvassing every IOC vote on offer. The Russians controlled a sizeable block of East European IOC votes and those of their client states worldwide.

'Samaranch always wanted to become president of the IOC, long before his time in Moscow,' recalls Christian Jannette. 'The Russians were thankful for what he could do for them. He was helping them a lot in that time. It was not easy for the USSR to organise the Games.

'One thing I must say: the Russians do not forget what you do for them. Horst Dassler did a lot for them and they never forgot it. Even before 1970 I remember the Dassler family being generous with equipment and so on even though the Russians had no money.'

The scene was set. Dassler was prepared to range all his contacts behind Samaranch – in the hope that there would be a payback.

The arrival of the amateur diplomat in Moscow raised eyebrows among the professionals. They had all been posted to the capital of the super power because they were the cream of their countries' foreign services. How would this fifty-seven-year-old reject from a collapsed dictatorship perform in such a rarefied atmosphere? He turned out to be surprisingly competent. In many ways it was not a difficult posting for a clever chameleon. Spain was not a major political player in Moscow. Samaranch could devote his time to his own image. His work rate was excellent.

The dedicated Francoist who for forty years had backed the campaign of extermination against communists in Spain, their jailing, torture and execution, turned a typical somersault. He ingratiated himself at every turn. The irony was superb. All his life Samaranch had fought against the 'Reds' – now he was going to woo them to win the ultimate prize in sport. On the anniversary of Spain's national day Samaranch appeared on Russian TV and delivered a three-minute speech of friendship – in Russian. He had worked hard not only learning the language but memorising the words. The man had no shame; whether it was the Catalan or Russian languages, the chameleon would tell people what they wanted to hear.

The new Spanish embassy on Paliashvili Street opened its doors to all; lavish 'Spanish nights' enlivened an otherwise drab Moscow. It was one of many ironies about Samaranch; his allowances from Spain were not great and he funded much of the entertaining for the comrades out of the fortune he amassed in Spain in the days when wages were held down and taxes were minimal for friends of the regime. The press reported that Juan and Bibis gave some of the better parties in town. Their wine cellar was reputed to be the best.

It was now, as part of the process of re-inventing himself, that Samaranch the amateur diplomat adopted the ambassador's title of 'His Excellency' – usually shortened to 'HE'. A dozen years after that brief envoy's post in Moscow, much of the Olympic world still refers to him, reverentially, as 'HE'.

The votes that gave Samaranch the presidency of the IOC were won in Moscow and in the back rooms of the Spanish organising committee for the 1982 soccer World Cup in Madrid. Although football's greatest tournament was still five years away FIFA president João Havelange was in difficulties. He had been elected on the promise that he would expand the World Cup final from sixteen to twenty-four teams. The Spaniards had agreed to stage the competition on the basis of only sixteen countries. There was no money in the budget for the extra squads.

Havelange could lose the FIFA leadership if he did not keep his election promise. He turned to the two men who could help; Horst Dassler and Juan Antonio Samaranch. Dassler could deliver the money. Samaranch, who had close connections with the World Cup organising committee, could deliver a change of plan.

Dassler and Nally had the marketing contract for Spain '82. In typical Dassler style he promised Havelange his support – and then told Nally to raise the extra money. 'At a meeting in Madrid,' recalls Nally, 'in the Palacio de Congresos, while we were in the gentleman's toilets, Horst quite casually told me that the going rate with the Spanish organising committee to cover the team increase was going to be an additional DM36 million – around £12 million. Needless to say, this wasn't money that was going to come from Adidas. This was money that I had to go out and raise from corporate sponsors.'

With the money pledged, Samaranch was now brought into play. In May 1979 the Spaniards announced that the tournament had been expanded to twenty-four teams. Havelange was safe. He acknowledged his debt to Samaranch on his re-election as FIFA president in July 1982 in Madrid. 'This new departure,' he said, 'was only made possible by the Royal Spanish Football Federation.'

In return Havelange would deliver for Samaranch the Latin, African and much of the Asian votes. These were the IOC votes Samaranch needed if he was going to become Olympic president. Dassler was confirmed as the kingmaker. He had sustained Havelange and now he would put Samaranch on the throne.

Samaranch's IOC victory seemed assured. Then at Christmas 1979 the Red Army went into Afghanistan. The Americans were powerless to act and President Jimmy Carter ordered a boycott of the Moscow Games. US diplomats around the world began to pressure their allies. The new Madrid government fell in line with the Americans and announced that Spain would not go to Moscow. Samaranch was distraught. The Russians would be furious and might well switch their support to another candidate for IOC president. Other IOC members might also withhold their votes from a member whose country had snubbed the Games.

According to sources at the Spanish foreign ministry Samaranch was stunned. 'How can you do this to me when I'm on the final leg of the race for the IOC presidency?' he appealed. The reply from Madrid was that if he went to the Games he would be fired. He was Spain's official representative in Moscow and was forbidden to attend the Games. Allegedly Samaranch pleaded unsuccessfully with his Government to allow him to resign. This would have brought him a huge sympathy vote at the IOC and helped counter the embarrassment of the absence of a Spanish team.

Samaranch returned hurriedly to Madrid. In the back rooms of the Spanish Olympic committee, which Samaranch had led for so many years, every old favour was called in. His lobbying worked and the Spanish NOC decided to ignore its own government and compete in Moscow. Samaranch's election bandwagon was rolling again.

In the first issue of the IOC *Review* for 1980 was a prophetic article by Horst Dassler. It was titled 'Sport and Industry'. Dassler knew what the result of the IOC election would be and he was already looking to his own business future with the Olympics. Dassler posed the question 'How can we avoid a situation in which industry takes control of sport?' The problem was 'short-term excessive advertising.' A much better idea would be long-term and more discreet marketing programmes. Dassler called it 'packaging'. The IOC could be the mediator. His own role in this was not specified. Never one to miss an opportunity, Dassler ensured that the photograph accompanying his article featured soccer players wearing Adidas strip.

On the morning of 16 July 1980, the IOC members trooped into the Soviet House of the Unions for the crucial session. The doors closed behind them as they sat down to cast their votes for one of four candidates to lead the IOC. The Canadian lawyer James Worrall was seen as the main rival to Samaranch. At a private meeting with Dassler he had been told, in a kindly way, that he had negligible support. Worrall could never be a member of The Club that Dassler was painstakingly assembling.

The other runners included New Zealand's Lance Cross and the Swiss leader of international skiing, Marc Hodler. The West German Willi Daume also stood and would have been a threat to Samaranch's plans – until his national team boycotted Moscow.

The effectiveness of Dassler's work over the previous years was repaid when the vote was taken. There was only one round: Samaranch crushed his rivals on the first ballot. He had made it.

The hatchet has been buried. Samaranch, who left Barcelona with the abuse of his fellow citizens ringing in his ears, is now lauded as the man who brought the Olympics home. There he stands on the rostrum. The leader of world sport. The chameleon has changed his skin for the last time. Perhaps we should be generous on this great day for Barcelona. Perhaps we should respect Samaranch for his astonishing achievement. In Moscow a dozen years ago he slipped the chains of his fascist past for ever when he took on the presidency of the Olympic Movement.

But pause a moment and think of the price the world has paid for Dassler's legacy. The Club, with its secrecy, its lack of democracy, its self-perpetuating élite, its ceremonies, protocols and medals appears to be not so very different from the *Movimiento* Samaranch so loved. Remember how he used to raise that right arm and give a cheer for the greatest survivor of our age.

CHAPTER 7

The Jewel in the Crown

The president of athletics was hosting a small dinner party at his Turin apartment, just across the street from the Agnelli home. He has always been proud of this slight association with the Fiat dynasty, the most powerful family in Italy. He is a patron of their soccer club, Juventus, and like the industrialists, counts himself among the leading citizens of the province of Piedmont.

One of his guests that night recalls, 'We had dinner, a lovely meal, all done by caterers of course. It was a fabulous apartment and I complimented him on it. He beamed and said "If you think this is fabulous wait until you see my home in Rome!" '

Dr Primo Nebiolo is the president of the International Amateur Athletics Federation, the IAAF. Impressed by the magnificence of it all, his guest inquired what was the secret of his success? In his gravelly voice the president confided, 'Every morning when I wake up, I lie in bed and for five minutes I think of nothing else except how I can improve my position today.'

Dr Nebiolo has undoubtedly improved his position in world sport over the last decade. At the end of the 1970s he was virtually unheard of outside his native Italy. When he first ventured onto the world stage Nebiolo was laughed at behind his back. With his long sideburns and ability to strike deals he was dismissed as a street hustler. His undisguised ambition seemed so out of place in the genteel, essentially amateur world of sport. The establishment linked his ambition to his name and commented patronisingly that 'Primo just wanted to be *primo.*'

Ten years on Nebiolo has shaved off his sideburns, put together a labyrinth of alliances and favours spanning the world of sports politics and clawed his way to the top of The Club. On the way he stabbed one of the world's most decent sporting leaders in the back, presided over the worst example of organised cheating ever seen in international sport, ignored the syringes littering the dressing rooms of his top stars and now controls a secret fund of $20 million which he extracted from the Olympic Games.

The Nebiolo entourage on the road can rival even president Samaranch's imperial processions. His preferred mode of travel is private jet, met by stretch limousine with police motorcycle outriders who then escort him onwards; preferably to the largest suite in the most prestigious hotel in town. Included in the Nebiolo royal party are likely to be his astute wife Giovanna, his personal secretary and also his personal press officer.

Nebiolo cannot risk being too accessible to the media. His press officer has the job of putting out Nebiolo's press releases and trying to distract inquiring journalists from the ever-increasing number of track and field scandals.

For the fun runner, the club runner, and the majority of international athletics stars, the organisation that Nebiolo heads appears to be a distant bureaucracy. The athletics federation is seen to organise some major competitions and provide judges and officials and make the rules. Beyond that it is little more than a worthy sounding name.

Athletics is the jewel in the Olympic crown and the athletics federation has become a very lucrative industry. The IAAF has earned around $80 million from TV and sponsorship in the four years since the 'Ben Johnson' Olympics in Seoul. Large amounts are spread around the developing world improving facilities for track and field. But there is still plenty left which is frittered away on excessive expenses and even more extravagant promotion of Nebiolo.

He can safely ignore the occasional jibe from informed journalists; Nebiolo never has to answer to a 'home' electorate. If the critics do beat too loudly from time to time on the IAAF front door, Nebiolo can be confident he will survive whatever the current scandal may be. In the world of track and field, Nebiolo wields absolute power. His predecessor, Adriaan Paulen, was a very different man.

★

Holland is a small nation with a big sporting tradition. Adriaan Paulen was one of its finest examples. He was a finalist in the Olympic 800 metres in 1920 and beat the 1924 gold medal winner Eric Liddell in the 400-metre quarter finals in Paris. He set a world record for 500 metres at the Bislet Games in Oslo and near the end of his running career he appeared before his home crowd in the Amsterdam Olympics of 1928.

Adriaan Paulen loved so many sports. When his running days were over he drove his car in eight Monte Carlo rallies, rode his motor cycle in the Dutch Grand Prix and played soccer for a local team near his home in Haarlem. But athletics was his first love and he combined his career as a mining engineer with backroom work as an official in the Dutch track and field federation.

Paulen was a brave and patriotic man. When the German army invaded his country he joined a cell of the Dutch resistance movement formed by friends at his local running club. When the miners where he worked downed tools he was one of the managers who refused to hand over the lists of the workers' names to the Nazis. For this he was thrown into jail and threatened with execution.

'The Germans locked him up with his colleagues,' says his daughter Iet Nieuwenhuys-Paulen. 'Every morning they played recordings through loudspeakers of prisoners being shot. It was only later that the prisoners discovered it was a cruel hoax. It was mental torture. When my father was eventually released, because the Germans desperately needed the coal, he went on fighting.

'He was a member of the secret sabotage teams which blew up the rail lines at night. In the morning he would meet with the German Army officers to explain that the coal could not be moved.'

His resistance colleagues conducted a campaign assassinating high-ranking German officers. Paulen, as a prominent member of the Dutch middle classes, was in constant danger of random arrest and reprisal execution. 'He sometimes used to sleep on the roof in case the Germans came for him,' says his daughter. 'He could have escaped but he chose to stay and fight.'

Another side of Paulen's war was controlling a twenty-kilometres section of the underground escape route for downed allied pilots. His secret report on the progress of the war was smuggled to his queen, in

exile in London. When the allied armies landed to liberate Europe
Paulen fought with the American 2nd Armoured Division, was made
an honorary colonel and later awarded the US Medal of Freedom. A
grateful Dutch nation gave him their highest award, the Order of King
Willem.

Three years after the war Paulen was elected to the athletic federation
council. Their world of international athletics was light years away
from today. All-weather tracks had not been invented, there was no
TV coverage and sponsorship was unknown. Little changed in the
next decade. 'We worked out of two rooms near Victoria station,' says
Fred Holder, the former treasurer of the IAAF. 'We were so short of
funds that we had only one secretary. She even had to pay part of her
own fare to attend the Melbourne Olympics in 1956 and to save money
she stayed with a local family.'

Despite these hardships, athletics flourished. Although there were
delays while undeveloped film was airfreighted around the globe,
sports fans could still thrill to see Kuts and Pirie duel in the distance
events, Al Oerter throw the discus for the first of his four gold medals
and Tamara Press win two golds for the women's shot – only to
disappear from competition when sex tests were introduced.

As a member of the athletics federation council, Adriaan Paulen was
there in the background encouraging the athletes and ensuring fair
competition. 'My father always travelled with the athletes,' his
daughter recalls. 'He loved being with the athletes and he loved
organising the events.'

The Olympics were beginning to generate large sums of money from
TV. As the business side of sport expanded, Paulen began to hear new
and unpleasant voices off the track. 'He was horrified in Munich
before the 1972 Games to be offered a huge bribe by a company which
wanted the contract for the new running track,' says his daughter. 'He
turned away saying the best product would win.'

TV changed the world of Paulen and the athletes for ever. Once the
Games were beamed out of Mexico by satellite in 1968 the world would
demand more and more live sport. Dassler was still busy in the locker
rooms doing cash deals to get the shoes with the three stripes on the
feet of the famous but he was beginning to glimpse the shape of the

future. Athletics was going to need money to organise new events and the athletes were going to demand it for themselves. If TV and the promoters wanted them to appear then they would have to be paid.

Once they had arranged the marriage of soccer and Coca-Cola, Horst Dassler and Patrick Nally turned quickly to the other major sports federations. Athletics, central to the success of the Olympics, was top of their list. 'I first met Adriaan at meetings of the European athletic congress in France in the mid-1970s,' recalls Nally. 'He was about to become the president of the IAAF. He was clearly the best man for the job of leading athletics. He'd worked his way through the ranks, he was a runner, he was well respected and of course he saw, as Havelange did with soccer, that there was a radical change needed in his sport.

'You have to try and picture a man who stood on his principles. He was very determined but he would sit and talk. Unlike the Nebiolos of this world, he would listen. Adriaan had a tremendous enthusiasm for everything. He would think nothing of driving for ten hours to get to a meeting. The extraordinary thing was that when he got tired he would stop, get out by the roadside and roll himself out on the ground and sleep. He was tough as nails. You had this extraordinary contrast of a strong, tough, decorated military man who could never be broken and yet was full of almost adolescent exuberance.

'His lifestyle was modest. He didn't seek the trappings of wealth, he never demanded fancy hotel rooms. I'll never forget those big solid old shoes that he wore, they were more like army boots. Adriaan dressed frugally and he had absolutely no wish to be flamboyant.'

Fred Holder has similar memories. 'Adriaan would come on a cheap flight to Heathrow for meetings, travel into town by underground and stay in a small hotel. He didn't see any need to spend the federation's money unnecessarily.'

When Paulen met Dassler he was introduced to the good life on the French Riviera. Contracts could be discussed in the most pleasant surroundings. 'Adriaan loved going in Horst's private plane and private boat. One of Horst's business associates owned what was reputedly the fastest boat in the Mediterranean,' recalls Nally. 'I remember going from Monte Carlo on the back of this boat with Adriaan and we were zapping along at a million miles an hour towards St Tropez.

'It was very helpful for Horst to be able to entertain people in this style and Adriaan loved it. He was like a kid with a new toy, sitting on the back and chatting away.'

At home in Haarlem his daughter Iet had now made him a grandfather. 'My father was once given an Adidas football. He refused to give it to his grandson and donated it to a local club he once played for. And he never took any of the free shoes. He said "If I do that, they will never trust me again. Once you have been bought, you are not free any more." '

TV was clamouring for more sporting spectacles and with Dassler harnessing Nally's marketing skills there was the promise of new money to pay for them.

One of the last acts of Paulen's predecessor Lord Exeter was agreeing to hold the first Athletics World Cup in Dusseldorf in the autumn of 1977. The recent history of athletics has been rewritten by Nebiolo's followers to suggest that he is the great architect of the explosion of events and the endless flow of sponsorship money. In fact the creation of new events outside the Olympics was supported by Exeter and put in place by Paulen. They built the roller coaster and Nebiolo has climbed aboard. It was Nally who found the money.

'Adriaan presided over that hugely successful world cup. At the end he ran a lap of honour with the winning team as they waved the cup above their heads. We were all so proud because that event, in 1977, was the first major international athletics event outside the Olympics.

'Adriaan knew that you couldn't turn the clock back. He saw that sport was becoming entertainment and the revenues were beginning to come through. He also knew that appearance money had been paid secretly to amateur athletes for years and that he had to make it legitimate. He constantly wrestled with his own conscience about how to get it under control while ensuring that it didn't destroy the sport. In his own words, athletics had to be cleaned up.'

Paulen and his new advisers had to move quickly. A number of star athletes in America wanted to earn openly from promoters and there was talk of following the tennis stars and setting up a professional circuit. They had been offered money from Dubai by a group who wanted to promote the country's image. Nally met them, suggested a merger and the result was a quantum leap for athletics.

'Together with Adriaan we created the Golden Series. The first event was the Golden Mile and it was run in 1978 in Japan. The stars were Steve Ovett, Henry Rono and the American Steve Scott. The trophy was a huge gold cup which cost nearly $40,000. Today it gathers dust in a safe in a London bank.

'After the first Golden Mile we created a whole series of Golden events – the Golden Javelin, the Golden Pole vault, the Golden Sprints and the Golden 10,000 metres. All these spectacular events were inserted into existing meetings, mostly in Europe. It brought in a lot of new money.'

After Düsseldorf and the Golden Series there was no turning back. The next breakthrough was to create track and field's own world championship. Traditionally the Olympics had been the athletic federation's own championships.

'The World Cup was the pinnacle for soccer and it was Adriaan who created the athletics equivalent, the World Championships. We started writing the rules and regulations together while flying from Japan to Los Angeles. Fred Holder and Adriaan were on the plane and Adriaan, typically, would not sleep in his seat. He just rolled himself up on the floor.

'When we weren't sleeping we spent the flight sitting on the floor with him writing the regulations. He was quizzing me: if we're going to be commercial how do we write regulations for these world championships in a way that will protect everybody's interests?

'Here's this man in his seventies sitting on the floor of a jumbo jet planning what became the ultimate championships in Helsinki in 1983. Of course Nebiolo took the credit because by that time he was in the seat and Adriaan was a broken man.

'Adriaan took the positive steps needed to develop the sport. With the new money we were raising he started the aid programme, he promoted the Golden Series, he organised the World Cup and he created the World Championships.'

Watching and plotting from Rome was Nebiolo. It was obvious that Paulen was an old man. He would not hold the reigns of power much longer. The IAAF with its growing wealth and influence was there to be taken. But if Primo was going to be *primo* in world athletics, deals would have to be done. This was where Nebiolo excelled.

Nebiolo's first taste of power was in the world of student sport. One of his colleagues who worked with him in the 1950s told us, 'He went after power in student sport because it was the only area available.' There was another reason. Nebiolo had appreciated the potential in a world divided by the Iron Curtain but occasionally united through sporting contact.

One of Nebiolo's official biographies recounts his rise in student sport. 'In 1961 Dr Nebiolo was elected president of the International Federation of University Sport. In this capacity he took dramatic steps which increased the role and importance of world university sports, becoming, among other things, the founder of the Universiade – second only in importance to the Olympic Games.

'As president, Primo Nebiolo came into contact with politicians and university representatives of the world, making the organisation an important element within the world of sport, and becoming one of the most important contributors to sport in the world.'

This was published in the 1980s alongside a picture of Nebiolo with the 'Butcher of Bucharest', the Romanian dictator Nicolae Ceausescu. The pair of presidents were engaged in amiable conversation at a student sports event in the Romanian capital.

Without the backing of the East Bloc the biennial Student Games might have folded years ago. The communists were happy to finance these events because they wanted to market communism. Whilst the rest of the world yawned, the East Bloc took the the student games seriously. So here was The Deal: Nebiolo would bring them the Games they wanted and in return he could count on their votes when he made his move in more important forums. Significantly, Nebiolo was elected to lead student sport at their 1961 Games in communist Sofia.

Nebiolo claims that student sport made him 'one of the most important contributors to sport in the world'. The fact is that TV and sports sponsorship have consistently sidelined the Student Games because they are not good value. A number of top athletes have appeared over the years but most of the young competitors never again grace a world stage. In recent years Patrick Nally has tried to help a number of cities to finance the student games. 'It's impossible to generate any real excitement and TV and sponsor interest when the athletes are not household names.'

Under Nebiolo's leadership the Student Games were staged in Tokyo in 1967 but two years later Lisbon had to cancel through lack of funds. In 1975 Belgrade had to cancel but meanwhile in 1973 Nebiolo had brought them to Moscow's Lenin stadium. Four thousand competitors turned up and Primo was *primo* again. Leonid Brezhnev had good reason to pour money into the student games. Moscow wanted to stage the 1980 Olympics and they needed a dry run to prove that they could organise such a large event.

The student games staggered on through the 1980s. They were cancelled in São Paulo in 1989. In 1991 they were staged in the north of England by the city of Sheffield. The city prepared itself for a £1 million loss but it turned out to be nearly £14 million. There was a personal loss of face for Nebiolo as well. An anonymous and lengthy letter calling for his overthrow was circulated amongst the games delegates.

The key section of the letter denounced Nebiolo as 'a totalitarian chairman of a democratic organisation who has used power politics during the "cold war" era. While acting as chairman for so many years he gained personal power to which he added some personal characteristics that should not be part of the world of university sport. He developed megalomaniac and extravagant behaviour.

'His expenditures on luxury hotels, restaurants, travel arrangements, cars and other personal expenses are outrageous. His behaviour, when he participates in a student event, is imperious and not befitting a person representing the students of the world. He has exerted his power to twist the decisions of student sport.

'We believe that this is not the kind of leader who fits the needs of an international sports organisation. We do not need a pompous and overbearing chairman who presents student sport to the public in ugly colours; nor do we need a totalitarian chairman in a world that is becoming more and more democratic and less and less involved in the East–West dirty politics. After so many years in power Dr Nebiolo should understand that it is time he resigned from his post.' Needless to say Nebiolo, in his sixty-eighth year, was re-elected unopposed to continue leading student sport.

The anonymous writer had spotted Nebiolo's strategy. 'Early on Nebiolo realised that in the East Bloc countries the minister of education could be as important as the minister of sport,' a long-time student sports leader explained to us. 'The minister of education controlled the students and mounting the Student Games was good politics for the East Bloc. So he would instruct his country's athletics officials to support Primo on the international front.' The backing of Moscow was essential and from the early 1970s Nebiolo could count on it.

The important role that Nebiolo had built for himself during the cold war years was demonstrated in Romania in 1981 at the Student Games. When Nebiolo arrived at Bucharest airport there was a government car awaiting him. Adriaan Paulen, who was then still the president of the IAAF, had to wait for the airport bus into town.

The balding, middle-aged student leader made erratic progress up the ladder of his own Italian athletics federation. From his modest powerbase in university sport in Turin he was elected to the ruling council of FIDAL, the Italian national athletic federation, but in the mid-1960s he dropped out.

He came back with a vengeance in 1969 when he took the presidency of FIDAL. He had been nominated by a group of young officials who wanted a change of leadership. These young Turks had no candidate for president, until somebody thought of Primo. He was energetic and ambitious. Nebiolo would hold the post for twenty years until successive scandals drove him from office.

Nebiolo's first decade at FIDAL was a success. He did a good job promoting Italian athletics. One of his triumphs was to take the first foreign athletics team to China and to welcome China's team to Rome. This bought him prestige in the West and, even more importantly, won the support of that part of the Communist Bloc not controlled from Moscow. In 1976 Italy awarded him the Grand Cross of the Republic.

The first step in Nebiolo's plan to take over world athletics was to be elected to the IAAF's ruling council. He did his deals with the Third World and the East Bloc and at the athletics congress held at the Munich Olympics in 1972 he was voted in.

Four years later, at the next congress during the Montreal Games, Nebiolo stood for vice president but was lucky to keep his seat on the council. Many people wanted to see a woman elected and two were nominated. But the feminist vote split and Nebiolo scraped in at the bottom of the list. If there had been just one woman candidate he would probably have been ousted – and that would have been the end of his ambitions.

At the same congress Adriaan Paulen was elected president of world athletics. He was seventy-three when he won in Montreal and he announced that he would serve one term and then retire at the Moscow Games in 1980. But as he became involved in planning athletics' first world championships, scheduled for 1983 in Helsinki, he longed to stay to see it through.

Dassler was becoming restless. Despite the progress he had made since 1976, he sought total control. This could never be guaranteed with a man of Paulen's stature and Dassler had good reason to worry for the future. Lord Exeter, Paulen's predecessor, had refused to deal with him after the scandals at the 1968 Mexico Games. The following year the athletics federation council had produced the drastic resolution that 'at future international competitions only shoes without identifying marks on them will be allowed'.

Later there was a meeting in London, chaired by Fred Holder, with representatives from Adidas and Puma. They promised to stop paying shoe bribes. In his farewell speech at Montreal Lord Exeter warned that athletes who wore the logos of sportswear suppliers risked turning themselves into tailor's dummies. It was his last shot against Dassler. But Dassler would get his way in the 1980s.

'Horst wanted to ensure that Adidas would be the exclusive equipment suppliers to the IAAF and he wanted to keep control of the lucrative commercial marketing rights. We had the contract up until 1983 but a new and unknown president might favour somebody else,' says Patrick Nally.

'Horst's concern was whether he really controlled Adriaan as much he wanted. Adriaan listened to him but he had a very independent attitude. Often round the dining table in Landersheim Horst and his political team would chat about what they should do. It went without saying that if there was going to be a major change in athletics then Horst was going to be involved in it.

'We debated whether Adriaan was the right man and who else might be put up to run. It was in Horst's interest to ensure that he selected a president who would be forever in his debt. Horst had conversations with Nebiolo's lawyer, Mino Auletta. He would talk to Horst about exactly what he could do for him. That was a big deciding factor in why the candidate should be Nebiolo and not somebody else. Needless to say, Primo was more than vocal in guaranteeing that it would all go Horst's way.

'Primo, being the sort of person he was, made it easy for Horst to do a deal. Nebiolo was a real wheeler-dealer. But there was a problem: how the hell were we going to get him to become the president of athletics without having to run against other and better candidates?'

Stage One of the secret war to impose Nebiolo on the IAAF was the choice of the battlefield. Elections were due in Moscow in 1980 and Dassler knew that Paulen would surely defeat the ambitious Italian. General Secretary Brezhnev and President Carter saved the day. The Russian invasion of Afghanistan was countered by the American Olympic boycott. Immediately there were doubts about holding such an important vote if some delegates were going to be absent. Nebiolo took his cue and with Dassler's influence in Africa, Latin America and the East Bloc managed to delay the election.

'The Moscow boycott was a godsend,' says Nally. 'Horst saw the potential very quickly. The following year Rome was due to host the third athletics world cup and so there was the opportunity to hold an extraordinary congress on Nebiolo's home ground. The thought was, let Paulen have another year, which seemed right because he was deeply involved in putting into place the first athletics world championships in 1983. In the meantime Horst could organise the coup.'

Fred Holder has similar memories; 'Nebiolo manoeuvred in 1980 to postpone the elections. It wasn't necessary to wait. Even though the US athletes did not go to Moscow their administrators did. It was a "windfall" for Nebiolo to get the vote moved to his home turf in Rome for 1981.'

Nebiolo left nothing to chance. On a campaigning visit to East Berlin he played to the fears of the communist bloc. He declared 'We are against the commercialisation of sport. If we want progress in sport, it is essential to develop amateur sport in every way.' His campaign manager in Landersheim must have laughed.

Stage Two, according to Nally, was to make sure there would never be an election. 'Dassler hatched a scheme. He wanted only two runners. When it was too late for other candidates to throw their hats in the ring, Paulen would be persuaded to pull out.'

★

'Adriaan wasn't in athletics for anything other than the sport itself,' says Nally. 'The tragedy is that he never had the chance to nominate a successor. Horst's plan evolved over many months. First of all he had to ensure that nobody else would run against Nebiolo and Adriaan because that could have thrown it out completely. Literally anybody else could have won and that would have ruined Horst's plans.

'This was like a military campaign. Adriaan's own standing was used to block any of the other major contenders from coming forward. Once we had made it very public that Adriaan was going to run all the other possible contenders, out of respect, declined the challenge. Nebiolo's chances against Adriaan were scoffed at.

'The next and most pivotal stage was to get Adriaan to agree to step down. Horst had to convince him that he was going to lose, which I don't believe that he ever would. Horst persuaded Adriaan that he knew the Africans and Asians better and that they were going to back Nebiolo. Horst convinced and cajoled Adriaan into thinking that he was going to lose.

'As the months passed these warnings became more pointed until Adriaan came to believe that unless he withdrew from the contest and did a deal with Nebiolo, he ran the risk of being completely ousted from international athletics.

'Horst told him, "Adriaan, this isn't going to be good for the sport or good for you if you to go out this way. Let's structure it now so that we can all work together to make sport work." It's sad really because it came across in such a genuine way, that it was in the interests of athletics and in the interests of Adriaan.

'The *coup de grâce* was presented in the early spring of 1981 at a meeting in a Paris hotel. At this meeting he was brought face to face with Nebiolo by Horst, to strike a deal.

'After everybody had shaken hands Adriaan said "Fine, I will stand down – subject to you agreeing these things," which gave him more than just an honorary position. It was a snowball job, it was a sell job, basically designed to convince Adriaan Paulen that it would be better for him to step down and that his own role in athletics would be secure.'

Paulen requested one more service from Fred Holder. 'He asked me to attend a meeting between him and Nebiolo. Paulen had already decided to stand down and at this meeting Nebiolo was going to repeat his guarantees about Paulen's future role with IAAF. Paulen was a bit nervous that Nebiolo might rat on these promises and he wanted me there as a witness.'

Betrayed and deceived by his friend Dassler, Adriaan Paulen wrote to the IAAF withdrawing from the race. It was a short letter. Discussions have taken place, opinions have been expressed ... it has become clear that a majority of our federations support Dr Primo Nebiolo, who is a perfect successor...

I greet you in friendship.'

'My father could be naïve, he always looked for the best in people. He was intelligent, but in some ways, he was not shrewd,' says Paulen's daughter. When we told her the true story of how her father was evicted from the presidency of the IAAF she could not at first believe it.

'Dassler did that? He conspired against my father? I knew there was something against my father to make sure that Nebiolo would be elected. But I never thought that it was Dassler because he was always very friendly to my father.

'Even after my father had stepped down he stayed at Dassler's home – so he could never have suspected. He told my mother that he stood down because there were too many people against him – but he never mentioned Dassler.

'He believed that something was going on behind his back to get votes for Nebiolo. My father did not want the indignity of losing. That's why he stepped down. His heart and soul was in track and field.'

CHAPTER 8

ISL Rules the World

Once upon a time in the early 1980s a man set up a little company to sell advertising off the back of sport. Moments later he had secured the multi-million dollar rights to the Soccer World Cup. The following year he was awarded similar rich privileges by the Olympics. Another year on, he captured world athletics.

One little company with no history, no experience and no track record had been given a monopoly of the world's biggest and most lucrative sports marketing contracts. This was one of the world's greatest business coups.

These contracts are invariably renewed. Some now run into the next century. They are not put out to tender. Competitors know better than to waste their time bidding. Sponsors queue up to throw hundreds of millions of dollars at this company for the right to link their 'brand images' to what's left of the beauty and purity of sport. Every time a sports fan turns on a television to watch IOC, FIFA or IAAF events they make this little company richer. Every time a particular brand of soft drink or roll of film is bought, the percentages trickle in. The man who founded the company and had the connections to bring off such a triumph was of course Horst Dassler. Once he had created The Club, Horst Dassler became its banker.

ISL Marketing can be found in a complex of offices above Lucerne's railway station. They have branch offices in half a dozen cities around the world. They employ just over 100 people. Annual turnover is estimated to be at least $200 million a year. ISL keep up to twenty-five per cent of that in commission for their services. We cannot publish the exact figures because ISL is not a public company. The sports they sell are very public but ISL is a name known to few outside the private world of sports marketing. They are understandably shy about discussing the millions that slip through their fingers. They speak a different language to that of most sports enthusiasts.

To a fan or to an athlete the biggest prize is still to watch or win an Olympic gold medal, a track and field championship final or a soccer world cup goal. To ISL the value of these events lies in the 'global opportunities' of 'marketing segments' that they can make available in 'packages' to manufacturers in 'product categories'. The eventual target may be the 'consumer' or it may be the more private 'business to business'. Whatever your company does, if you are very rich, you can buy a piece of the Final, the Championship or the Games.

When these sports are staged in historic and beautiful cities like Rome or Barcelona, the 'ultimate in corporate hospitality' can be arranged for valued clients of the multi-national sponsors. Put another way, you don't have to watch the sport if you don't want to.

Within a year of the end of the Barcelona Games the worldwide annual sponsorship budget will exceed $5 billion. In return, the sponsors will demand the right to 'shape' the world's great sporting events to become more efficient for television in its pivotal role as a purveyor of 'sponsor imagery'. What the majority of us naively call the Olympics are already referred to in the pseudo-scientific world of marketing research as 'communication tools'. Not a word of this appears in the Olympic Charter.

The five linked rings are now one of the world's more valuable commodities – in monetary terms. Just a quarter of a century ago they had a much rarer value. They could not be bought. IOC president Avery Brundage dispatched constant circulars from Lausanne denying competitors and federations the right to carry commercial logos on their clothing. He even set up a Commission for the Protection of the Olympic Emblems to prevent the rings being exploited by advertisers. It has been replaced under Samaranch by the Commission for New Sources of Financing, which is charged with selling off the emblem for the best price the market will bear.

The new breed of businessmen-IOC members became concerned that they were too reliant on their TV income. Prudence, they insisted, required that money was raised from elsewhere. The result, as seen by one Olympic commentator, is that the 'IOC's image has been systematically raped by the corporate world.'

'Horst always said that he got the basic idea for sports marketing from watching a Wimbledon final in the early 1970s. The players, Nastase and Smith, both contracted to Adidas, were dressed in plain whites with only very discreet company logos. With so much televised attention on this match, Horst started to consider these players as mobile billboards, awaiting corporate branding,' says ISL vice president Paul Smith. In Dassler's book, those plain whites were a sin against nature. The partnership with Patrick Nally was born. Over the next eight years the two men transformed the funding and appearance of soccer, athletics and the Olympics. The federations were turned on their heads and a new breed of president arrived at the helm of world sport.

In 1982 Dassler and Nally parted company. 'I was at a point of conflict,' says Nally. 'I didn't know whether I was in this to help Horst and Adidas or to represent the best interests of Coca-Cola and Canon and my other clients. The people who were getting the benefit of the money were the federations and the person who was getting the political kudos and manipulating it all for his own companies was Horst.'

When the partners split Dassler hurriedly set up ISL. He took the marketing rights to international soccer with him and ISL have held them ever since. FIFA later awarded him options taking the contract into the next century.

It was going to be bottles of bubbly all the way; sometimes in small, six ounce bottles but more frequently in bright red cans. Coca-Cola, who had provided the money and the image to keep Havelange in power, would now fuel Dassler's plans to take over world sports marketing. ISL would rule that world, all the favours accumulated over the past decade would be called in and Coke would foot the bill.

The Atlanta corporation was crucial to Dassler's new company. Nally watched, almost in awe. 'When we separated it meant that Horst had to get control of the Coca-Cola company because he needed that credibility, that image. So he spent a long time getting Coke on his side, to utilise the muscle and the money of the Coca-Cola company.'

ISL's Paul Smith admits that Coca-Cola's name has a 'halo effect'. That halo was draped around the shoulders of soccer's new marketing programme. The previous name of 'Inter-Soccer' was retained and the events for sale included the 1984 European Championships Finals in Paris, the European Cup Finals and culminated in the 1986 Mexico World Cup.

Sponsors were offered 'A complete communication package based on product category exclusivity and continuity over a four-year period. The programme for each of seventy-five matches includes stadium advertising, official supplier's titles, the use of mascots and emblems and franchise opportunities.' If they were prepared to pay nearly £7 million each they could, in 1986, own their share of 'the biggest single televised event in the world' with 'unparalleled exposure far in excess of other sports'.

But was it a fair price? Nally thinks not. 'When we created Inter-Soccer, we built into the budget the payments Spain needed to increase the tournament from sixteen to twenty-four teams. Havelange needed to fulfil his election promises and Samaranch was on the brink of the IOC elections in Moscow and needed Havelange's support. So there was a bigger overhead in 1982 than was needed in 1986.

'But after Spain Horst didn't bring the prices down, if anything he put them up. Coca-Cola coming back into the Inter-Soccer programme at the price Horst demanded, legitimated this whole over-priced programme.'

Next to fall to ISL was what Dassler once described joyfully as 'the least-exploited property', the Olympic Games. They had the perfect image for marketing. Every national Olympic committee had the right to licence the five rings in their own countries. Dassler's plan was to move away from local selling to global selling.

Private conversations were held with the IOC and in March 1983 Samaranch announced that ISL had been appointed to manage its new fund-raising programme. The competition never got a look in.

The *New York Times* report of this business coup covered all shades of opinion. Mark McCormack's International Management Group said that it had expressed interest, but was never invited to bid. Patrick Nally was quoted saying, 'That ISL, out of nowhere, gets one of the biggest sports contracts in the world clearly identifies that Dassler is in a position to get the contracts he wants.' Canadian IOC member Dick Pound said, 'ISL was picked by osmosis.' Samaranch commented, 'Dassler has been close to the IOC but I don't see any problem, and Dassler, no doubt with a broad smile on his face added, 'What I do is best for the Olympic movement. I have no conflict of interest whatsoever.'

'Isn't it strange that none of the big marketing companies which had been in business for many years even got a sniff, a word or were even asked to tender or put up an alternative package to ISL?' asks Nally.

Another two years would pass before the contract between ISL and the IOC was signed. Dassler had achieved a breakthrough. He now had the right to run a global marketing scheme for the Seoul Games. But if it was going to work he had to persuade all the 150-plus NOCs to sign away a large part of their rights to market the five rings in their own countries. Even Samaranch was sceptical and in private said to Dassler, 'Convince me that you can go out and get all of them.'

Dassler was uniquely placed to achieve this goal. He was the best-informed man in sport, the best-connected and the man who made sure that he was always owed favours. Now they were clawed back. Five months after receiving Samaranch's blessing a team of ISL executives met up with the Mexican Mario Vazquez Raña in Caracas at the Pan American Games. Raña was a key player. He headed the worldwide organisation of national Olympic committees, the ANOC. Together they successfully lobbied the Latin American NOCs to sign up with Dassler's marketing company. That was a sizeable start. But the new Olympics marketing plan was a non-starter without the agreement of the major economic powers: America, Germany, Great Britain, France, Japan and Australia. One by one Dassler promised them money until he had enough support to go back to Samaranch. The contract was finally signed in March 1985 and for the first time TOP – The Olympic Programme – was unveiled.

TOP raised about $100 million for the 1988 Games but it is doubtful if ISL made a profit. Buying out the rights of each NOC, by guaranteeing them more cash than most could ever raise themselves, was a costly affair.

To Dassler's rescue came the world's biggest advertising agency. 'Dentsu is enormous,' says Nally, 'a monstrous company which has infiltrated nearly every part of Japanese commercial life, the press, publishing, TV and advertising.

'When I was working with Horst I sold the soccer package to JVC, the Japanese electronics manufacturers, and also to Fuji Film. In Japan, the system is that you go through an agency. I selected Hukuhodo, the number two agency in Japan and Dentsu's sworn rivals, to be our partner with JVC and with Fuji .

'What I didn't realise was that by doing this I woke up this slumbering giant, this Rip Van Winkle called Dentsu. Both JVC and Fuji Film are high profile companies, neither had ever worked with Hukuhodo before. Heads were rolling at Dentsu because this was the most dreadful thing ever to have happened.

'When Horst and I parted company, I discovered that there were all these telexes from Dentsu to Horst at Adidas France in Landersheim, trying to buy their way in to ISL. They were offering silly money, because they wanted to get JVC and Fuji Film out of the clutches of Hukuhodo and back into Dentsu.

'Suddenly Horst had got the answer to his financial problems. Here was a vast Japanese company, wanting to buy their way in with him, who were prepared to pay almost any price to get what they wanted. They offered Horst vast sums of money and they bought half of ISL.

'Events in Japan were just Horst's luck. I created the perfect partner for him. Dassler of course made hay out of this. He told Dentsu, "Sure, I know how to solve the problem Nally has created for you. You will have to move immediately and here's my bank account in Switzerland, please send me millions of noughts." And that is exactly what happened.'

With Dentsu's money behind him, Dassler's energy and ingenuity triumphed. 'There was no one executive at ISL who could get the national Olympic committees to sign their rights back to the IOC in favour of a global marketing programme. It had to be Dassler himself,' says Nally. 'Samaranch could not have done it – he didn't have that kind of money to give away – so Horst had put Samaranch completely in his debt again.'

Nine multi-national companies – Coca-Cola, Visa, Brother, Federal Express, 3M, Time-Life, National Panasonic, Kodak and Philips joined the first TOP programme for the 1988 Olympics and contributed more than $100 million – less ISL's commission. But that was only seed corn. All they got for that payment was the right to use the five rings anywhere in the world.

The Olympics are unique in the world of major sporting events. No advertising boards are allowed to disfigure the stadium. Much is made of this by the IOC. They say that commercial messages are kept out of the stadium to maintain the purity of the Olympic ideal.

'This is misleading,' says Nally, 'The real reason that no advertising signs appear in the Olympic stadium is because the US networks pay so much for the TV rights. They want clean pictures so that they can then sell the commercials themselves. If you take NBC, which has paid something like $400 million for the rights for Barcelona, it would need to sell something like $600 million plus of advertising spots on the networks to break even or make a small profit. NBC couldn't do that if there was advertising already around the stadium.'

Having paid their millions to join the Olympic élite, the nine TOP sponsors had to spend even more money finding ways of incorporating the rings and the logos of Calgary, the venue for the 1988 Winter games, and Seoul in their packaging and buy advertising in print and on TV. Visa put the rings on their credit cards and produced aggressive 'knocking ads' pointing out that Games locations were the one place in the world where 'they *don't* take American Express'.

The rival green card was a sponsor at Los Angeles in 1984 but bridled when asked for four times as much. American Express commented, 'We refused to pay ISL $15.5 million for Seoul. The price was just way beyond what we could expect to gain in any commercial benefits.'

Campbell's Soup, who paid $500,000 to sponsor the Sarajevo winter Games in 1984, were near speechless when ISL invited them to join TOP and sponsor the 1988 Calgary Games. Director George Mahrlig said, 'I won't ever forget the price they were quoting. The ISL salesman, with a straight face, asked me for fourteen times as much – $7.2 million.' Campbell declined.

Time and its stable mate *Sports Illustrated* won the right to produce special Olympic souvenir issues. It seems an odd situation. Has a major publishing group tied itself so closely to the Olympic movement that it has jeopardised its ability to produce critical journalism?

Brother typewriters concentrated more on the 'business to business' exploitation of the rings. They took key dealers and customers to Seoul and paid for the privilege of their clients meeting each day's gold medal winners. What the Olympic champions thought of being paraded to press the flesh with the guests of big Brother has not been recorded. Around 17,000 corporate guests bought special privileges in 1988.

There was one more major favour for Dassler to call in. After the Helsinki Athletics World Championships the IAAF marketing contract was up for grabs. The negotiations would take place during the Los Angeles Games. Was there a price to be paid for the ending of Adriaan Paulen's reign and instituting Nebiolo's regime?

Bidding for the IAAF contract was a new kind of experience for ISL, one they had not encountered with FIFA and the IOC. There would actually have to be a competition. There were two contenders. Patrick Nally held on to this contract after his split with Dassler. He wanted to continue the partnership that had been so successful in raising money for the first championships in Helsinki in 1983. Dassler wanted to take the contract for himself.

The two rivals had to make their presentations to the recently inaugurated IAAF marketing committee. One member of the committee recalls, 'Nally made a very professional presentation and was followed by ISL. They said they could offer a large guarantee, maybe $20 million over the next four years and on that basis it was agreed that they would have the contract. But for some reason it was another two years before the contract was actually signed.'

Nally says now, 'ISL got the IAAF contract – suddenly they seem to have done a better deal than us who had been the incumbents for many years and who created all the programmes. It was a farce.' ISL now had the big three.

ISL have found Nebiolo a lot more difficult to deal with than Samaranch. The president has cost the IAAF money on occasion. In the run-up to the 1987 Rome Athletics Championships Nebiolo insisted on an emblem for the event produced by someone in his retinue. 'It was a dreadful logo,' an insider at the IAAF told us. 'It was ugly. It didn't mean anything. We all hated it but he would not listen because he insisted that IAAF's logo had to be unveiled before FIFA's logo for the 1990 soccer World Cup in Rome. The emblem died the death. Earnings were zero.'

The Dassler relationship with athletics flourished. In 1986 Nebiolo concluded a deal with Adidas to provide sportswear for the IAAF. The federation's magazine carried a page of advertising dressed up as a feature on the science behind the manufacture of Adidas shoes. The athletics contract with ISL was renewed in 1988 and again in 1991. Paul Smith admits that while Dassler was alive, ISL was highly involved in sports politics. 'Since Horst's death,' he says, 'ISL has become just another marketing company.'

ISL have one more major contract. In 1989 they secured a deal with the international basketball federation. The deal is limited because the prime territory, America, is already wrapped up but the global marketing possibilities are expected to explode in 1994 when top flight American professionals will compete in front of the cameras at the World Basketball Championships.

Basketball is what the men in suits call an 'advertiser-friendly' sport when televised. The court is small and the play confined and ISL assure customers that just two advertising boards will be in vision for as much as thirty per cent of the 'screen time'. There are other benefits on offer. Advertisers will be able to buy the right to have their names included in the title of some individual matches. This is known in the trade as 'upweighting their message' and gives the TV commentators a longer name to pronounce.

In the spring of 1988 the chairman of Coca-Cola, Roberto C. Goizueta, travelled to Lausanne where Samaranch invested him with the Olympic Order. The IOC president revealed that this honour was due because the company had 'a profound sense of a positive concept of life'. Coca-Cola was the first to sign up for the next TOP bonanza which will peak in Barcelona. Samaranch himself flew to Atlanta to sign the contract. With all the openness and honesty that now characterises the Olympics, neither side was prepared to reveal how much the company paid. Informed guesses put it at around $30 million. Coca-Cola have to pay more than other sponsors because the soft drink market is one of the world's most competitive.

The other companies, making up the 'TOP 12' at Barcelona are predictable. Kodak has again paid a fortune, if only to exclude their rivals Fuji Film. Equally determined to buy in are the massive Japanese companies of Brother, National Panasonic and Ricoh. Philips from Holland are in but cannot compete in product categories sold to Panasonic. The rest of the Barcelona sponsors are *Time* magazine,

Mars sweets, Bausch & Lomb – the makers of Rayban sunglasses – Visa, the EMS parcel delivery group and 3M products. In 1989 Bob Helmick's United States Olympic Committee named 3M's president as 'The Corporate Executive of the Year'.

Have the Olympics been 'raped' by the corporate world? Paul Smith of ISL says not. 'The public does not think the Olympics are over commercialised. The commercial element is well controlled. The TOP companies have a long-term vested interest in ensuring the Games are not damaged.' The long term has now become the short term. The IOC has conceded a major change to the traditional four-year cycle of the Games. From 1994 the winter and summer events will alternate every two years. The most pressing demand for this has come from the American TV networks, suffering under the burden of paying out nearly $1 billion in one Olympic year to buy both Games. Sceptics believe another reason is that sponsors would prefer their cash injections to yield a high profile with consumers every two years rather than peaking every four.

In its publicity material ISL appears to be simply the meeting point between the ethical content of sport and the very reasonable, benevolent requirements of business. Inside the company it has been two years of warfare since the majority of the Dassler family-owned Adidas shares were sold to the French entrepreneur Bernard Tapie in mid-1990.

Dassler's four sisters – Inge, Karen, Brigitte & Sigrid – were attacked in the German media for selling their eighty per cent of Adidas shares cheaply. His daughter Suzanne and son Adi retained a part of their Adidas holding. The family also own fifty-one per cent of ISL, Dentsu holding the remainder. While they appear united at not wanting the marketing company to decline in the same way that Adidas fell from world leadership in sportswear after Dassler's death, the two generations of the family now speak to each other only through lawyers. With Adidas gone, ISL is their only milch cow.

Six months after the sale of their Adidas shares and just before Christmas 1990 the four sisters struck at ISL. Sigrid's husband Christoph Malms was appointed president of the holding company, Sporis AG, and immediately afterwards to head ISL. Almost immediately it became clear that he could not work with Klaus Hempel and Jürgen Lens, the two men Horst Dassler picked to run the business. Hempel, the chief executive officer, was used to running the company without interference and reported his decisions to the family-dominated board after they had been taken. Malms wanted to be a hands-on boss.

In January 1991, Hempel and Lens left suddenly. Their departures were announced in the kind of corporate non-speak that suggests harmony and usually obscures the sight of executives wrestling on the boardroom floor. A press release was issued from ISL's Lucerne office. It announced 'significant changes to the company's executive structure'. Hempel and Lens had of course left by 'mutual agreement to pursue other business activities and personal interests'. ISL was in good hands because the core executives were still in place.

The next day a more discreet letter, signed by Hempel and Lens, went out to their best contacts in the sports federations. It made clear they were both still very much in the business. It told their old clients, 'We intend to capitalise on our past experience in event marketing.' The letter ended on a diplomatic note. 'Meanwhile we would appreciate your continued support of ISL.' Connoisseurs of corporate rows could smell the rich perfume of a negotiated pay-off.

It remains to be seen if Malms or Dassler's son Adi have any of the great man's political skills. What they do not have is the profound knowledge of everyone and everything who matters in world sport. Dassler was a brilliant and intuitive man who exploited his knowledge for Adidas and ISL. Hempel and Lens worked alongside him through the years and even if they lacked his vision, they knew the politics of sport intimately. Dassler took a lot out but first had to put a lot in. It is open to question whether his successors at ISL can maintain his record.

Patrick Nally is sceptical about the record and future of ISL. 'The relationship with FIFA, the IOC, the IAAF and basketball is all because of Horst. The infrastructure was so solidly built. He was with the people who now lead world sport from their very earliest days. He put most of them in place.

'When their hands are eventually prised off the leadership positions the legacy of Horst will blow itself out. Then the rationale for ISL may be questioned. When we started, the federations had no staff, they had no specialists. Now they've got their own marketing people and many of them are very good. They won't need an agent. The federations needed ISL because they needed the Horst politics, the money, the credibility and all the things to get them where they are now. Now of course they know how to do it themselves.'

Not surprisingly, ISL's Paul Smith disagrees. 'We are specialists. We understand the subtleties and nuances of sports marketing. Just as major companies use advertising agencies, instead of their own in-house people, we are confident the federations will want to go on using our skills.'

This summer the corporate guests will frolic on the cruise liners moored in Barcelona port. Consumers worldwide will be encouraged to drink Coke not Pepsi, take their snaps with Kodak not Fuji, watch the Games on a Panasonic TV not a Sony and charge it all to Visa, not American Express. These are some of the TOP sponsors. ISL's market research claims it is worth their while; 'Any company sponsoring the Olympics takes on Olympic qualities.'

'The public are no longer as naïve as they were,' Nally believes. They know the reason that you're promoting your company to be associated with the Olympics is not because you've got some unique Olympic endorsement, because you've been selected for your quality or your image; it's because you're the one that paid more money that anybody else.'

CHAPTER 9

Flotsam and Jetsam

The Samaranch who went to the IOC in 1966 would have found himself at ease among the many other members from authoritarian or undemocratic backgrounds. All his adult life he had given whole-hearted support to a police state based on an ideological system which claimed it was acting in the best interests of the majority.

Moving to Moscow after the collapse of the Franco dictatorship and the heady onrush of democracy in Spain must have seemed like a welcome step back into history. The Russians were as easy to deal with as the Castilians from Madrid; they enjoyed absolute power and would reward those who helped them.

Warped by his own lack of experience of active democracy Samaranch misjudged the strength and longevity of his new communist allies. Since he came to power at the IOC he has recruited and sustained many East Bloc members who are dinosaurs from another political age.

Today the IOC is top heavy with the now discarded political appointees of the old East Bloc regimes. They represent nothing but their own will to survive in a harsh new world without privileges at home. If Samaranch lacks the will to seek their resignations he will offend the new, democratically elected national Olympic committees of the Eastern republics, who want no truck with 'their' IOC members.

The contrast with the changes in the rest of the world order is glaring. As corrupt regimes fall their ambassadors and their delegates to the United Nations go home in ignominy. Not so at the IOC. This handful of discredited IOC members may stay in power until they die.

111

They are now the creatures of the IOC leadership. Without honour or reward in their own countries, they will stay on the everlasting gravy train, inspecting candidate cities, attending IOC sessions and making trips to the Games and other major sports events.

The East Bloc countries have always had an uneasy relationship with the Olympic movement. For forty years after the 1912 Stockholm Games the Russians boycotted the Olympics. They came back at Helsinki in 1952 winning their first ever gold medals. They captured twenty-two and came second only to the Americans in the medal count. From then on sport became a front line political activity. The Russians, the East Germans, the Czechs, Romanians and Bulgarians poured scarce resources into providing élite sports facilities and training regimes to try and beat the West. By 1956, the Russians topped the medals table. They stayed ahead of the Americans in three of the next five Olympics.

Meanwhile the Soviet Union remained a closed camp. The only foreigners who were truly welcome were fellow travellers and piratical capitalists like Horst Dassler. 'I was always very impressed by Horst in Moscow. He never talked about politics,' remembers Christian Jannette. 'His only politics were the politics of Adidas. Even when we had dinner with people who were on the Central Committee, I never heard Horst talk for one minute about politics. He spoke business, he spoke about sports organisation but never about politics.'

The Adidas boss brought two special gifts. The Russians were grateful for the free sportswear he donated to their teams but they were desperate for access to Dassler's unique commodity – knowledge. The isolation of the East Bloc, and their habit of travelling with a phalanx of KGB minders, cut them off from any understanding of sports politics. From the early 1970s Dassler became their educator and their political chaperon. They realised that their bloc vote gave them immense power but they didn't understand how to wield it.

'Whenever Horst travelled to Eastern European countries he received the VIP treatment,' says Patrick Nally. 'Our ability to move within that world was very easy. It meant that we could fly into Russia, get off the plane and never have our passports checked. It wasn't just Armand Hammer who was doing that, Horst was doing it all the time.

'Horst spent a lot of time in the sauna with the key politicians talking about who was to be elected and who wasn't and what roles the Eastern Europeans could play in the federations. The Eastern European countries gave Horst very little in the way of business but they were extremely important to him from the political perspective.'

Dassler wanted two major paybacks from the Russians; he wanted to be able to manufacture behind the iron curtain and he wanted to be involved in the business of the 1980 Games in Moscow. In both cases he was pushing against an open door. The Russians needed better quality product for their domestic market – until recently the generic term in eastern Europe for a pair of trainers was 'adidas' – and they wanted the chance to export some of it for hard currency.

A new team was assembled in Landersheim to handle the Olympic challenge. Nally was closely involved. 'Horst selected a number of people, like Christian Jannette. He lived in Russia between 1976 and 1980 as the Olympics were building up.

'There were regular visits to Moscow all the time and my role became greater as the 1980 Games came closer. Russia needed things like textiles and clothing and we made commitments to support them. Horst hadn't got masses of budget to pay for it so I had to find other companies to help that effort.

'The negotiations were difficult but Horst succeeded in winning some marketing rights in Moscow. He got a deal where he clothed not only the athletes but the officials. We put together a package at West Nally, going round signing up sub-contractors.

'What seemed like a great success at the time was persuading Levi's to supply 64,000 pairs of jeans. We took their executives to Russia several times and they were very impressed with Horst's political contacts. Levi's, like Coca-Cola, planned to use the Olympic Games as a way of getting manufacturing plants established in eastern Europe. Blue jeans were a hot ticket item.'

Nobody had foreseen the American boycott at Moscow. Samaranch, while first vice president of the IOC, had cultivated his communist contacts at the expense of the Americans. From his point of view it had made sense; the Americans were insignificant players in Olympic politics. They had little understanding of the machinations in Lausanne and in the international federations. Samaranch's diplomatic skills failed at the first big test. His attempts to reverse the American-led boycott were unsuccessful.

When the Russians revenged themselves in Los Angeles Samaranch, now IOC president, pleaded once more. Again, his entreaties fell on deaf ears. He had been practising Olympic politics for eighteen years but he was quite unable to get the East Bloc to see that they would regret their boycott. There were well-known divisions within the communist countries and the truth was that nobody but Brezhnev wanted to stay away from Los Angeles.

Despite the years as Spain's ambassador to Moscow Samaranch never learned to appreciate the nuances of communist bloc politics. He failed to win his former friends round.

It was not as if Samaranch had failed to appease some of the most ruthless dictators in the communist bloc. He continually courted the emperors of the East. Honours were liberally bestowed in both directions. Even after they turned their backs on Los Angeles he proceeded to reward them as if they had been the stars of the Games.

When the IOC met in East Berlin in 1985 Samaranch was welcomed by Manfred Ewald, the ultimate apparatchik of the East German sports movement and the driving force behind his country's doping programme. Ewald already possessed the Olympic Order. 'The GDR closely identifies itself with the humanistic content of the Olympic idea,' announced Ewald and everybody clapped politely. With their GDR hosts footing the bill it would have been impolite to ask what role steroids played in the Olympic idea and how many citizens had been shot that year crawling under the wire to the West.

The hypocrisy continued: Erich Honecker, the former East German leader, now indicted for crimes committed by his murderous regime, opened the IOC session. For this Samaranch rewarded him with the highest honour at his disposal, the Gold Olympic Order. Awarding the Gold Order to such tyrants did not simply disgrace the Olympic ideal; it mocked the legions of decent, ordinary people who had often given a lifetime of service to sport.

One other notable qualified for Olympic Gold that year; the butcher of Bucharest, Nicolae Ceaucescu. He was rewarded for ignoring the Russians and sending a team to the LA Games. It is inexplicable that the IOC president, who claimed to be a widely travelled diplomat, could not have known of the appalling misery inflicted on Romanians by the

Ceaucescu dictatorship.

What was the message that went out to ordinary Romanians, watching the ceremony played at full length on local TV? That the civilised world did not care about their plight and their poverty behind the sealed border. To see their cruel leader rewarded for sending athletes to America whilst they were shot if they tried to leave the country must have seemed odd.

At the sporting level, Samaranch would surely have been aware that facilities in Romania were pitiful. He was also conferring Olympic respect on a country with a reputation for doping many of its leading competitors.

Samaranch seemed to have a gift for picking out the most unspeakable dictators to honour with the Olympic ideal. Two years after the Berlin follies he went to Bulgaria and sought out the dictator Todor Zhivkov and presented him too with a Gold Olympic Order.

There must have been late night sessions in Moscow and Washington when thoughtful counter-espionage officers pored over Samaranch's itineraries of the 1980s. Who, they must have wondered, was he was really working for? The CIA must have evaluated the possibility that the IOC president was really a secret agent of the Comintern, regularly going 'home' for orders and to hand over the micro films.

Similarly, the KGB must have leafed through their immigration files. From 1981 to 1987 Samaranch remorselessly visited the East Bloc. Was he reporting back to the Americans, they must have asked themselves at the Lubianka.

As the communist system creaked slowly to its end Samaranch was regularly photographed in Moscow, Albania, Poland and Pyongyang. His travels only diminished as the walls fell. The sports power of the East is smashed; the doping camps are closed, performances are levelling off and the bloc vote has dissolved. The sports barons of the East are mostly sacked, discredited and their empires stripped of their secret hard currency accounts. The East are now the supplicants and must tip toe with their begging bowls to Lausanne.

They will have the best seats with the best view of the events in Barcelona. They will travel in the best limousines. They will be in the best hotel. They can give your city the Olympics. They are the East

Bloc rejects, the flotsam and jetsam of the Brezhnev era, the IOC members for totalitarianism.

Meet Shagdarjav Magvan from Mongolia. He's a trade union boss and former wrestler. Born in 1927, he was fifty years of age when selected to join the IOC. The next year the communist party promoted him to run a porcelain factory. His native language is Mongolian and he also speaks Russian. He is one of the few IOC members who has never been appointed to any of their many commissions. He will stay on the IOC until he reaches the compulsory retirement age of seventy-five in the year 2002. Only then will Mongolia be eligible for a new member. Even then, though without voting powers, Magvan will remain an IOC life member until he dies.

Then there's Marat Gramov from Moscow. He is one of Samaranch's major disasters. Gramov was the hard-driving bureaucrat who organised the East Bloc's boycott of the LA Games. This did not not bother Samaranch when he selected Gramov to join the IOC in 1988. Gramov was a Deputy of the USSR Supreme Council and President of the Soviet national Olympic committee.

His appointment to the IOC was a clear signal that Samaranch had no understanding of the pressures building up in Russia. Three years as ambassador and the endless trips back over the next eight years apparently taught the IOC president little. The choice of Gramov has left the IOC ill-represented in the new world of the democratic East.

Within a year of his appointment Gramov was forced from his position as Soviet Sports Minister. By continually postponing meetings of the Soviet NOC he held off the inevitable until April 1990 when he was ousted from his last position in Soviet sport. Today Gramov is a sports nobody. This does not prevent him touring the world at the expense of the IOC and receiving the homage of candidate cities. Gramov will remain a full member of the IOC until the year 2002.

The USSR's other IOC member since 1971, Vitaly Smirnov, has fared better. He was a member of the Moscow Soviet but has managed to distance himself from the old guard and has replaced Gramov at the Soviet NOC. He has been a vice president of the IOC and is secure as a full member until the year 2000. He has reached out to the new world of sport with alacrity, arranging with Germany's Mercedes car company to accept two of their limousines for his use in Moscow. Mercedes are backing Berlin's bid to host the Games in the year 2000.

1 Juan Antonio Samaranch smiles after his election as IOC president in Moscow, July 1980.

4 João Havelange, president of FIFA, world sport's longest-surviving power broker.

facing page:
2 *(top)* Primo Nebiolo: 'It is all for our great family of sport.'
3 *(bottom)* Horst Dassler receives the highest Olympic honour from Samaranch in October 1984.

5 Dr Un Yong Kim and his wife with the Samaranchs.

6 Kuwait's Mr Sport, Sheik Fahd Al-Ahmad Al-Jaber Al-Sabah.

7 Robert H. Helmick, who abruptly resigned from the IOC after his commercial dealings were revealed.

8 Mario Vazquez Raña takes the oath of Olympic membership. Only thirteen members voted for him.

9 Out with the old, in with the new: retiring FIFA President Sir Stanley Rous congratulates his successor João Havelange in 1974.

10 Lord Killanin, the last of the part-time presidents, hands over power to Samaranch in Moscow in July 1980.

11 IOC President Samaranch honours Romanian President Nicolae
Ceaucescu, the Butcher of Bucharest.

12 Former French premier Jacques Chirac with Havelange and
Samaranch. His oratory threatened to overturn the Barcelona bid and win
the Games of 1992 for Paris.

13 Samaranch, in the fascist Blue Shirt and white jacket of the *Movimiento*, is watched by General Franco as he is sworn in as a national councillor in 1967.

14 A Blue-Shirted Samaranch greets his leader just a year before General Franco's death. Behind the dictator is Spain's future king Juan Carlos, also wearing his Blue Shirt.

Gramov and Smirnov were the IOC's representatives in the USSR, a country which no longer exists.

As Romania struggles to emerge from the trauma of the Ceaucescu era their man in Lausanne continues to be the Russian-speaking Alexandru Siperco. He was active in Romanian communist politics for many years. Born in 1920 he is now a life member of the IOC.

Poland finds itself in a similar position with the Russian-speaking Wlodzimierz Reczek who joined the IOC in 1961 and is now a life member. Czechoslovakia is represented by another fluent Russian speaker, Vladimir Cernusak, who will stay a member of the Lausanne set until 1996.

Bulgaria's IOC member, Russian-speaking Ivan Slavkov, appears to be overcoming the handicap of being son-in-law to the former State president Todor Zhivkov, recipient of the Gold Olympic Order. Slavkov was Deputy Minister of Culture under the old orthodoxy and head of Bulgarian TV. He is a personable man in his middle years and is highly thought of by Samaranch. When his father-in-law's government collapsed he was held under house arrest and then imprisoned, accused of a range of crimes from arms trading to misappropriating funds from Sofia's unsuccessful bid for the 1994 winter Olympics.

The accusations have been subsequently dropped and now he has been re-elected president of the national Olympic committee in the only country in the East Bloc where the Communist Party is still a major force. He will remain a full member of the IOC for the next five Olympics – until the year 2015.

Yugoslavia's senior IOC member, the Russian-speaking Slobodan Filipovic, has been struggling since 1989 to distance himself from his former comrades in the leadership of the country's ruling party. His opponents accuse him of backing the government militias in Montenegro when they fired on demonstrators. Filipovic has denied this, claiming that his former comrades forged minutes of party meetings to discredit him. He has been fighting off a campaign from Yugoslav sports leaders to have him recalled from the IOC because he has no backing in his own land. Samaranch has gone out of his way to support him. Filipovic will remain a full member of the IOC until 2014.

Yugoslavia's junior IOC member, Boris Stankovic, joined the IOC in 1988 and has been general secretary of the international basketball federation since 1976. He was active in the world of Monte Carlo sports politics with Dassler and kept a distance between himself and the communist Party at home. He will sit on the IOC until 2000.

Hungary's Pal Schmitt has the best international reputation of the East Bloc IOC members. An Olympic fencer, Schmitt represents the independent strain of Hungarian politics that the Russians sought to crush. Since joining the IOC in 1983 he has been active on a number of key commissions.

The collapse of East Germany caused a problem for the IOC. The new, united Germany had too many members. Russian-speaking Gunther Heinze, formerly an apparatchik in the GDR's dope-driven sports establishment, agreed to retire early. He remains an honorary member.

The last IOC representative of a monolithic and repressive Communist party is China's Zhenliang He who joined the IOC in 1981. He is an Olympic vice president and on the IOC executive board. He will be a member of the IOC until 2004.

CHAPTER 10

Olympia's Black Gold

One special night in January 1987 The Club met at an exclusive Paris restaurant. The host was Horst Dassler and his guests included Samaranch, Havelange, Nebiolo, America's IOC member Bob Helmick, UNESCO Secretary General Mahtar M'Bow and a smattering of other IOC members.

Also invited was an IOC member who believed that he too was a member of The Club's inner circle. As he was rich enough to buy them all, nobody disabused him of this notion. He had one other distinction. He was almost certainly the only man in the room whose mother had been a slave.

Sheik Fahd Al-Ahmad Al-Jaber Al-Sabah, from Kuwait's billionaire ruling family, had only three more years to live before his death in mysterious circumstances at the hands of the Iraqi invaders. But his achievements were unique in sports history.

Liberally dispensing his petro-dollars Fahd had corrupted a major slice of the Olympics, trampled on the Olympic Charter and made the ideals of the movement a byword for cheating and racism. None of this could have come about without the blessing of Samaranch and the other Club members.

Sheik Fahd was born in 1945 before Kuwait's oil deposits made the country the richest in the world and when it was still normal for the sheiks to avail themselves of slaves and concubines. His father, Sheik Ahmad Al-Jaber Al Sabah, was then the ruler of Kuwait and among his favourite concubines was a woman taken from the nomadic tribes of wild Baluchistan. The Kuwaitis did not turn their backs on children

119

born to slaves and when his mother gave birth to the young Fahd it was accepted that he would rank equally with the Amir's legitimate children.

Being the child of a slave was not a bar to advancement – the mother of Kuwait's current Prime Minister Crown Prince Saad was a negro slave from Somalia. Nevertheless the young Fahd was sometimes taunted because he was not a pure-blooded Al Sabah.

A Kuwaiti friend from his childhood days recalls, 'Fahd resented the jibes because of his mixed background and he grew up to be unruly and volatile. He was not stupid but neither was he as shrewd as many others in his family. After slavery died out in Kuwait in the 1950s he looked after his mother but he always had a complex about his background and it may have driven him to over-achieve.'

A colleague who knew Fahd in Kuwait in the early 1980s told us, 'Fahd was the only brother of the Amir who wasn't trusted with a ministerial position. It rankled. Sport was the only way he could get himself noticed.'

When interviewed by the IOC's *Review* Fahd claimed that he had been a university student but he did not say what course he had studied or what class of degree he was awarded. This was another of the gentle myths that rich and powerful Kuwaitis were allowed to get away with. He may have registered at Kuwait University – as any Al-Sabah could – but he was not a scholar.

Like many of the Al-Sabahs he was given a senior rank in the Kuwaiti army. Unlike many of his relatives Fahd wanted to be seen as a man of action. Whilst his family's contribution to the defence of Kuwait in August 1990 was to set new world records for high-speed driving across the desert to sanctuary in Saudi Arabia, Fahd had proved that he did not lack personal courage.

In his early twenties, without telling his family, he went to South Lebanon to fight with the PLO against the Israelis. The admiration he received in the Arab world for that bold gesture gave his life meaning. As he rose in the world of sports politics Fahd never missed an opportunity to tighten the sports boycott on Israel, progressively excluding them from world competition.

The Olympic movement, like most sports organisations, divides the world into continental divisions. The Asian area is the largest and most populous. It stretches for thousands of miles from the Eastern seaboard of the Mediterranean through to Mongolia in the North, takes in China, India and Japan and then scoops up Thailand, the Philippines and the Koreas. It is a mix of ethnic and religious groupings, poverty and riches and varying degrees of sports development.

Those countries with a history of Western-style sport banded together in Delhi in 1949 and formed the Asian Games Federation. The founding group was dominated by countries emerging from the collapse of the British and other colonial empires – Burma, Ceylon, India, Indonesia, Pakistan, the Philippines, Thailand – and Israel. The Federation's purpose was to stage a regional games every four years on the pattern of the Olympics and the Pan-American Games.

The international sports federations had no reason to worry until the early 1960s when Indonesia staged the fourth Asian Games in Jakarta. The organisers announced that they would not give visas to competitors from Israel. They were only following the lead set by Samaranch's Mediterranean Games. This time the IOC stood firm and suspended Indonesia. They were reinstated a year later in time for the first Asian Olympics in Tokyo. The pressure to discriminate against Israel had come from the Arab states in the Gulf, eager to register their support for the Palestinians.

Israeli athletes were allowed back to compete at the Asian Games in Bangkok in 1970 but it would be for the last time. The Gulf states were flexing their political muscles. Once the Arab world had failed militarily to drive the Jews into the sea, they opted for a policy of creating a sporting ghetto. The expulsion of Israel from Asian sport would grow in direct proportion to the increasing wealth of the Gulf Arab oil states. Their campaign was to distort sports politics and sport itself throughout Asia.

Fahd, like many sons of rich royal families, diverted himself at first with his Army rank and a prodigious appetite for sporting activity. He played all sports until his increasing girth pushed him into the ranks of the administrators. He then proceeded to collect Kuwaiti sports federations the way small boys collect stamps or car numbers. Over the next few years he was to control Kuwait's fencing, soccer, basketball, volleyball and handball organisations. Most important of all, he became president of Kuwait's national Olympic committee, a position that was in the gift of the Al-Sabah family. Also at their disposal were the endless revenues from the oil fields.

Those funds, which might have been ploughed into improving the social, economic and sporting conditions of the poorer Arab states, were spread as thickly as required across the Asian region to buy votes. Fahd, the former competitor, soon discovered that there was more glory to be had as a sports leader. Little Kuwait was about to make a huge impact on world sports politics.

It was a permanent struggle for the Asian Federation to fund and organise their regional Games until a tidal wave of cash began to flood down the Persian Gulf and all the way to the South China Sea. It washed away the principles of a majority of the sports leaders in Asia. They were offered all they might desire; funding for events, for new sports facilities, for conferences, for air tickets to attend those conferences and of course personal bribes. There was only one condition. The Gulf Arab states demanded that in due course the Asian Games Federation would be abolished. It would be replaced with their own organisation. Asia acquiesced.

The building blocks were laid at the 1974 Asian Games in Tehran. Fahd and his allies in Saudi Arabia offered to pay for the next Games in Thailand. This guaranteed them the influence required to take their plan forward another step.

On the eve of the 1978 Games in Bangkok the organisers announced that Israel would be allowed to attend. But there was a catch. When the Israelis read the small print they found out that they could only send officials to the opening and closing ceremonies. No athletes would be permitted. The IAAF was offended by this blatant anti-semitism and refused to recognise the track and field events, imposing three-month suspensions on athletes who took part.

Mr Sathiavan Dhillon, general secretary of Singapore's national Olympic committee and a key player in Asian sports politics, agreed to talk to us. We had heard that he had fought the Arab takeover where he could. But on the record he told us, 'Sheik Fahd was a great sports leader and a personal friend of mine. We met years ago in Bangkok when we were re-drafting the constitution of the Asian Games Federation and to see how the 1978 Games could be hosted in Bangkok without problems from the IAAF over the exclusion of Israel.

'After much debate and discussion we took a stand that, irrespective of what the IAAF would do to Asia, we would bar Israel from taking part. That position was carried and the IAAF took certain sanctions – but they were very cursory.'

Having defied the IAAF it took another four years for Fahd to put the new organisation together. His efforts were lubricated with a further torrent of cash. In a twelve-month period from late 1980 Kuwait volunteered to stage and fund future Asian Games and pledged $15 million towards the cost of the next Games in Delhi in 1982. Their allies in the Arab Emirates chipped in with a promise that they would fund the Mediterranean Games in Casablanca in 1983.

Fahd had another reason for dispensing this largesse. Having discovered how easy it was to take over Asia his next ambition was to join The Club. He found no more difficulty buying his way into the IOC.

The capitalist, conservative Kuwaitis sought out Israel's enemies. Sports agreements were made with the communists of Hungary, China and the USSR. More oil money was applied to the Olympic pressure points and in March 1981 the new IOC president Samaranch toured the Gulf states. He was accompanied by Fahd who argued that the Arabs were entitled to a new IOC member and who better for the job than himself?

Throughout the summer of 1981 Fahd was widely tipped to join the IOC and at their September session in Baden-Baden he was elected. The Israelis, denied an IOC membership in case the rich Arabs were offended, could only watch powerlessly.

Only one nation tried to come to their help as the ghetto walls were raised. At the IAAF special congress in Rome in August 1981, where Nebiolo took power, Japan backed Israel's plea to be allowed to leave the Asian area. Israel wanted to join the European area. Here they would not be discriminated against and would be able to attend international meetings. The Japanese proposal was defeated. Instead, the IAAF recognised Palestine.

The scene was now set for a successful Asian Games in Delhi at the end of 1982, to be crowned by the creation of Fahd's own personal Olympic organisation. He had the Gulf Arab votes and he was confident of more from Bangladesh, India, Pakistan and Nepal. With the addition of China, Mongolia and North Korea, who would follow him because of his campaign against Israel, he had a majority locked up. Israel did have friends in Asia but they did not have the courage to speak out.

The Indian organisers came up with novel grounds for excluding the Israelis. They insisted that they could not provide adequate security. As the Israelis always travelled with a squad of armed bodyguards, it was a thin argument.

Fahd and the Arabs made no secret of their plans and in the May of 1982 the IOC executive board authorised Samaranch to talk to the Indians about the exclusion of Israel. He was too late. The money had already been paid. Two months before the Delhi Games the Israelis asked Samaranch, directly, at a meeting of the international federations in Monaco, to try again. Samaranch came up with one of his 'diplomatic' solutions.

A month before the opening ceremony the Delhi Games organisers announced they would withdraw their application for Olympic patronage and so there would not be the customary visit by the IOC president, signalling approval of the event. However there would be a private visitor to the Games, by the name of Juan Antonio Samaranch, but he would only attend for a 'very short period'.

During his 'short and private' visit Samaranch managed to fit in meetings with President Singh and Premier Indira Ghandi and India's Sports Minister. He held a press conference and then visited a range of sports facilities. He was presented with a ceremonial key to the athlete's village, was entertained by the Games organisers and India's two IOC members and attended a dinner for 500 people. His visit was given extensive coverage in the *Review* with no reference to the blatant contempt for the provisions of the Olympic Charter going on behind the scenes. Despite the IOC having withheld recognition from the Games, ten IOC members turned up, accompanied by athletics president Primo Nebiolo.

The Games over, the politics were concluded in the back rooms. The Asian Games Federation was buried and up sprung its replacement, the grandly named Olympic Council for Asia. Israel, banned from Delhi, could not apply for membership whilst every state on her borders was admitted. The budget for the new organisation was set at $1 million a year although the OCA, as it is known, had no funds.

Sheik Fahd pledged to find the money and, not surprisingly, was elected as the first president.

Singapore's Mr Dhillon told us, 'The whole creation of OCA was aimed primarily at Israel. It was a political issue. If you study the history of Fahd you will see that he was a great supporter of the Palestinian cause.'

Another leading Asian sports official, reluctant to be named, told us, 'The destruction of the Asian Games Federation was masterminded by the Arab oil countries. It was an unfortunate thing, there was nothing we could do about it, but Israel was excluded from membership of OCA.'

He also told us how Fahd won crucial votes. 'The Arabs did not sit in a group at meetings and they tried to avoid secret ballots. They spread themselves out around the hall, close to the people that they had bribed. When it came to the vote they would give their people a push and up would go the hands. On one occasion one of their people raised both hands and when the votes were counted we found that we had more votes than delegates!

'We heard on the grapevine that they had paid bribes. This is an open secret. The oil money was irresistible to people from the poorer countries.'

Mr Dhillon from Singapore was less certain about bribery. He told us, 'There is no proof of this. Although I have often heard stories, I cannot openly say that it happened. Those who take bribes don't talk about it. Some people think there was bribery to buy votes but there is another view; that Sheik Fahd financially assisted poorer nations to send delegates to meetings by paying air fares and paying them allowances. In other words, it was an assistance, not a bribe. I urge you to say that he helped the poorer nations to be represented – this should not be taken as a bribe.'

Only one thing might have prevented Fahd taking control of the OCA and that was his astonishing behaviour four months earlier at the soccer World Cup in Spain. He had spent nearly $4 million preparing his team for the largest world cup ever and was determined that they would qualify.

Kuwait's progress through the regional play-offs was, on occasion, controversial. They were in the Asia-Oceania Group and the competition was arranged so that Kuwait played all their qualifying matches at home. It can only be a coincidence that Fahd had recently been elected treasurer of the Asian Football Confederation. On their home ground Kuwait beat Thailand, Malaysia, and South Korea.

Then they went to Auckland to meet New Zealand who had declined to lose the home advantage and turned down the offer of an all-expenses-paid trip to play in Kuwait. The match statistics of thirty-three free kicks and two penalties to Kuwait against ten free kicks to New Zealand enraged the home crowd who pelted the officials with cans. Kuwait won by two goals to one.

In Spain Kuwait drew with Czechoslovakia and then met France. The game ended in disaster. France scored their fourth goal eight minutes from time but the Kuwaitis claimed they had let the ball go through because they had mistaken a whistle from the crowd for the referee stopping play.

Fahd stormed on to the pitch to protest and was roundly booed. Afterwards one commentator wrote 'To be fair, the Sheik only treats people like dirt when they disagree with him.' Kuwait was fined £7,000 and Fahd censured for 'unsporting conduct'. The sad thing was that Kuwait's soccer players had reached a creditable standard for such a small country, even playing their way into the quarter finals at the Moscow Olympics.

Fahd's version of the soccer dispute in Spain appeared in a new magazine called *Continental Sports* which was launched from Paris in late 1982. The editor was an Ethiopian refugee, Fekrou Kidane, and it was suggested that Fahd provided the finance. Two months after Fahd's display in Spain Kidane wrote, 'The press, which feeds off sensational news, rancorously seized the opportunity to make him pay for the increase in oil prices. He was criticised because he was the brother of the Amir of Kuwait.' According to Kidane, it was all 'latent racism'. Kidane also wrote that at the World Cup politicians had been given better seats than IOC and FIFA members. This sounded suspiciously like a Fahd tantrum.

Late in 1982 the German Sunday paper *Welt am Sonntag* carried a story about Rudi Gutendorf, formerly of the Bundesliga. He accused Fahd of trying to fix the result of the previous year's match between Kuwait and Nepal. Gutendorf, who was then an adviser to the Nepal Football Association, claimed that two of the Sheik's officials offered

him a $240,000-a-year job coaching with the Kuwait Football Associa-
tion if he could arrange for the Nepal team to be defeated by eight clear
goals.

Allegedly Kuwait had to win 8-0 to qualify for the Final of the Asian
Junior Championships. At seventy-two minutes Kuwait were winning
4-0. Then a brawl started which Gutendorf claimed was initiated by a
Kuwaiti player. The game was terminated.

The soccer scandals only served to enhance Fahd's reputation in Kuwait
for standing up to the big countries. Over the next three years he
embarked on increasingly costly ventures, all paid for out of state funds.
Even though no income taxes are levied in Kuwait, many leading
citizens eventually became concerned at the amount of money Fahd
claimed he needed to fund his Asian empire building.

The first decision he had to fix was the location of the OCA
headquarters. Japan and other Far East countries were unhappy at
Fahd's demand that the OCA should be based in Kuwait, on the very
fringe of the region. Votes were duly bought and the OCA was
established in Kuwait City.

But Fahd still faced problems over the future of the OCA. It would
not be a credible organisation unless it was given formal recognition by
the IOC. The issue was on the agenda at the 1983 IOC session which,
fortunately, was held in Delhi. Again, the vote had to be got in. Fahd
came up with a novel idea.

The seemingly bottomless Kuwaiti exchequer was raided and Fahd
announced that he would stage the first ever Afro-Asian Games in
Kuwait in 1985. This would provide lavish hospitality for the sports
officials of both continental areas and even more hospitality for those
IOC members who wander the globe constantly receiving gifts, first-
class air tickets and five-star accommodation.

Samaranch himself was persuaded to stop off in Kuwait en route for
Delhi for a joint meeting of the OCA and the African Olympic
committees to discuss the proposed event. With its new Arab member
lobbying vigorously in the corridors and Israel's friends silent, the Delhi
session bestowed the IOC's blessing on the OCA; an organisation whose
sole reason for being was a contradiction of the fundamental
requirements of the Olympic Charter. The needs of the Asian vote were
not forgotten; in October 1983 the Asian Athletics Championships were

held in Kuwait.

To his own astonishment Fahd discovered that he was on the verge of personal bankruptcy. Like many other foolish Kuwaiti speculators he had become a player in the country's unofficial stock exchange, the Suq-al-Manakh. As oil prices had risen, so had stocks and shares. Assuming that the prices would continue to soar Kuwaiti speculators issued post-dated cheques in the expectation of taking their profits before the payments fell due.

The only thing to fall was the share values and Fahd found himself in debt to the tune of $1billion. Fortunately he was in good company. Many other members of the Al-Sabah family had gambled and lost and the total deficit was believed to be a stupendous $90 billion. The Government – in effect the Al-Sabahs – agreed hastily to a rescue package to bail out some of the biggest losers. The political opposition to the Al-Sabahs, mostly merchant families who had amassed their own fortunes through financial acumen, was not amused.

Fahd had his own plans to restore his fortunes. Unabashed by losing a billion dollars he embarked on a spending spree which brought his family near to the edge of political ruin. A Kuwaiti source told us, 'He demanded money from the state for sports projects, deliberately overestimated the costs and then helped himself to the surplus.

'This way he killed two birds with one stone. He won more personal prestige for his achievements in sports politics and he also enriched himself. He inflated the budgets and stole millions of dollars. There's no question that the Government knew. He would declare the bribes in private because, after all, the rulers – the Amir and the Prime Minister – were his brother and his cousin!

'They tolerated the bribes paid throughout Asia because they brought prestige back to Kuwait. And while his vanity was being satisfied he kept quiet. He was a volatile man and he threw tantrums when he did not get his own way.

'He was clever at knowing how to bribe people, whether in Kuwait or abroad. He would check the guy out personally to see what he most wanted, whether it was donating facilities which would give a sports leader prestige in their own country or a personal bribe to buy a vote.'

The cavalier way in which Fahd helped himself to the state's money raised the ire of the Kuwaiti opposition. They resented the fact that he did not work and lived by stealing from the oil revenues which were supposed to benefit the whole of Kuwaiti society.

The first move against him had come in 1983 and was launched by Ahmed Al-Saadoon, the Speaker of the Kuwaiti parliament. At this time Fahd's collection of Kuwaiti sports federations included boxing, handball and soccer.

Al-Saadoon proposed a bill which prevented any Kuwaiti being the president of more than one federation. This was tantamount to a declaration of war on the Al-Sabahs by the opposition. The local press, at that time a free one, ran stories critical of the temperamental sheik. He was often known as 'Mad' Fahd and there were allegations that he had fixed the results of soccer games in Kuwait. The battle was carried on in the Kuwait elections of 1985. The Al-Sabahs retained control but could not assuage their critics.

The new parliament launched an investigation into Fahd's financial affairs but he declined to produce accounts. Other members of the ruling family also came under suspicion of misappropriating funds and in the middle of 1986 the Amir suspended the constitution, closed down the parliament, ordered strict press censorship and resorted to ruling by decree. Since then there have been no elections and no more embarrassing questions in parliament. Even the *diwanias*, traditional discussion groups, were broken up by the police until the time of the Iraqi invasion.

With the country's democratic forum abolished, sport in Kuwait became even more politicised. There are three leading families in Kuwait and the ruling Al-Sabahs are permanently at odds with the other two. Every Thursday, the traditional day for soccer matches in Kuwait, political battle was joined in the Al-Arabi stadium across the road from the British Council offices. The Al-Sabahs controlled the Al-Arabi Club and two others. The opposition funded three more teams and when they clashed there was the chance to inflict a surrogate defeat on the government.

The scandals of the Al-Sabahs were widely reported in the foreign press but ignored in the IOC's *Review*. Over the years it has run an occasional series under the headline 'Influential figures in sport'. Fahd was interviewed and proclaimed, 'I am a volunteer, I work twenty-four hours a day, seven days a week, four weeks a month, twelve months a

year as a volunteer for sport. Thank God I do not need a job.' The IOC
was helping to maintain the myth.

With democracy safely abolished at home Fahd campaigned vigorously
for it abroad. If he was going to keep the support of the
underdeveloped countries at the world's sporting forums he needed to
be seen to represent their concerns.

Before long *Continental Sports*, which so often seemed to reflect
Fahd's views, was attacking the IAAF and its voting system, which
gave more votes to the older, established sporting nations. Primo
Nebiolo was accused of 'presiding over a federation where demagogy
and cynicism reign'. This of course was absolutely true, but Fahd was
showing a lamentable ignorance of the real world of sports politics. Far
from ignoring the smaller nations Nebiolo was desperate to achieve a
one-nation-one-vote system so that he too could dilute the power of the
major players, some of which were bitterly opposed to him.

Pandering again to the third world, Fahd began a hypocritical
crusade to maintain 'the purity of the Olympics'. He sent letters to
countless organisations claiming that the admission of professional
athletes would lead to the 'total destruction' of the Games. He invited
sports officials to 'join hands with us to stop this devastating tendency'.
It was a good ploy; many poorer nations who faced severe difficulties
providing facilities for their athletes feared the new professionalism
would set unreachable qualifying standards. There was no mention of
Fahd's huge inducements to Kuwaiti soccer players to win
competitions.

Fahd's motive was nothing to do with altruism. His next ambition
was to win a seat on the IOC executive board in the elections due at the
Istanbul session in 1987. African support was swung behind him and
Fahd achieved twenty-eight votes but was defeated by Chiharu Igaya
from Japan. It is significant that in a secret ballot and with no
inducements available, much of the Asian sentiment went to Igaya.

The following year saw the Games in Seoul. This was the serious
business of sport and although they were in Asia, there was little role
for Fahd. His only noteworthy contribution was a protest to
Samaranch when Israel's capital was shown on the Seoul scoreboard as
Jerusalem. The Israelis countered by pointing out this had been the
case for the last 4,000 years.

As his life neared its end it became obvious that Fahd had achieved little positive outside Kuwait. His 'successes' on the international scene were hollow and when the hype was stripped away, any progress Asia had made in sport was despite Fahd's efforts rather than because of them.

His last flamboyant whim was the First Peace and Friendship Games in Kuwait in November 1989. This was organised by the Islamic Sports Conference under its president, the Amir of Kuwait. Iraq attended and in the soccer competition played a goalless draw with Iran which was some achievement after eight years of war. Samaranch attended, flanked by Havelange and several IOC members. They praised the 'spirit of fair play and mutual respect' and then listened while Fahd recited a poem he had written for the occasion. Kuwait set out to show its Arab brothers just how much money could be wasted on sport, providing five-star hotels for the competitors and limousines for the journalists. The event was chronicled in the *Review* by none other than Fekrou Kidane who not surprisingly concluded that it was an 'unqualified success'. He was also able to disclose that a committee had been set up to plan future Games. By acclamation, they had voted Fahd its chairman.

IOC president Samaranch toured the Middle East again in February 1990. He was met in Amman for the last time by Sheik Fahd who accompanied him throughout the region. They ended up in Kuwait where Fahd had funded a conference on 'Apartheid and Olympism'. This was an odd topic to discuss in Kuwait bearing in mind the millions of dollars Fahd had spent successfully discriminating against Israel. But it helped to keep African support.

Two months later Fahd set his sights on FIFA. At a meeting of the Asian Football Confederation he was appointed to be their regional vice president on the FIFA executive. One commentator described it as a 'rather peculiar' election and he won by seventeen votes to sixteen. Fahd's campaign was described at 'vehement'. In true Olympic tradition, he paid for a chartered Boeing to deliver the voters to the meeting in Bali.

It was Fahd's last sporting triumph. On the night of 2 August 1990 Saddam Hussein's troops rolled into Kuwait City. There are many versions of his death and the truth may never be established. The official story from the Al-Sabahs is that Fahd died heroically fighting

against the invader. His family would not know as they had fled
already.

The most widely believed version is that his family could not find
him as they prepared to flee because he was spending the night at an
establishment known locally as 'the bordello'. Allegedly he came out
on to the street at dawn and seeing the armoured columns went to the
royal Dasman Palace to find out what was happening. He started
arguing with the Iraqi troops and a sniper shot him in the neck.

What would happen to the OCA with its leader and paymaster gone?
Delegates who attended its congress in Beijing two months later were
taken aback to find that the Arab contingent had arrived with Fahd's
young son Ahmad at its head demanding that he replace his father!

While the Kuwaiti resistance fought bravely against the invaders the
Al-Sabah family had installed themselves safely at the Saudi resort of
Taif. Ignoring the priorities of war Ahmad, aged twenty-five and with
no experience of sports administration, had himself 'elected' president
of the Kuwaiti Olympic committee. When he tired of exile in the
restricted culture of Saudi Arabia, he moved to London to plan the
campaign to inherit his father's positions.

The Asian members of the OCA were outraged. If they could have
voted straight away for a new president, the Arab power might have
been broken. 'We are not a monarchy,' said one. The usual persuasive
tactics of the Arabs were brought to bear in an attempt to defer an
election until they were sure they would win. Ahmad told journalists,
'I did not want the voting to take place in Beijing because I did not
want to endanger the unity of Asian sport, although I know I have a
majority of twenty-four on my side.' He was right. The usual measures
were taken and eventually the OCA congress voted to defer the
presidential issue until a meeting six months later in Saudi Arabia. But
the previous control had weakened and through 1991 new meetings
were planned and then cancelled because the Fahd faction had not yet
assembled a rigged ballot.

For the first time many of the other Asian delegates talked to the
press. One Asian NOC president said bluntly, 'They have bought us
and cheated us.' Meanwhile the OCA was established at a new address.
Its magazine *Horizons* – full of pictures of the late Fahd and his
ambitious son – was published from the sleepy English seaside resort

of Eastbourne where Fahd's personal assistant Abdul Muttaleb Ahmad had taken refuge.

The young Sheik Ahmad turned up at the IOC session in Birmingham in June 1991 hinting strongly that the IOC would be well advised to appoint him to his father's seat. President Samaranch welcomed him. Numerous IOC members went before the camera of a Kuwait TV team to say what a loss Fahd was to the Olympic movement.

In August 1991 David Miller of the London *Times* reported from Seoul that the OCA was likely to split into Asian and Arab groupings. He referred to the late Fahd's 'unceasing, altruistic work that cemented the unity of OCA' and then wrote that the South Koreans, like many Pacific Asian countries, were tired of the Arab hegemony. They told him that 'meetings are postponed, agendas never sent, accounts of Solidarity Fund allocations are allegedly lost, the money unaccounted for'.

These criticisms may have annoyed the Arabs but it did not deter them in their search to find a way to impose the young Sheik Ahmad on the OCA. Their problem was that the OCA rules specifically forbid anyone under the age of thirty-five taking the Presidency. This appeared to debar the twenty-five-year-old Ahmad. After a careful reading of the OCA constitution they discovered a clause ruling that the qualifications could be waived by a simple majority. All that was needed was enough votes.

Last autumn, as the delays continued while attempts were made to line up enough votes behind Fahd's son, one South East Asian official told us, 'The OCA has been drifting without any central power. I think that OCA should change its form and go back to the old Asian Games Federation. The over-concentration of power in the president has caused many bad side effects.

'It will be a lamentable thing if the Arab countries push for the son – just for the sake of power. That's why the East and South Eastern Asian countries should now stick together. We must speak in unison for the development of the OCA. We have to fight against irregularities and other wrong doings.'

The diplomatic Mr Dhillon from Singapore told us, 'I say that a great man was lost and we miss him a lot and at the moment the place is in a quandary about who should take up the leadership. So there are discussions because many people want to change the format of the leadership. They don't want a leader to remain too long in the presidency – maybe an eight-year term.'

In an attempt to head off a takeover by young Sheik Ahmad and his Gulf millions, the national Olympic committees of East Asia – China, Japan, Korea, Mongolia, Taiwan and Malaysia – met in Tokyo on 15 September 1991 and discussed the situation for nine hours. They all signed a resolution which was highly critical of the way Sheik Fahd had run the OCA as his occasional plaything. The document said, 'OCA has fallen into disarray. Many irregularities and anomalies have arisen. The main issues are over-concentration of power in the presidency, administrative problems in the Olympic solidarity programme and weakness in procedures for agendas and implementation of decisions of the Bureau and General Assembly.'

They pleaded that a special meeting of the OCA, fixed for a week ahead in Delhi, be postponed until the organisation's planned general assembly in Japan three months later. They were backed, belatedly, by IOC president Samaranch who sent a telegram urging that the OCA listened to the Far East nations.

They were ignored. The Kuwaitis had bought enough votes and were keen to place their young sheik on his throne. A week later, on Saturday 21 September 1991, the OCA delegates met in Delhi and elected Sheik Ahmad unanimously.

Man Lip Choy, General Secretary of Korea's national Olympic committee, was still angry when he talked to us a few days later. Most of the sports politicians we had spoken to in Asia demanded guarantees of secrecy before disclosing their true feelings. Not the courageous Mr Choy. He insisted on going on the record.

'For nine years Sheik Fahd did nothing and although there were strong feelings among the East Asian countries, like China, Korea and Japan, they could not speak up because they were afraid of the Arabs.

'There has been a strong feeling that there should be a new leadership because the Arab countries are small countries, not that we ignore them, but they have little sport and no women's sports. If they did something to improve the sports quality standard of Asia we wouldn't mind but they have done nothing.

'We have eighteen or twenty countries in South East Asia. In the

Asian Games, not many Arab countries participate – maybe they send five people. There's also problems with the solidarity fund from the IOC. We have to produce a programme and they just don't do it. As for money, they submit no financial accounts for the OCA, nothing.

'The Western Asian countries are practically all bribed. They pay off delegates – from $25,000 to $50,000, sometimes as much as $100,000. Every time the elections came they paid off and then watched for the hands to go up.'

Mr Choy named a list of Olympic officials that he says have taken bribes. Then he told us about the oddities of the Delhi meeting which elected Sheik Ahmad. Inevitably, even with more than half the delegates bribed, the issue of Ahmad's age came up. Surely, some argued, he was ten years younger than the minimum age of thirty-five required by the rules? This was dealt with adroitly by Mr C L Mehta, the longtime general secretary of the OCA and a close associate of the deceased Sheik Fahd.

Mr Choy explained, 'Sheik Ahmad did not say anything. The Indian General Secretary Mehta said "He may be thrty-two, he may be thirty-five." That's what he said. The father was forty-five when he died. I think Mehta was saying there was no way to verify Ahmad's age.

'I told Sheik Ahmad in India, before the election, I told him straight "Listen my friend, I knew your father, I visited your house twice. I liked your father first but for the latter part, he didn't do anything. Now you are the one who is trying to break the constitution and this is not a royal kingdom. You have a long way to go. You prove you are good and in another four years, if you prove you are good, then I will support you." Ahmad didn't say anything.

'We will take action but I think the Japanese are a little chicken with the Asian Games coming up. The Chinese are hoping to win the Olympics for the year 2,000 so they do not say much. As for us, we want justice.

'If they don't listen and continue unjustified domination by the Arabs then I think we feel very strongly that we should not be participating in the OCA. It's just a monarchy now, that's exactly what it is.

'I shall never attend an OCA meeting again. I have told my staff this is not the Olympic movement. I will personally stay away. Under that kind of environment there is no future. This is the dirty business of power politics.'

We asked Mr Choy, what view did the IOC take of this crisis at the OCA? 'I don't know,' he replied. 'Samaranch should know about it because Zhenliang He from China was in Tokyo with us and then he went to the IOC executive board meeting in Berlin and will have reported to Samaranch. He's the guy who made Sheik Fahd an IOC member and he's the one who has got to straighten out the problem. I think the IOC should now threaten not to recognise the OCA. If Samaranch would do that, it would help a great deal.'

A leading Olympic official in another East Asian country told us, 'President Samaranch does not support Ahmad but he wants us to remain united. There has been pressure from the IOC for a peaceful election and harmony.

'Ahmad has no experience of sports administration, no proper command of English, no proper knowledge of sport and he lacks everything – he is a jack of no trades. There was a slight chance to beat Ahmad but now we have a monarchy in the OCA. Like father, like son.'

But the new monarch's inheritance is already crumbling. The East Asian countries – the major sporting nations of the OCA – have had enough. In November 1991 they announced the first-ever East Asian Games, which will be staged in Shanghai or Beijing in May 1993 and every two years after. The behaviour of Sheik Ahmad and his backers was viewed as so outrageous that formerly antagonistic nations like Taiwan and China and North and South Korea formed themselves into an alliance to rescue sport in the region. Ahmad's Asian empire without China, Japan, the Koreas, Taiwan and Hong Kong loses credibility. The announcement of the new regional event came simultaneously with the IOC *Review* reporting that Sheik Ahmad has been 'unanimously elected the president of the OCA'.

Sheik Fahd was not a bad man. But surrounded by sycophants and cushioned by wealth he never had the opportunity to discern what Olympic values really were. Prestige in his own community was gained by making life difficult for the Israelis. Yet he was not a rabid Jew-baiter. Uri Afek of Israel's national Olympic committee told us, 'Sheik Fahd would speak most courteously to our people at meetings.

However it is clear beyond doubt that he headed every attempt to remove Israel permanently from all activities in Asia.'

Fahd was a victim of his corrupt family who abolished democracy in their own country rather than have their accounts audited. He was also a victim of the IOC who pandered to his power and never dared assert that theirs was greater and had more moral force.

The Olympic Charter proclaims that the IOC 'fights any form of discrimination affecting the Olympic Movement' and that it is 'dedicated to ensuring that the spirit of fair play prevails'. Samaranch and the IOC membership ignored their own rules. It is difficult not to believe that they were reluctant to cut themselves off from the benefits that Fahd's OCA lavished on them, publicly and privately.

The IOC should have refused to recognise Fahd's racist OCA and given its member countries the stark choice of stopping using sport as a political weapon against other countries, or be expelled from the Olympic movement.

It is hardly surprising that an IOC led by a man who tolerated discrimination against Israel in the Mediterranean Games was quite prepared to tolerate an OCA whose *raison d'être* was to exclude Israel from world sport. When the IOC recognised the OCA in 1983 they sent a signal to the world; Olympic principles could be abandoned when the applicant was rich beyond dreams.

CHAPTER 11

The Bumps on the Logs

Every Olympic Games has a slogan. In 1988 Seoul chose 'Harmony and Progress'. It was very popular with Korea's military leader, Chun Doo Hwan. When Seoul was awarded the Games he announced that the role of the Olympics was 'to restore order'. In Korea that meant tear gas, rubber truncheons and bullets. They were extensively applied to the population during the seven years it took to organise those Seoul Games – the Olympics that president Samaranch praised for 'bringing people together in peace for the benefit of mankind'.

The Koreans came up with a second slogan: 'The world to Seoul, Seoul to the world.' That meant 'Let's do some business.'

Every Olympic Games has a mascot. Seoul chose the noble tiger and turned it into a woolly toy wearing an odd, alpine-style hat.

Every Olympic Games has an official emblem. At Seoul this was a 'modification' of a traditional Korean design. The original symbolised the harmony of man, heaven and earth with the universe. The PR men re-designed it to symbolise 'progress through world understanding and peace'.

Peace is a very popular word in Olympic-speak, although there is no record of any war being averted or nations being brought permanently closer by the Games. When the Olympic flame finally went out, the Seoul Games were pronounced a 'tremendous success', a return to the 'Olympic ideal'.

The Seoul Games were conceived from a desire by a military junta to obscure their brutal image and to find new markets for their dynamic economy. The Koreans were fortunate to bid at a time when few cities wanted to risk boycott and bankruptcy. They won the contest because of mistakes by their rivals, Dassler's genius in organising the vote and the remarkable political skills of Dr Un Yong Kim. Dr Kim is a quiet, stocky business-like lawyer who looks exactly what he is; a man trained to kill with his bare hands. Today Dr Kim is a senior member of The Club, sits at Samaranch's right hand and is a candidate to inherit the President's mantle in Lausanne.

Dr Kim is not forthcoming about his background. At one time he admitted having been Deputy Director of the presidential security forces. This team protected President Park Chung Hee who ruled the country with great brutality and no democracy for nearly two decades. He was assassinated in 1979, after Dr Kim had moved on to greater things.

Dr Kim's profession was later altered on his IOC official fact sheet to 'Deputy Director General of the President's Office'. Dr Kim studied at three American universities and was an envoy to Washington, the United Nations and to London. In 1973 he founded and became president of the World Taekwondo Federation. Taekwondo is taught to all ranks of the Korean armed forces. Initiates learn to smash bricks with their bare hands.

Taekwondo has received considerable state backing in Korea. There has been speculation that with his mix of considerable intellect and martial arts skills Kim was and may still be, a senior figure in the Korean CIA. At an IOC meeting in Atlanta in 1991 the organisers were surprised when Dr Kim went off to spend a day at the US Army's Fort Benning 'to be with his buddies'.

We turned to former CIA intelligence officer Philip Liechty who served in Korea from the late 1960s. 'You have to understand what kind of people were recruited to the Presidential Protective Force, President Park's personal bodyguard,' he told us. 'It was a time when there were several carefully planned paramilitary assassination attempts on the president, attempts by teams dispatched from North Korea, and so he surrounded himself with proven killers. The important thing is that the man who protects the president in a country like that has to have demonstrated that he is willing to kill without hesitation for his boss, to do anything the president asked him to do.

'They insisted on people totally loyal to the president, with no wild ideas about Western-style democracy, people who would give their lives to protect the president, who would do whatever he told them to do, who believed that he was the best thing for the country.'

CIA officer Liechty also opened our eyes to the role of the 'sport' of taekwondo. 'I am aware of a lot of allegations, many of which I consider very reliable, that during President Park's era the Korean CIA used taekwondo schools as bases for operations and cover for its overseas officers, particularly here in the US. There was a period when some of these people were allegedly involved in kidnapping and covertly removing Korean students, protesters against the Park regime, from the US back to Korea. There's much evidence of this and similar operations in which the KCIA was involved back in the 1970s.'

So, we asked, what could have been Dr Kim's role in the Korean secret service? 'I have never come across Kim but my assumptions are that he must have been very much involved in Korean intelligence activities over the years,' says Liechty, 'either as an operational officer or at least as someone who was friendly towards the KCIA and who was co-opted into Korean operations intended to exert influence in areas where he had overseas positions. Based on the information he has provided about his background with the Korean embassy in the US, his education at American universities, his founding of the World Taekwondo Federation, and his position in the Presidential Protection Force I'd say there has been little doubt as to his past involvement in Korean overseas intelligence activity. That's the mildest way I might state my opinion as to his possible background in intelligence'.

Dr Kim had unique credentials among the Seoul organisers. He was the only Korean who had managed to step outside his own country on to the world sporting stage. He had formed an association with a New York entrepreneur called Don Kalfin. Kalfin ran the Sanshoe company, a huge importer of shoes from Korea. Kalfin in turn was involved with a group from California who were planning to stage the first World Games in 1981. These Games were a showcase for all the non-Olympic sports and some felt that Kalfin saw himself as another Dassler in the making, mixing shoe sales with sports politics. With Kalfin's sponsorship, Dr Kim became president of the World Games.

The Games ran into financial trouble and the organisers turned to Patrick Nally. 'The money wasn't coming in and I got called in to see if we could help. It was very difficult for us because it was fairly late in the day but I put up more than $100,000 so that the Games could actually take place.

'Kim was a mystery man in those days. Nobody knew quite what his power or his influence was within Korea. He started talking to me a great deal. I think he realised that Kalfin and Sanshoe weren't the only people who could support him. He was obviously anxious to develop as a bigger figure in the international sports world.

'He invited a lot of sports leaders out to Seoul in the 1970s. This was another strand of the Seoul Olympic bid. They needed to convince the international sporting community that they could put on the Games. My first visit was amazing. I was taken to Dr Kim's taekwondo hall in Seoul where he staged magnificent displays for his guests. In all my years of travel I have seen nothing like this.

'I was ushered into a VIP box, seated in a luxurious, embroidered armchair and then watched hundreds of teenagers and young adults performing taekwondo exercises. I have never seen the movement of so many human bodies in one place for such a small audience.'

In 1980 Dr Kim's career took two major steps forward. The IOC 'recognised' taekwondo, the most aggressive and dangerous of all the martial arts, and he was elected to the council of the General Assembly of International Sports Federations – known as GAISF. 'Kim started rubbing shoulders with the more important international presidents and began to appreciate what the possibilities could be in the system,' says Nally. 'And through me he also met Horst.'

The favourite to win the nomination for the 1988 Olympics was the Japanese city of Nagoya. They were backed by the powerful Toyota car company. Japan had already staged a summer and winter Games successfully. The chances of Melbourne, Athens and Seoul were not highly rated; Korea was seen as an unstable military dictatorship in constant danger of war with it's communist brothers to the north.

Dassler weighed up the bidders in terms of how he could benefit. Melbourne and Athens never got a bandwagon rolling so when it came down to a race between Nagoya and Seoul, Dassler knew which way he wanted the vote to go.

'Seoul was much more attractive than Japan for a number of reasons,' says Nally. 'Firstly, Horst couldn't control the Japanese. They were very independent minded. Horst would have spoken to them about being co-operative but the meeting wouldn't have gone well. They were too arrogant, they were always too confident that they would win the Games.

'Korea was different; they were co-operative and they manufactured nearly everybody's sports equipment and sports shoes. A lot of Adidas product was made there and Dassler knew the Koreans well. Politically it was an important country for him.

'The victory of Seoul over Nagoya was a victory for Dassler in his own eyes because he proved to himself that with his political team, his Colonel Hamoudas and his Chowdrys, he could put the machinery together. It was the first time that Dassler could prove to himself that he had been decisive in choosing an Olympic city.'

Another Dassler associate told us, 'In the run-up to the vote Horst was saying to us that Nagoya would win. But at the last moment he swung behind Seoul and would have talked to people. Yes, the Japanese were arrogant and Horst could not get on with them.'

When the vote came in Baden-Baden in late 1981 it was overwhelming. Seoul crushed Nagoya by fifty-two votes to twenty-seven.

However, there was one embarrassing problem which had to be swept under the carpet. The Koreans did not just make everybody else's clothes and shoes to order – they made almost as much again illegally. They were crooks. Korea had a counterfeiting industry churning out an estimated $10 billion a year worth of imitations. Howard Bruns, president of America's sporting goods manufacturers association said, 'Brand-name piracy has become highly sophisticated in South Korea. You can buy labels and identification tags for every well-known brand in the world.' He was backed up by the world federation of the sporting goods industry, which claimed that Korea was the biggest single source of counterfeit goods in the world. They were not amused when Korean Government officials looked them in the eye and insisted, 'There is no counterfeiting here.'

What made the situation worse was that the Koreans, always so protective of their own domestic market, wanted to use the Olympics as a Korean goods showcase. They had no intention of putting on the world's greatest sporting festival for the world's biggest TV audience and then have foreign brands highlighted. The Korean soccer federation led the way when it banned its players from wearing foreign brands. The country's ruling sports body, the Korean Sports Association, announced that 'using foreign goods is shameful'.

★

When the euphoria of winning the Olympics wore off the Koreans had to face some hard facts. However much outside help they had received in winning the nomination, they now had to build a team who could organise the Games, and also find the money. It helped that in a society controlled by the military they could get decisions made quickly. Unfortunately, packing the Seoul Olympic organising committee – known as the SLOOC – with military men was a disaster.

Dr Kim had his own idea of what constituted the ideal Olympic organising committee. According to him, it should contain 'bureaucrats, the military, police, intelligence agents, sportsmen, press and broadcasters, diplomats and even businessmen'. Within a year of awarding the Games to Seoul the IOC were becoming concerned that this collection of spooks, policemen and paper-pushers were not up to the job.

The SLOOC leadership were regularly sacked or, to save face, moved to nominal posts. New names came and went until the IOC were unsure who had responsibility for what. Fortunately, the lower levels of management were efficient. Their ability to divert national resources ensured the facilities were built.

The Koreans had assumed that these costs would be recouped from a grateful world, eager to shower them with massive TV payments. There was shock in the New York offices of the three big American TV networks – ABC, CBS and NBC – when the Koreans announced that the price for the US TV rights to the Games was $1 billion. This was four times the record sum of $225 million paid for the previous Games in Los Angeles.

'Traditionally the summer Games are valued at about two and half times the winter Games,' an adviser to the Koreans told us. 'After Calgary, for which ABC paid $300 million, the Koreans came up with the number of $700 million. Then in their hierarchy that figure went up and became not a possibility but a probability, then it became the target and finally it became the only figure they would accept. They developed this self-created and unreasonable expectation, totally devoid of any market considerations and totally devoid of what was going on in the TV industry in the US at that time.'

US TV executives said publicly that the Seoul cash demands were 'far beyond reality'. When the Koreans dropped their sights by $300 million an NBC executive commented drily that '$700 million is not a figure you can arrive at after doing the financial analysis'.

IOC vice president Dick Pound who was on Lausanne's negotiating team recalls, 'The problems were acute because the Koreans had totally overestimated the value of the rights and had created an expectation that had no possibility of being achieved.

'That was then coupled by suspicion, when they got the numbers that were so much lower than they had expected, that they were being jerked around by the Americans – because they were Koreans. Maybe this big giant was trampling on them because they were a small Asian country and they had not really analysed what the market would be.

'The third feature was that ABC was way over extended on its Calgary coverage and was not really a serious bidder. CBS had not been in the Olympic broadcasting business since Rome in 1960 and their corporate culture was such that they were not prepared to pay very much for rights although it turned out that they were in the same ball park as the other two.'

But the Koreans were deaf to the arguments from America. When it was pointed out that each network had an annual budget of only $2 billion the Koreans still suspected they were being cheated.

One of the American TV negotiators told us, 'The numbers the Koreans were floating were insane. They dug in and said that's what they thought it was worth. NBC offered $325 million and revenue sharing and ABC and CBS both offered $300 million. The Koreans were clearly stunned by these offers and it was only then that we discovered that their team did not even have the freedom to negotiate.

'They had come from Seoul with instructions that they could accept any number over 500. So we sat there at noon in Lausanne and they couldn't do anything because they had to wait hours until it was morning time in Korea before they could call up to get further instructions. Dr Kim was there, but he said nothing. He just sat there and slept in the chair. They had a whole bunch of bumps on logs doing nothing.'

Eventually Samaranch got through to the Korean government and urged them to accept NBC's offer of $325 million. Reluctantly, they agreed. By the time they got back to the meeting NBC had withdrawn the offer.

★

There was consternation at the IOC. They were quite happy to accept the NBC bid. Samaranch became worried that the Koreans' greed might upset the good relationships with the US networks. He emerged from the Château de Vidy in Lausanne to announce, 'As far as an organising committee is concerned, the relationship to the TV companies ends with the end of the Games. For the IOC the relationship continues and we will always depend upon their goodwill. The IOC has no interest in pushing the fees up endlessly.' The message from Lausanne to New York was clear: the IOC was pulling the rug from underneath the Koreans.

When that message filtered back to the government in Seoul they pulled the rug from underneath their negotiating team. The Seoul sports minister was recalled and Dr Un Yong Kim was promoted to chief negotiator.

He had trained with the best. 'I used to have an office in Japan and Dr Kim had watched me and my colleagues doing TV deals,' recalls Patrick Nally. 'He would watch us selling rights and its clear now that he learned quickly. He started off raw and innocent and eventually became the chief TV negotiator for SLOOC. He was clever and he assimilated what we told him. He is cool, calculating and capable, he learned quickly and has taken every single advantage that he could.'

Dick Pound, leading the negotiations for the IOC, remembers that the last round of the TV negotiations was bitter and acrimonious. 'The detail of the contract negotiations was excruciating. NBC wanted guarantees that all the money they spent in the years before the Games could be recouped if anything went wrong. They insisted that the guarantee offered by the Korean Central Bank was not good enough – they wanted a letter of credit that would be accepted by a consortium of American banks.

'Everything they said was insulting to the Koreans so it took months to negotiate it. We didn't know the afternoon we were leaving for Lausanne to sign the contract in March of 1986 if we had a deal. It was that tough.'

They shook hands on a minimum of $300 million – $25 million less than the Koreans had turned down earlier. To save face in Seoul NBC offered a share of profits that could take the payment up to $500 million

– but everybody knew it would never happen.

The real power behind the Korean organising team was now Dr Kim. He was given the title of vice president but he was the brains behind every major decision. Once he had concluded the US TV negotiations he sold the rest of the TV rights around the world. He was appointed to head all international relations, was made Head of Protocol and finally asked to control the organisation of the sports events themselves. Dr Kim had become the 'Dr Fixit' of the whole Games.

He had an even greater ambition. He wanted to join The Club. 'Whatever issue came up, he was saying "yes" to everyone, so he would be invited to join the IOC,' says one IOC member. In November 1985 a vacancy came up at The Club. Korea's existing member Chong Kyu Park died of cancer and less than a year later Dr Kim was taking the Olympic oath in Lausanne. Nine days on, in Monte Carlo, he was elected president of GAISF. It was a remarkable rise in world sports politics.

Dr Kim's elevation to The Club was against a background of near civil war. By 1987 the mood in Korea was similar to that in the Philippines where 'people power' overthrew the corrupt Marcos dictatorship. In Seoul and all Korea's major cities the middle classes, housewives, workers and students went on the streets to demand free elections and an end to President Chun's authoritarian rule. Early in the year he announced that there would be no constitutional reform until after the Games. The street protests turned to fighting.

Chun was forced to abdicate and who should come to the fore but his right-hand man Roh Tae Woo, the godfather of the Games. He had championed Korea's bid and gone on to head the organising committee. At the end of the year he was elected state president.

The North Koreans were incensed when Seoul won the Games. They called on the rest of the communist camp to boycott Seoul in a gesture of fraternal solidarity. Could the 1988 Games be in jeopardy? Samaranch was galvanised into action. The amateur diplomat who had rubbed shoulders uneasily with the professionals in Moscow now sought to bring some substance to the 'HE' that the IOC always put before his name. From 1985 until the eve of the Games three years later Samaranch threw himself into endless shuttle diplomacy, hopping from one communist capital to another, visiting Pyongyang regularly and entertaining delegations from North and South Korea at his official residence in Lausanne.

Breathless media reports appeared around the world suggesting that Samaranch was a super-diplomat, fighting to save the Olympics from destruction. Superficially, it looked like the real world of power politics. Even eminent commentators, who might have known better, praised Samaranch's political skills.

It was a charade. The Russians and the East Germans made fraternal noises but there was no way they were going to pull out of another Olympic Games. The American boycott had reduced the competition in Moscow in 1980, the East Bloc had stayed home in 1984. If they did not go to Seoul then their athletes would be be out of Olympic competition for a dozen years. They could not allow sixteen years to pass – from Montreal to Barcelona – before they met the Americans again in an Olympic stadium. A boycott was unthinkable. Generations of young stars would come and go before the East Bloc could return to Spain in 1992. Morale in the training camps would be fatally damaged and invaluable propaganda from the inevitable haul of medals sacrificed.

Much as the powerful communist countries loathed the right-wing military regime in Seoul, they were not going to do more than humour Kim Il Sung and his absolutist regime in North Korea.

Most important of all, Gorbachev now held power in the Kremlin. Perestroika and glasnost were entering the Western vocabulary as Gorbachev set about sweeping aside the old order. The USSR was now in the business of building solid bridges to the West.

The one worrying incident which could have damaged the Seoul Games was the Russian shooting down in 1983 of a Korean passenger jet which overflew Soviet airspace. Two hundred and sixty-nine people, mostly Koreans, were killed. In an effort to calm the anger and grief, Horst Dassler hosted a private dinner in Beverly Hills during the 1984 Los Angeles Games for Russia's two IOC members and SLOOC's President Roh.

The prickly image of North Korea did cause legitimate concerns about the security of the Games. In November 1987 a North Korean terrorist team planted a bomb on a Korean Airlines flight from Baghdad to Seoul and 115 people died.

The American public was shocked. The phones started ringing at the US State Department as the anxious parents of athletes likely to go to Seoul asked what Uncle Sam was doing to protect them.

Clayton McManaway, who was then working in counter-terrorism at State, told us, 'We set up special briefings by the Bureau of Diplomatic Security for all American athletes before they departed for Korea. Then my office co-ordinated all the American government support for the Korean government's security for the Olympics.' McManaway soon left State and joined one of the world's more discreet private security companies, the Fairfax Group, based in Northern Virginia across the Potomac from Washington. They had been hired by NBC to guard their vast expedition of reporters, technicians and hardware in Seoul.

Former FBI man David Faulkner, who also works for Fairfax, said, 'After the bombing of the aircraft we were pretty sure that the North Koreans had other events planned but they got caught, and therefore couldn't carry them out. That's what most people involved believed.'

The biggest problem for the NBC staffers was trying to do their job. Seoul is surrounded by military installations and that caused headaches for the cameramen. 'We wanted a particular high camera position,' recalls Faulkner. 'But if you panned the wrong way you were going to pick up something they didn't want you see. So the Koreans had armed soldiers on the top of the building to make sure your camera went from here to here and not any further. They were holding the NBC people at gun point on one occasion and threatening to shoot them!'

There was never any real danger that the North Koreans would try to sabotage the Games, once they got under way. Thousands of their East Bloc comrades were in Seoul as competitors or officials and would be likely victims of any terrorist attacks. The US government organised three high-profile military exercises and filled the seas around Korea with warships. It was an obvious signal to the North Koreans to back off.

Running up to the Games the Americans had been concerned that Pyongyang might attempt a terrorist mission. Thousands of miles away in Kenya, the CIA took considerable risks to persuade a North Korean intelligence officer to defect on the eve of the Games. They wanted to know if any sabotage acts were planned.

The South Korean authorities left nothing to chance. They used the 1986 Asian Games in Seoul as a dress rehearsal for the Olympics. The police detained an astonishing 263,564 people during the run up to those Games. They explained that it was part of a 'social purification programme'. The exercise was repeated on the eve of the Olympics and thousands of dissidents were incarcerated in camps outside Seoul. No doubt it was explained to them that their detention was all part of 'Harmony and Progress'.

When it came to winning medals the Seoul organisers dedicated themselves to progress at the cost of harmony. Eighteen months before the Games the Korean sports minister produced a report for his government predicting that the host nation would win more than a dozen gold medals – including three in boxing. Once that rash commitment had been made, a lot of face was going to be lost if the medals were not won.

The prediction that Korea would have successes in the boxing tournament was based on more than optimism. The groundwork was laid over the two years running up to the Olympics and little of it was done in the boxing ring. The result would be the most disgraceful TV pictures from the Games, embarrassment for the hosts and headlines about corruption.

Since 1986 world amateur boxing has been presided over by Professor Anwar Chowdhry from Pakistan, once a highly paid member of Horst Dassler's political team. Over the years amateur boxing has held many meetings courtesy of Adidas at Dassler's French Landersheim base. Adidas were official suppliers to the boxers in Seoul and there was a huge scene at the ringside when one boxer turned up in front of the cameras wearing a rival manufacturer's kit.

Professor Chowdhry does not draw attention to his former Adidas connections. In a recent profile in his federation's magazine, running to many hundreds of words, his payments over the years by the German sports manufacturing company were never mentioned.

Chowdhry was elected to head boxing at the federation's annual congress in Bangkok in November 1986. At the same congress, Seung-Youn Kim of South Korea was elected an Asian vice president. Kim, who had led the federation's business committee, is reputed to be among the world's richest men. He is known worldwide by his

nickname 'Dynamite' because his father was a munitions manufacturer. Kim – not related to Dr Un Yong Kim – who had headed the
Korean Amateur Boxing Federation since 1982, was appointed to take
charge of the Olympic boxing tournament.

In the period before the Games the Koreans attempted to bribe some
of the Olympic boxing judges. One of the biggest problems in amateur
boxing is ensuring that the judges are capable of scoring a contest
correctly. The pool of potential Olympic judges and referees were
invited to Seoul in March 1988 for a seminar.

One federation member who was present told us, 'Everyone was
entertained lavishly, given piles of presents and taken to night clubs.
Anybody who was going to be a judge in the boxing tournament later
in the year could have anything they desired. A number of officials
were very worried because obviously when they came back to judge at
the Games, the Koreans would expect to be repaid.'

One judge, New Zealand's Keith Walker, who would later make the
world's headlines, commented that the level of gifts was 'phenomenal'.

The pictures every TV viewer will remember from Seoul came in the
bantam-weight contest between Korea's Jong-il Byun and Bulgaria's
Alexandr Hristov. Referee Keith Walker twice warned the Korean for
using his head dangerously but even then some commentators thought
that he had been too lenient. After three rounds the judges voted
Hristov the winner by 4-1. All the experts thought it a fair verdict. But
to the partisan Korean spectators another medal opportunity had
slipped away. The Chamsil gymnasium erupted. Korea's chief coach
and another official climbed into the ring and began punching referee
Walker. They were joined by reinforcements who began pulling
Walker's hair out.

He managed to escape, made for the airport and fled to New Zealand
as fast as he could. The defeated Korean staged a sitdown protest,
staying in the ring for sixty-seven minutes. The TV pictures of the
recalcitrant loser went round the world. Korea lost even more face.
David Faulkner, who was minding the NBC commentators, recalls,
'NBC played the tape over and over and the Koreans said they were
making something out of nothing. We had to provide extra security for
NBC commentators at the next few boxing matches because the
crowds tried to intimidate them.'

Professor Chowdhry had to admit that it was 'the most disgraceful incident' he had even seen. There would be worse before the tournament was over. To placate the angry media it was announced that Korean boxing president Seung-Youn Kim had resigned.

The world's TV cameras moved on but the boxing scandals continued. A day later American light welter-weight Todd Foster knocked Korean Jin-chul Chung to the canvas and assumed that he had won the bout. Chung complained he had stopped boxing because he heard the bell in the adjacent ring. Senior boxing officials ruled immediately, to the disgust of the Americans, that it was a no-contest. In the re-match later that day Chung was knocked out in the second round.

Despair began to set in when the Yugoslav heavyweight Havrovic was judged to have lost to his Korean opponent. Observers thought that the Yugoslav had won all three rounds.

The pictures that told the real story of the Seoul boxing came on the last night of the tournament. They showed Korea's light-middleweight gold medal winner Park Si Hun lifting the man he had just defeated, America's Roy Jones, in the air.

Both boxers were victims of one of the worst examples of cheating ever seen at an Olympics. On his way to the final Park had defeated the Italian Vincenzo Nardiello. This had surprised many observers who were sure that Park had lost. Nardiello beat the canvas in anger when the 3-2 verdict went against him.

There was worse to come. In the final Jones battered Park round the ring for all three rounds. In the second round the Korean was forced to take a mandatory eight-count. At the end of the contest the NBC computer credited Jones with landing eighty-six punches and Park just thirty-two.

The Russian and Hungarian judges gave Jones the gold medal by huge margins. But Jones lost. The three other judges took the opposite view.

American coach Ken Adams rushed over to the president's table and shouted at Chowdhry 'I don't believe this. You wouldn't dare give the decision to the Korean!' Chowdhry never looked up.

British referee Rod Robertson, who was watching the fight, called the result 'disgraceful'. West Germany's Heinz Birkle said it was 'criminal' and Scotland's Frank Hendry thought it was 'shocking'. Korea's boxing president described the score-sheet as 'fair'.

Officials from every country, including some from Korea, alleged that the three dissenting judges had been bribed. The world's press summed up the verdict. They used words like 'stench' and 'corrupt'. Gold medallist Park said he was ashamed to be the victor and lifted Jones in the air to make it clear who *he* thought had won.

To the credit of the host nation, 50,000 Koreans phoned the local TV station to protest that their man should have lost. The three judges who voted for Park, Larbi of Morocco, Duran of Uruguay and Kasule from Uganda made excuses. They claimed that if all the judges had voted for Jones they feared that a unanimous verdict against the Korean would produce a riot. Nobody believed them. It must be one of the few occasions in the controversial history of boxing when both fighters, the world's media and a billion or so TV spectators were certain the judges were wrong.

One official took journalists to one side and told them they had to understand the Moroccan judge Larbi's predicament. The result had been fixed way in advance and Larbi, a simple schoolteacher, would never work again if he scored against the Korean. Chowdhry, ignoring the universal condemnation, continued to appoint all three judges to officiate in the remaining Olympic finals.

The following year the international boxing federation met in Nairobi. On the agenda was the question of what to do about the three judges who had brought boxing perilously close to being evicted from the Olympics. The federation's referees' and judges' commission decided that the three offenders should be banned for life. They prepared to pass their views on to President Chowdhry.

Word reached Chowdhry. One of his closest associates approached a member of the commission and said, 'The president feels we should not announce the decision. We should have a further meeting.' More private meetings were held. Finally, the three judges were suspended for two years, nearly half of which had already passed. Later in 1989 the discredited Larbi turned up for a tournament in Moscow as manager of the Moroccan team.

All demands for an investigation of the Seoul scandals have been ignored by President Chowdhry. In an attempt to rectify the damage with the world's media, Chowdhry's old chum and Dassler political team mate, Colonel Hassine Hamouda, has been recruited to improve amateur boxing's image.

Chowdhry proclaimed later, 'There is scope for further improvement to make judging foolproof.' Nobody had ever said the three judges were fools.

The Korean boxing president S-Y Kim did indeed resign his position – but for only a year. Then he turned up in Moscow, was warmly welcomed by Chowdhry and remains a boxing federation vice president for Asia. Samaranch made muted criticisms of boxing immediately after Seoul but the sport remains on the Barcelona agenda because American TV viewers want to see their boxers in action. The Olympics would lose a lot of dollars if boxing was banished.

As the Seoul Olympics came to an end the Koreans began their round of saying thank you to all those who had helped make their Games such a 'tremendous success'. A formal list was drawn up of people to receive presents. At the top were the IOC members and their wives, then came the presidents of the international federations, the rank-and-file officials and judges. Bottom of the list were the athletes. The value of the gifts started at $1,100 at the top and went down to $110 for the athletes. The Seoul organisers knew who really mattered in the Olympics. The total bill came to $4.5 million.

Horst Dassler, the man who deserved the biggest thank you, had died the year before the Games. State President Roh, who had led the Games bid, invited Dassler's children Suzanne and Adi to Seoul to receive his personal thanks. Roh handed over Korea's Order of Merit in memory of their father. Dassler's long-time confidante, Huguette Clegironnet, was later received by President Roh.

At the Birmingham IOC session in 1991 we spoke briefly with Dr Un Yong Kim. We asked him about his relationship with Dassler. 'I did not have any dealings with Dassler, I only know he was a great supporter of the Olympic movement,' insisted Dr Kim. 'I have no personal knowledge of him. We had no direct dealings with him.' Then he managed to cram almost the whole dictionary of Olympic-speak into one sentence as he terminated our meeting. 'The Olympics is the greatest festival of mankind and all the youth get together for friendship and world peace.'

'Dr Kim was part of the Seoul bid committee in Baden-Baden, he worked with Horst to get the Olympics into Korea and ultimately got himself an IOC membership,' says Patrick Nally. 'Kim was one of that handful who were politically astute and could see exactly what they were going to get out of it. But Kim was not a Dassler prodigy like Nebiolo, Havelange or Samaranch. He dealt with Dassler, he made agreements with him but to be fair to Kim, he learned very fast and came through from obscurity to the IOC in record time.'

'I think he is a combination of fighter and spook,' one IOC member told us. 'There's great speculation that he runs the Korean CIA. He certainly trained with them. He's pretty opaque. He's very ambitious. He's got this network of taekwondo which is totally supported by the Korean government and that's his job. He's everything you would fear about somebody from that part of the world, in a position of power.'

Dr Kim is now a leading contender to replace Samaranch and become the next Olympic president. He would be a fitting choice; like the Spaniard he rose to high office in a totalitarian state which routinely murdered dissidents and used sport to put a gloss on their poor image. Both have survived as their countries have embraced democracy and have moved away from their roots to concentrate on the international sports politics scene.

It is a fair question to ask whether someone with Dr Kim's background is a fitting person to be on the IOC at all. He would no doubt be pained by such a suggestion. After all, his Korean predecessor on the IOC, Chong Kyu Park, known as 'pistols' Park because he was also vice president of the world shooting union, was from a similar background. 'Pistols' Park was Kim's boss at the Presidential Protection Force and president of the Korean national Olympic committee but had to resign 'for political reasons' after the assassination of his president in 1979. 'Park was totally loyal to his President,' said former CIA man Philip Liechty. 'He was a deadly and very dangerous man. He was Korea's Number One Thug.'

'Pistols' Park was nominated for Olympian membership by President Samaranch. It takes all sorts to make up the IOC.

CHAPTER 12

Twenty Million Dollars

This is the untold story of how the Seoul Games were nearly destroyed long before the flame arrived from Olympia. The threat was not from North Korean terrorists; it was not from an East Bloc boycott. It came from one of the most senior members of The Club. He held the Games of 1988 to ransom and sweated the Koreans until they were on their knees. He then allowed them to pay him off with tens of millions of dollars.

The long and drawn-out negotiations to sell the TV rights to the American networks concealed a subterranean drama. The plot was built around the finals of the key sports in Seoul. The sub-plot was their timing and the main character was athletics.

The most exciting part of the Olympic Games is the finals when medals are won and lost. It is then that the world tunes in to TV.

Traditionally, the finals of the biggest Olympic sports are held in the late afternoon. At Seoul, this posed a problem. Because of the time gap between Seoul and New York, finals staged in the afternoon would come up 'live' on US TV screens late at night or in the early hours of the morning. This spelled financial ruin. If the finals were not brought forward to earlier in the day there would be small TV audiences in America.

The Games would be of little interest to advertisers. The Olympics would go for a song to the networks. Finals at midnight – or recordings shown the next day – would see the value of the Games plummet.

The American networks needed the key finals in every sport to be concluded by late lunchtime in Seoul. That would put them in evening prime time in the USA and guarantee them big advertising revenues.

The decision to change the finals times could only be taken by each international federation. They planned their own events within the overall framework of the Games.

The key federation, the one which provided far and away the most hours of TV, was of course athletics. Club member Dr Primo Nebiolo, the president of track and field, is a shrewd streetfighter. He knew that he controlled the one commodity that the Koreans, the Olympic committee and the networks wanted most badly.

The athletics federation produced a schedule with finals as late as 5pm, Seoul time. Nebiolo made it clear that he could not have his athletes upset by changes in the schedule. Then he stood back and waited.

In the autumn of 1984 Samaranch summoned Nebiolo to Lausanne. They had to talk about the finals times. What would persuade him to change them? Nebiolo told Samaranch that if he agreed to move the late afternoon finals to the middle of the day, he would want a bigger share of the TV revenues from the IOC.

Samaranch held the line and refused. He could see angry protests coming from the other federations if Nebiolo got his way. So Nebiolo then demanded the right to hold his own separate negotiations with the US networks. Samaranch blocked this too.

The Koreans were then brought back to the negotiating table and several other federations agreed to make the changes required. Some asked for modest compensation – believed to be up to a ceiling of $200,000 – and the Korean organisers agreed to pay.

The moment that the Koreans rather than the US networks or the IOC offered to solve the problem with cash, Nebiolo realised that he could pull off a once-in-a-lifetime coup. His sport now held the key to the success or collapse of the Games. The Koreans were vulnerable to a shakedown and the longer Nebiolo postponed an agreement the more pliable they would have to be.

Nebiolo's athletics council met in Canberra in October 1984 and he persuaded them to stand fast; it was their right to hold finals up until 5pm and nothing would be conceded. The Koreans went specially to Canberra to lobby the IAAF. But their style was abrasive and they played into Nebiolo's hands. As the Korean negotiating team left Australia they realised that the TV value of their Games was haemorrhaging.

The game of poker ran on into 1985. To keep to their timetable of preparations for the Games the Koreans had to commit themselves to more and more spending without knowing if they were going to get the money back from the sale of the US TV rights.

The IOC seemed unable to grapple with the issue. The *Review* ran an article claiming that the networks had offered to 'double the sums it pays to the organisers if the finals in the major Olympic sports take place in the morning'. The reality was that the sums would be more than halved if the federations did not alter the schedules.

The Koreans were quoted saying, rather desperately, that temperature and humidity levels made it preferable to hold the finals in the morning.

Nebiolo chipped in, tightening the screw on Seoul, with his interview for the *Review*. He said that he had consulted with all the leading track and field nations and they did not want to alter the timetables. He went on, 'Finals in the morning would not allow the athletes to realise their potential. We are governed by the interest of the athletes.'

In March and April 1985 the networks put more pressure on the Koreans. TV executives briefed the New York media that because the Games were being staged later than usual, in September, the Olympic transmissions could clash with college football, major league basketball and the host of high-rating programmes launched for the new autumn schedules.

Advertising Age noted that having dropped from their demand of $1 billion, the Koreans were still asking $500 million for 'mostly delayed-tape telecasts'. One commentator wrote that 'September is the time people send their children back to school and get down to the business of watching the final dash to the Baseball World Series, the beginning of the national football marathon and the thrills and agony of a new prime-time TV season.' Steadily, the value of the Games was being talked down. The networks knew that whatever was published in New York would be read in Seoul the next day. The rack was tightened another notch.

At the end of May Samaranch washed his hands of the Seoul finals problem. 'The question of timetables for the competitions at Seoul is to be settled between the organising committee and the international federations,' said the president. 'The fact that each federation is now free to negotiate timetables has taken the heat out of the problem of morning finals.' This was a clear signal to Nebiolo to do whatever he wanted – as long as he brought forward the finals.

Nebiolo appeared to play his tactics brilliantly. The Koreans were nearly on their knees. Now it was time to Go for Gold. He sat in Rome holding court and the Koreans came to him, to try and get a deal.

There were several meetings between the IAAF and the Koreans. The media were briefed regularly about the lack of progress. Then came the meeting that has never been reported. Somebody who was in the room told us about the crucial moment when the log-jam cleared.

According to the source a Korean negotiator, at last realising the calibre of his opponent, asked in desperation 'What do you want in return for changing your finals' times?' It was the moment to strike. Now they really were on their knees. Nebiolo's eyes lit up and he replied, tersely, '$20 million'. The Koreans collapsed. Just one cheque to Nebiolo for $20 million would put them back in the business of collecting hundreds of millions from NBC. It was an investment. They agreed to find the money.

Nebiolo had grandiose plans for the $20 million. If he could keep it seperate from the IAAF then he would have unbelievable riches to dispense and his powers of patronage would be enormous.

The Seoul organisers persuaded a Korean sportswear company to sign a sponsorship contract with the athletics federation. They agreed to provide the cheque for $20 million; $5 million more than Visa paid for total worldwide exclusive sponsorship of the Olympics. The cheque for $20 million was placed in an account at the Bank of Monte Carlo.

Monte Carlo had become a hub of sports politics intrigue since Dassler and Nally had moved there a decade earlier. The ruling Grimaldi family were grateful for the trade that Dassler, the association of international sports federations and the crowded calendar of sports meetings brought in.

Now Nebiolo offered another sporting organisation that would bring in even more cash. But Nebiolo wanted something in return. He wanted 'royal' patronage. That was no problem. The heir, His Highness Prince Albert, was available.

At the end of the first week of May 1985 Prince Albert and his retinue were received in Lausanne by IOC President Samaranch. The reason given was that Prince Albert had just been elected president of the Monaco track and field federation. This is not one of the larger federations in world sport. The faithful *Review* reported the visit in its usual way, describing the playboy Albert as 'a man of the sea' because he was organising a yacht race to New York. Samaranch and his noble guest went off to dine in the city's finest restaurant, the Girardet, where, according to the press release, they discussed 'the development of sport in the Principality'. The most important development, for the Monaco economy, would not be revealed for another year.

A week later, in East Berlin at the 90th IOC session, Prince Albert was admitted to The Club. Another 'aristocrat' had been added to Samaranch's collection.

Everything was now in place: the cheque for $20 million had been delivered safely to Monte Carlo, Prince Albert had joined The Club. A month later, Nebiolo's athletics federation council met in Athens and kept their part of the secret deal with Seoul. All the important finals, including the 100 metres and the 1,500 metres would be concluded by late lunchtime in Seoul.

Now NBC could start talking serious money, their executives begin selling advertising. Nebiolo must have laughed hugely to himself. He had won the jackpot in the sporting world's biggest game of poker. And he'd done it with an empty hand!

'If the Koreans had told Nebiolo that his $20 million demand was outrageous and that they would never pay, he would have shrugged his shoulders and conceded the finals times they wanted,' a source inside the IAAF told us. 'What the Koreans didn't know was that the IAAF council had decided that they dare not risk alienating the US networks for much longer.

'Remember that Primo wanted them to pay big money for the Athletics World Championships in Rome in 1987. He couldn't afford to be seen as the guy who left the Olympics destitute. Secretly, the decision had been taken that it was time to change the schedule. If the Koreans had not been so naïve, so out of their depth in this kind of negotiation, they could have sat tight and saved themselves a lot of money.'

Nebiolo had played the most almighty game of bluff. Fortunately for him, the Koreans only knew one way out of trouble – to pay up.

★

Dr Un Yong Kim had led the TV negotiations for the Koreans and was a
key member of the Seoul team dealing with both international relations
and organising the sports events of the Games. It was Dr Kim who had
headed that delegation to Rome which sought Nebiolo's agreement to
re-scheduling the athletics finals. 'Dr Kim developed in co-operation
with the sports associations,' reported *Sport Intern* magazine, 'schedules
for Seoul which are also acceptable to the American TV companies
without the sports associations losing face.'

We assumed that Kim would know how the problem of the finals
times had been resolved. It seemed unlikely that he would have been
ignorant of a deal that saw a sum as large as $20 million leave Seoul for
Monte Carlo. We were wrong.

'I have no idea about that. I am not involved in money, only in
organisation,' Kim told us. 'NBC did not set the times for the Seoul
finals. We did. We just set what we felt were the best schedules. For
Japan and Europe the time zone was OK. For the US it was either live in
the early morning or at midnight. But the decisions on the times were
taken by the organising committee. They were not taken by the
federations either. We just studied the times and set the best schedules.'

'We Koreans are a very proud people. We are very nationalistic and
we don't take kindly to being told what to do. We just say "go to hell!" '

We had spoken with Dr Kim at the 1991 IOC session in Birmingham.
We parted apparently on good terms. A couple of hours later we were
approached by the IOC press chief, Michèle Verdier. Ms Verdier was
not happy. Indeed she seemed quite shocked that any journalist might
want to ask for information other than that provided by her own press
statements.

'Dr Kim has complained to me about you,' she said. 'You didn't ask
him about the session. You asked about other things.' This it seems is
not acceptable behaviour in Olympic circles.

After the Seoul Games, Dr Kim wrote a book about his experiences.
He had this to say about the immense problems of the finals times.
'Athletics was the most difficult to adjust'. And that was all.

Nebiolo invented his very own charity with the $20 million from Seoul.
It was to be called the International Athletics *Foundation*, known for

brevity as the IAF. It would be based in Monaco. Its purpose was to help the IAAF, the athletics *federation*, promote the sport throughout the world. The Foundation appeared to duplicate the aims of the Federation with money raised in the name of the sport.

The first the worldwide membership of the IAAF learned about Nebiolo's charity was in the pages of their *Newsletter*. This was because the Foundation had been set up by Nebiolo's inner cabinet. The subject was never brought before a full congress for discussion. Nebiolo's much-vaunted 'family of athletics' were excluded from any democratic involvement in whether the Foundation should be set up at all, discussion about the source of the money and who would control it. It was a Nebiolo ambush and it succeeded.

The IAF is registered under the laws of Monaco. Its statutes give the impression that it is a big organisation. It has a general assembly, a council, an executive committee, an assistant general secretary, a general secretary, a vice president and a president. It sounds impressive. Closer examination reveals that there are less than thirty individuals involved. The membership is confined to Nebiolo's IAAF Council, which currently has twenty-five members.

Virtually all power in the Foundation is vested in the president – who is of course Dr Nebiolo. He is the only person who can nominate new members, he is the only person who can sign cheques and the only person who can 'take any measures he deems necessary' and tell the Foundation later.

Nebiolo also 'holds all powers to act on behalf of the Foundation' and 'in particular the power to appoint the lawyers'. One lawyer he has chosen to appoint is his old friend from Milan, Mino Auletta, who draws an annual fee of $30,000 from the Foundation. Auletta also earns considerable fees from Nebiolo's athletics federation. They pay him around $100,000 a year for keeping his eye on the federation's contracts with ISL and Adidas. Auletta has replaced a London firm of City solicitors who previously undertook this work. Auletta has received in the region of $1 million over the last five years. The size of his fees have caused rows within the federation.

The first meeting of this new Foundation, in July 1986 was 'honoured by the presence of His Highness Prince Albert of Monaco. The council invited His Highness to become the honorary president of the Foundation and were delighted when His Highness graciously accepted the invitation,' reported the athletics *Newsletter*.

And now the good times rolled. At Christmas that year Prince Albert 'graced' the first public function of the new Foundation devoted to the development of athletics. The venue was the Hotel de Paris in Monaco and the function was 'The First World Athletics Gala'. Nebiolo and his Prince awarded a new decoration, the 'Prestigious IAF Gold Star of Athletics' to all the year's world record breakers. Applauding were several hundred of what Nebiolo refers to as 'members of the athletics family' – trusted officials, friendly journalists, TV executives and sponsors.

Their night of self-indulgence cost a mere $500,000. 'The moral aim of this institution is to help clean up high-level sport,' announced Nebiolo. He did not explain how such an aim could be reconciled with the origins of the money paying for the champagne that night.

The costly gala has been held every year since. Invitations read: 'In the presence of the President of the International Amateur Athletic Federation, Dr Primo Nebiolo, and of His Royal Highness Prince Albert of Monaco, the World Athletics Gala will be held in the Sporting Club, Monte Carlo.'

Unfortunately, Prince Albert does not qualify to be addressed as 'royal'. In the quaint world of etiquette he is only 'serene'. This may not disturb Nebiolo overmuch. He has signed up a prince to give credibility to the Foundation and one day his prince will rule the tax haven.

Nebiolo appointed himself president and he remains in that position for life. Should the Foundation be closed down for any reason, there is no requirement that the $20 million or more in the Monte Carlo bank account goes back to athletics.

Nebiolo has never revealed the source of his Foundation's money. Indeed he goes out of his way to keep it secret. When asked he says, 'It's anonymous only because the people making it wanted it that way. The money is only spent on developing our sport.'

At the IAAF offices in Hans Crescent, off London's Knightsbridge, we were given a copy of a glossy brochure that was about to be distributed. It stated that the initial funding – from one single donor – was indeed $20 million. When we expressed surprise that there could be one individual or company in the world capable of donating such a

vast sum, there was consternation. The brochure was snatched from
our hands.

Later we were told that that this had been a proof copy and that it
had now been pulped. This was surprising; it was obviously a costly
piece of work. The explanation was that they had made a mistake.
There was more than one donor and so the brochure was being
reprinted. Technically, this is true. Adidas have recently made a
$50,000 donation and one or two other sponsors have made modest
payments. Sources within Adidas accept that Nebiolo's Foundation
does not need the extra money but that it is very helpful to be able to
give the impression that the funding is from more than one source.

Nebiolo's athletics Foundation typifies much of what is wrong with
The Club. Over the last two years the Foundation has spent $516,000
on worthy projects. In the same period of time they have spent $1
million on two annual galas in Monaco. The extravagant event is
repeated every year. So far in the region of $3 million has been spent
on these annual junkets.

Then there are the fees paid by the Foundation to its professional
advisers, the cost of travel, hospitality, hotel suites and other expenses
which are not disclosed. Questions about what actually happens to that
mountain of money in the Bank of Monte Carlo are answered with the
bland reply 'autonomous projects which are overseen by the IAF
council and monitored by the IAF secretariat'.

One senior IOC member said to us, in confidence, 'Nobody talks
about these payments to the federations because it's embarrassing. It is
always couched in terms of "We have to think of the kids getting up at
3am to warm up – its the good of the athletes we are most interested
in." Then you find that they've done the opposite and a couple of
hundred thousand dollars have landed somewhere.'

The eminent Olympian gave us his personal opinion. 'We don't
know much about how the Foundation was funded except to say that
in that part of the world, and in the twilight area in which Nebiolo
works, there was an exchange of value.'

CHAPTER 13

The Cheats

Primo Nebiolo's finest year should have been 1987. But the dark side of his character triumphed and what were intended to be twelve months of achievements for sport, and even more prestige for himself, are only remembered because he presided over the worst example of organised cheating in the history of modern sport.

If that was not bad enough, he then refused to admit that it had happened. We can now reveal the secrets of the conspiracy to steal a medal from an American long jumper at the World Championships in Rome in 1987 and award it to an Italian. Only one question remains to be answered. When did the president first know?

The new year began as Nebiolo preferred it. At the end of the first week of January 1987 he chaired a meeting of the IAAF council in Rio de Janeiro, one of his favourite cities. The guest of honour was his old friend, FIFA president and Brazilian IOC member, João Havelange.

Then he flew to Paris to pick up yet another award. Just before the month end Nebiolo was at the Inter-Continental Hotel for what the press handout described as a 'glittering occasion'. It was the annual awards of Colonel Hamouda's *Champion D'Afrique* magazine. Dassler was of course the host and Samaranch was there to present the 'gold medals' in front of 200 guests to UNESCO General Secretary Mahtar M'Bow, Havelange and Nebiolo.

It was the perfect platform for Nebiolo. Fêted and well fed, he could take time to reflect that he had organised 1987 so that he would grace the centre of the world sporting stage all year long. He had pronounced that 1987 would be 'The Year of Athletics' and it would begin, formally, in the spring when he would preside over the first ever IAAF indoor world championships in America.

Through the summer would be the build-up to the second athletics world championships to be hosted at the Olympic stadium in Rome. On the eve of the championships Nebiolo would chair the congress of the IAAF where he knew he would be 're-elected' as president without any opposition.

The Year of Athletics should also have been the year of Luciano Barra. Barra is one of Italy's top sports civil servants. An employee of the Italian Olympic committee, he has for many years been one of the the main driving forces behind the success of Italian athletics and Nebiolo's rise to power. Outside Italy he was applauded for his skills in organising and marketing major track and field events.

Barra was also general secretary of the Italian athletics federation (FIDAL) and was one of the 'Young Turks' who had backed Nebiolo to become its president in the late 1960s. He had put in his years as a sports official travelling the length of Italy by bus and train, staying in modest hotels and always urging local organisers to promote the sport in their regions.

He acted as the brake on some of Nebiolo's wilder schemes and as his boss strutted the world stage, Barra was always a discreet pace behind, making sure that the rhetoric was translated smoothly into action. When Nebiolo was installed by Dassler as president of world athletics in 1981 he created a new position in the IAAF of 'assistant to the president'. Barra filled it.

Now Barra faced his biggest test yet; staging the largest and most complicated athletics meeting the world had ever seen. Nobody doubted that he had the skills to ensure that the 1987 World Championships in Rome would be successful. What neither Nebiolo nor Barra foresaw was that so large would be the workload that the assistant could not have the time to keep control of his erratic and ambitious boss who longed only for Italy to win medals.

The first indoor world championships in Indianapolis were projected as yet another triumph for Nebiolo, another first in the development of the sport. But the Italian contingent came back from America with bitterness in their hearts.

The championships had been organised with Nebiolo's power base in mind. Every one of the 170-plus member federations were invited to send one male and one female athlete whether or not they had reached any qualifying standard. Inevitably this increased the number of eliminating heats and dozens of no-hopers had their brief taste of world-class competition and then went home.

Inviting these inexperienced athletes was not a mark of sporting charity; it was a cold-blooded political decision. Even nations with just one competitor could also send an official paid for by the IAAF. They were the ones that *really* mattered. It was the officials not the athletes who would cast crucial votes when Nebiolo needed them. Although there are a lot of lunches in Nebiolo's IAAF none of them are free.

The indoor championships were staged under the massive Hoosier Dome in Indianapolis. More than 20,000 spectators turned up, making it the biggest-ever indoor athletics meeting. Nebiolo declared his 'great pleasure' that eighty-four countries were competing. His insatiable desire for world records, to boost the TV value of his events, was satisfied. Ben Johnson, his steroid-enhanced muscles gleaming under the arc lights, set a new mark of 6.41 seconds for the 60-metres dash.

For all the successes, the Italian officials were furious. They had gone to Indianapolis with high hopes of a good medal placing for their star long jumper Giovanni Evangelisti. Carl Lewis did not compete so his main rival was the American Larry Myricks. Evangelisti was not on his best form and by the end of five rounds his best jump was only 7.91 metres. For the last time, he squared up at the end of the runway and then hurled himself towards the pit, determined to go for gold.

The Italian officials were certain that it was a clean jump. All eyes had turned to the huge video screen and they swore that it showed Evangelisti's foot well behind the take-off board. When the American officials hoisted the red 'foul' flag the Italians seethed. They were convinced they had been robbed of the gold medal. They watched grimly as Larry Myricks took it with a leap of 8.23 metres. The incident opened a wound that would not heal.

The disputed jump by Evangelisti in Indianapolis in March was not forgotten by the Italian team officials. Whilst their energies were concentrated on organising the World Championships in August, five months ahead, there was still time to reflect on what had happened in America. In Rome it would be their turn to supply the officials at the long jump pit.

Some of those officials gathered at the championship headquarters late in August to finalise plans for the judging. The topic for discussion was an astonishing one: whatever the cost, Italian athletes were going to win medals.

They discussed a number of events but, with the decision in Indianapolis still rankling, they agreed that as long as Evangelisti turned up to jump, they would guarantee him a distance of around 8.40 metres.

News of what was being planned by the FIDAL officials leaked slowly through the organisation and reached Mrs Anna Micheletti, a secretary with FIDAL, who told her husband Renato Marino, the chief coach of one of the most prominent clubs in Italy. He in turn mentioned it to his friend Sandro Donati, an Italian national sprint coach. Donati had become increasingly concerned about the way Nebiolo ran FIDAL and what he saw as a lack of official action against rampant doping in Italian athletics. Marino decided to attend the stadium with binoculars and pay close attention to what happened around the long jump pit.

At the IAAF congress in Rome, on the eve of the championships, Nebiolo was installed for a further four-year term as president by the acclamation of the delegates. Then he moved to broaden his power base even further.

For nearly a decade the smaller athletic nations had been chafing at the IAAF voting system; they wanted each member nation to have only one vote and it suited Nebiolo to encourage their resentment. Up until 1984 the 170-odd member nations had been divided into four groups. Depending on the size of their role in world athletics countries had eight, six, four or two votes at congress. At the Los Angeles Games IAAF congress the system was simplified into three groups.

In the run-up to the Rome congress the Russians backed the demand from the smaller nations for a simple one-nation-one-vote system. Their willingness to sacrifice their powerful position was transparent; they had so many client states that they could always assemble a large block of votes when needed. By backing the little nations against the big ones, they could claim to be progressive reformers.

In the glow of goodwill and self-satisfaction in Rome that August Nebiolo saw his chance to rid himself forever of the shackling votes of the Western European nations who were all in the first division and were often unhappy with his style. He recommended that the congress move to a simple franchise; the one-nation-one-vote principle was presented under the guise of a democratic revolution. Nebiolo tightened his dictatorial grip on the IAAF.

Nebiolo knew only too well that he would always find it easy to keep the small nation support. The federation's soaring income enabled him to fund more and more of the cost of transporting athletes – and more importantly their voting officials – around the globe to events and congresses, TV and marketing and technical seminars.

The unspoken deal he offered to federations from remote places like Vanuatu, the Cook Islands, Nauru and even the Northern Marianas Islands in the Pacific Ocean, Aruba and the Turks and Caicos Islands in the Caribbean or Bhutan, Macao and Laos in Asia was clear; their officials would be offered a regular flow of air tickets, rooms in premier hotels and hefty expenses in US dollars in return for the loyalty to keep Primo *primo*.

It was a master stroke. The more that the developed and powerful sporting nations were to attack Nebiolo for his excessive expenditure, the more they would drive the officials on specks of rock around the world, all with the same one vote, into his arms. Most satisfying of all, it looked so democratic.

As well as being 'The Year of Athletics' 1987 was also promoted as the seventy-fifth anniversary of the IAAF. A lavish book was produced, its theme *One Hundred Golden Moments* in athletics. A commemorative film was commissioned, 8,000 gift packs were prepared for competitors, officials, sponsors, TV executives and the entire circus which accompanied the president. Specially commissioned awards and medals were presented throughout the year to 'Members of the Athletics Family, VIPs, guests and Heads of State'. For public consumption, Nebiolo opened an exhibition at the Foro Italico to mark the seventy-fifth anniversary of the IAAF. This too was called 'One Hundred Golden Moments'.

At a dinner before the championships Nebiolo pulled Carl Lewis to one side. He told him he wanted a world record – any record. 'This is going to be the greatest meet of all time,' he said. Nebiolo then repeated himself to Ben Johnson. The Canadian was the star of Rome 1987 and so he remained for another thirteen months.

In June, Johnson went on a last two-week steroid cycle, waited for his system to excrete all trace of the drugs and travelled to Rome. There, on the opening day of the championships, he beat Lewis in the 100 metres and set an astonishing new world record of 9.84 seconds. 'I watched the Canadian officials twitching until Johnson's dope test was through,' one IOC member who was present told us. With his star property pronounced clean, Johnson's agent immediately started negotiating millions of dollars in sponsorship.

Lewis, like most other competitors and officials on the track circuit, knew that Johnson was a monster created by drugs. Just before the 100-metres final Lewis had been told of a deeply incriminating conversation between Johnson's coach Charlie Francis and the American coach Chuck DeBus. Francis was heard to comment – 'I'm just going to say that Ben had gonorrhea.'

This was virtual proof that Johnson was taking the drug probenecid to mask any residual trace of his steroids. One of the legitimate uses of probenecid is to increase the effectiveness of penicillin in the treatment of venereal disease. Francis was well prepared to argue away any positive test result.

Lewis says he was perplexed: he did not know whether to denounce Johnson or rely on the officials to catch the cheat. The problem was that Lewis did not trust the track and field officials in his own country or worldwide. Lewis later announced that he knew of at least one other gold medal winner in Rome who was on dope and that another champion had visible needle marks on his upper thigh.

There was little doubt who would win the gold and silver medals in the long jump. Carl Lewis and the Russian Robert Emmiyan had out-leaped everyone that year. Lewis was so keen to win the jump that he even withdrew from the 200 metres to give himself sufficient rest. The contest would be for the bronze medal. Evangelisti, Myricks and the Cuban Jefferson were likely to be the main contenders.

It was not expected that there would be any disputes over the judging of the long jump. The three official technical delegates to the Rome World Championships were Georg Wieczisk from East

Germany, Artur Takac from Yugoslavia and Hassan Agabani from the Sudan. They were all senior members of Nebiolo's IAAF council.

Ten minutes before the contest began Luciano Barra and Takac arrived at the long jump pit and insisted on moving the press photographers back because, they claimed, they were obstructing the TV cameras and disturbing the athletes. But there was one camera that was overlooked by everybody. At the far end of the long jump pit there was an unmanned static camera which captured head-on each competitor's dash down the runway. The feed from the camera ran straight on to video tape. It was unlikely to be used during live transmissions because all it showed was the action in the pit, but the tape could be used later, with pictures from the other cameras, for editing together montages of the jumps.

The judges, mostly from Sicily, and the two English technicians who monitored the Seiko electronic measuring device, waited for the action. The Seiko machine has replaced the traditional tape measure. A reflecting prism on a spike is placed in the sand where the contestant's heels land and a beam of light is 'fired' from the machine positioned near the take-off point. If it is operated properly it gives out two 'beep' noises as it measures the jump.

At half past five in the early evening Evangelisti, who had drawn first, opened the competition to the cheers of the predominantly Italian crowd. He raced down the runway and was foot faulted. The crowd groaned. The American Larry Myricks followed and also faulted. Then Lewis soared into the air with a massive 8.67 metres. It wasn't beaten that evening and that was the gold secured. Emmiyan's first jump took him to a respectable second place at 8.30 metres.

Half an hour later the next round began. Evangelisti led off again and got on the scoreboard with a modest leap of 8.09 metres, putting him in fifth place. Myricks could only manage to land 5 centimetres behind. Lewis jumped a massive 8.65 metres and Emmiyan faulted.

In the third round the Italian increased his distance to 8.19 metres but was overtaken by Myricks at 8.23 metres. Meanwhile Lewis proved again that he was the best in the world by equalling his first round jump of 8.67 metres.

Evangelisti led off into the second half of the final but failed to reach 8 metres. Myricks jumped a moderate 8.19 metres and Emmiyan secured the silver medal with 8.53 metres. The fifth round was even more depressing for the Italians; Evangelisti faulted again. Myricks, landing at 8.33 metres, seemed certain to have taken the bronze.

It was now or never. If Evangelisti was to overhaul Myricks his sixth and last jump would have to be something special. He positioned himself at the end of the runway and paused to psych himself up. Before he could explode forward, the William Tell overture rang out over the loudspeakers, signalling the medal ceremony for the women's shot put. The Italian made a gesture of irritation and turned back. He would have to wait until the end of the awards before taking his last jump.

The organisers had made elaborate plans for the medal ceremonies. All officials were ordered to stop what they were doing and stand to attention facing the winners' podium. Every eye and every TV camera swung towards them as the three women walked out into the arena to collect their medals.

So hardly anyone noticed a slight flurry of activity among the judges around the long jump pit. The judges had forgotten about that TV camera at the far end of the pit. The images were locked onto a video tape running in the studios of RAI, the state TV service, alongside the Olympic stadium.

The medal ceremony came to an end and Evangelisti prepared for his final jump. It was his last chance for the bronze. Even as he rose into the air the spectators and the trackside statisticians knew he had failed. Evangelisti rose out of the pit, shrugged his shoulders as if to say, 'I gave it my best shot', and walked off. 'It was a good-looking jump,' reported *Track and Field News*, 'but there was no roar from the crowd. He walked away, looking discouraged.'

Judge Sergio Maggiari stepped into the pit and put the measuring spike by Evangelisti's heelmark. Judges Mario Biagini and Paolo Pellegrino, who were waiting to smooth out the sand after the jump, knew not to move until they heard two 'beeps' from the Seiko measuring machine. They waited – but the machine made only one 'beep'.

They realised that something was wrong and Pellegrino moved quickly and put his rake by Evangelisti's heelmark, to make sure that it would be measured properly. He called to Biagini not to make any move to level the sand. To Pellegrino's astonishment Chief Judge Marco

Mannisi protested and simultaneously Judge Tommaso Aiello rushed over shouting, 'erase, erase'. Obediently, they smoothed out the sand and the true length of the jump was lost forever.

Biagini did not appear to be completely surprised by this strange turn of events. He turned to Pellegrino and pleaded, 'Paolo, please, I know you. Keep calm, this thing is bigger than both of us. When you get out of here it is better to pretend that you noticed nothing, keep your mouth shut.'

The result flashed up on the scoreboard. Evangelisti had leapt 8.38 metres. The stadium erupted. He was in third place and on course to take the bronze. As the rest of the competitors took their final turns, the partisan crowd whistled and booed anybody, including Myricks, who might upset the result. The American did indeed turn in a substantial leap, which the judges measured at 8.20 metres, and which bettered anything Evangelisti had achieved in the previous five rounds. But according to the judges' measurement, he could not match Evangelisti's unexpected recovery. 'It felt further than 8.20 metres,' Myricks said later, 'there was something screwy about that last round.' Evangelisti took the bronze and the American was reduced to fourth place.

Many in the contingent of American sports journalists in Rome thought something was wrong with the long jump result. And they were not alone. A reporter from Finland protested to all who would listen that Evangelisti had been given a better distance than he deserved. The jump also came under other expert scrutiny. Seated in the stand opposite the pit were a group of British sports fans and track statisticians. One of them was Alf Wilkins from London. 'We thought the jump was about 7.95 metres. We just couldn't believe the result. We were certain it wasn't 8.38 metres. Even the Italians sitting near us weren't excited at the jump, until the result went up. Everybody was talking about the jump in the restaurants that night. It was greeted with derision.'

Wilkins is a member of the association of track & field statisticians. They refused to recognise the jump, categorising it as 'doubtful'. This was an astonishing verdict to pass on a result achieved at a world championship, run by the IAAF and in the presence of its president.

Two days after the long jump Renato Marino, who had been watching through his binoculars but had not spotted exactly how the Evangelisti

result had been rigged, was in a Rome bar. There he encountered the
director of the championships, Paolo Giannone, with his wife. Over a
pizza Giannone announced that he was was annoyed by a story about
himself in the newspapers. Luciano Barra had told a journalist that he
had received an apology from Giannone for allowing the women's shot
put ceremony to disturb Russia's Sergei Bubka as he was about to
attempt the pole vault world record.

Giannone insisted that it had not been he who gave the signal to go
ahead with the ceremony. He had been out on the field checking the
'regularity' of the long jump.

'Regularity!' Marino exploded, 'You mean irregularity.' Giannone's
wife turned to her husband, 'You see,' she said.

'He is an expert and he noticed it.' Giannone replied.

'Look, I didn't notice it because I happen to be an expert,' said
Marino. 'Everybody in the stand realised what had happened.'

'You must understand,' replied Giannone, 'we were told that
Evangelisti had to get a medal.'

CHAPTER 14

Scandal

The first casualty of the simmering long jump scandal was Nebiolo's political ambition in Italy. It was not enough to be president of world student sport, Italian athletics and the international federation; the remaining position of power he coveted was that of president of the Italian national Olympic committee. The presidency brings control of an annual sports budget of $750 million and all the power that implied. With that clout Primo really would be *primo* in Italian sport.

The vacancy occurred when the president, Franco Carraro, joined the government of the socialist leader Bettino Craxi. Only the thirty-nine presidents of the individual Italian sports federations were eligible to stand and vote. Nebiolo was already a vice president, as befitted the leader of a major sport, and he calculated that he had plenty of favours to call in. He quickly counted his likely votes and threw his hat in the ring.

The election was called for 12 November 1987, two months after the end of the Rome World Championships. The date came too late for Nebiolo. His hopes of victory were destroyed a week before the election. The sports journalists at RAI, the state TV service, had been as troubled as most other reporters by Evangelisti's amazing recovery in the last round of the long jump. They came up with the idea of applying one of their favourite video tools the 'Telebeam' – devised for analysing how goals were scored in soccer – to tapes of the long jump.

They showed the results on the main evening news. Their astonishing conclusion was that Evangelisti's last jump was no more than 7.90 metres. Nebiolo's assistant Luciano Barra was invited on the programme to comment. He asserted, in his calm way, that so great

174

was the difference – about half a metre – between Evangelisti's recorded jump of 8.38 metres and the suggested 7.90m that it could not be fraud. Nobody, he claimed, would dare to cheat that much. It must have been a technical error. This was the first split in the Nebiolo ranks. Whilst the president was adamant that there was nothing wrong with the result his assistant, who was also the general secretary of FIDAL, was conceding that it could not be right. The point was taken keenly throughout Italy but nowhere more so than at CONI, the Italian Olympic committee.

The election for a new president was held at CONI's stylish offices next to the Olympic stadium at the Foro Italico. It was big news in sports-mad Italy. The country's leading serious newspaper *La Repubblica* thought it important enough to publish a major feature, by Vittorio Zambardino, reporting the contest between Nebiolo and the other candidate, Arrigo Gattai, the skiing president. 'Nebiolo's longest day started at 6am,' the report began, 'when he received a phone call at home from Marchio, president of the boxing federation. "They did it. They've stitched us up. We've lost." More phone calls. A word of advice: "Withdraw and save face." But Primo wants to see this one through to the end.

'At 8.20 he's the first president at CONI. His famous suntan is showing cracks. He perfunctorily salutes the other presidents. His hands are in his pockets as he nervously strides back and forth, knowing he's beaten but not understanding why. A few cold hand shakes. Nebiolo's not smiling. He walks down the hall of lost ambitions. His eyes are bloodshot, staring furiously at the traitors.'

Carraro arrived and the sports presidents gathered to hear his farewell speech. Carraro did not miss a chance to turn the knife in Nebiolo and the rumours about the long jump. There was a reference to 'morality in sport'. Then there was a delay before the vote.

'Someone trying to be funny says, "Anyone who wants to buy my vote should step forward," ' the *La Republica* report continued. 'Nebiolo is glued to his chair, gnawing at his glasses. At 10.30 Giorgio di Stefani announces the results: "Gattai 26, Nebiolo 13". Nebiolo is more than depressed, he's 1.65 metres of mourning. He whispers, "I suppose I've got to congratulate him." His face is an anguished mask, his lips are drawn in a clown's smile as he shakes Gattai's hand. "Its only right. The best has won." His tragic sarcasm is obvious.'

The argument about Evangelisti's jump was turning into a scandal. Three days after the CONI election *L'Espresso*, Italy's most popular news magazine, published the first of a series of articles that ran to the year end, investigating what had really happened at the long jump pit. They had picked up clues that there had been some kind of conspiracy amongst the judges to fake a medal-winning result for Italy. The magazine had also commissioned its own computerised analysis of the TV pictures of the jump. These, like the Telebeam, showed that Evangelisti must have landed far short of the result he was given. They also cast doubt on the measuring of several of the other jumps. The story was developed by the rest of the press and the pressure increased.

Something would have to be done. Luciano Barra announced that he would conduct an inquiry into the long jump result for FIDAL. The Italian sports press appeared placated. The headline in *Corriere dello Sport* was 'FIDAL will throw light on Evangelisti's Jump.' The officials at FIDAL asked RAI to make up a video cassette of all the jumps. When it arrived, everything looked normal. It was several weeks before anybody thought to ask if anything had been captured on tape during the medal ceremony. The RAI technicians remembered the unmanned camera positioned at the end of the jump pit, which had run all evening on to video tape. They promised to search for the tape.

In the first week of December *L'Espresso* published the ultimate in independent evidence. It showed, yet again, that the jump result was false. This information must have been leaked from the Italian athletics federation and if that was the case it was likely that Nebiolo was already aware of it.

The headline on the article was 'The German Proof'. The long jump had been scrutinised by a team from the Sports Institute of Cologne led by Dr August Kirsch, also a member of the IAAF council. They had developed a three-dimensional form of measurement using electronic monitors along the side of the long jump runway and pit. Because the readings from the monitors were made as the athletes competed, the evidence could not be challenged. Kirsch's version of the long jump result was stunning.

Every competitor, with the exception of Evangelisti, had jumped further than the judges claimed. Kirsch confirmed that Evangelisti had only cleared 7.91 metres on his final jump. The difference from the judge's measurement of 8.38 metres was unbelievable. Revenge had been fully exacted on America for the result in Indianapolis five months earlier.

What would Nebiolo and the IAAF do now? The federation council was due to meet in Monte Carlo in mid-December to tidy up the year's affairs and then enjoy $500,000 of entertainment at the International Athletics Foundation's 'World Athletics Gala'. Concerned that Nebiolo might forget his duties the Milan sports paper *Gazzeto dello Sport* chose this moment to accuse him of being responsible for the Evangelisti long jump result.

The scandal could not be omitted from the council's agenda in Monaco. Barra had already conceded in public that the result must be incorrect. Kirsch's evidence could not be argued with. Two separate electronic examinations had condemned the measurement and the Italian press was bubbling with disclosures. At the very least the bronze medal award would have to be cancelled; it no longer had any credibility. Nebiolo would not hear a word of this. What he did have on his side was that the story had not spread beyond Italy. Bluntly, anyone who did not read the Italian press might not know of the scandal.

Justice lay in the hands of Nebiolo, his council and the federation's three technical delegates at the Rome championships. They were East Germany's Georg Wieczisk, Yugoslavia's Artur Takac and Hassan Agabani from the Sudan. Sudan has been ravaged for a decade by military dictatorships, civil war and famine. Athletics activities are rare and the capital, Khartoum, is crumbling. With little for him to do Agabani, a wealthy businessman, spends much of his time at his seaside home in Morecambe, Lancashire.

He had cherished the hope that the IOC would select him to replace the Sudan member General Gadir, who was imprisoned for four years by the military regime. Gadir has now been released and reinstated at the IOC. Without his membership of the IAAF council, the travel and the hospitality at the Olympics and other major events, life for Agabani would be dull.

Artur Takac had a distinguished career as an athlete. During World War Two he escaped from Yugoslavia to Switzerland and later joined up with the French resistance. As international sport flourished he became a full-time official, creating a good living for himself and his family. Takac has been involved in the organising of ten summer Olympics and four winter Games.

Takac was involved in the organisation of Nebiolo's 1986 Student Games in Zagreb. He is also president of the technical committee of the Mediterranean Games. Wearing yet another hat, Takac is a paid adviser to the IOC. He is on the council of the IAAF and active in the European Athletics Association.

The third technical delegate in Rome was Georg Wieczisk. His whole life had been spent under the austere East German regime. There were obvious bonuses to his membership of the IAAF council with its freedom to travel the world and enjoy a Western life-style. These 'three wise men' were in a delicate situation when they convened under Nebiolo's chairmanship in Monaco. They might not have been aware of every story published in Italy but if they were serious about their interest in athletics then surely they had heard on the grapevine that the result could not be fair or honest.

The report of Luciano Barra's investigation was placed before the council meeting. Much of it was predictable. Olivetti said their results computer was faultless. Seiko insisted that their measuring device was accurate. Contradicting this was the report from August Kirsch's Cologne Sports Institute which showed that the jump was only 7.91 metres.

With Nebiolo in the chair the result was inevitable. He would not accept that there was anything wrong. Evangelisti's last jump and his bronze medal were upheld. Casting around for a justification, Nebiolo played the Maradonna card. 'When we saw the video tape of Maradonna in the World Cup helping the ball into the net with his hand against England we realised he had cheated – but with us it's also too late, I'm sorry.' The IAAF statement in December said 'The men's long jump competition was correctly conducted and the official result is not to be changed.'

Confident that the jump scandal was buried, Nebiolo turned to the distraction of the IAF Gala. Ignoring the rage over the Evangelisti scandal, IOC president Samaranch flew in from Lausanne in a private jet and stood shoulder to shoulder with Nebiolo at the Gala.

The scandal could not be contained. Nebiolo had failed to take into account the determination of sprint coach Sandro Donati. He had already complained to the Rome police, who had launched an inquiry. Donati pondered the IAAF council decision over the Christmas holiday and then went to the Foro Italico and laid a formal complaint with CONI about the judging of the long jump.

To Nebiolo's horror the scandal was suddenly spinning out of control. He could manipulate the IAAF but not CONI; he was not short of critics at the Foro Italico. In January 1988 CONI appointed a five-man committee to investigate the scandal and restore the good name of Italian sport.

There was incontrovertible evidence that the long jump result had been rigged and the Italian public discovered it in the pages of *L'Espresso* in early February 1988, after the CONI inquiry had begun. The measurement of Evangelisti's last jump had not been deliberately exaggerated as most sceptics had assumed. It had not been measured at all!

The truth had been captured by the unmanned TV camera at the end of the pit. It had been running all the way through the medal ceremony that had delayed the sixth and final round of the competition. For months the video tape recorded from that camera had lain forgotten. Now *L'Espresso* had obtained one single, damning frame from the sequence. Then the full tape was shown on Italian TV.

The images were startling: history had been made that night. As the medal ceremony got under way, judge Tommaso Aiello had glanced around him conspiratorially. Believing that all other eyes were on the ceremony, he surreptitiously placed the optical prism in the sand. Then he moved away from the pit, out of vision of the TV camera, for about a minute. He was seen to return and remove the prism from the sand. He had recorded a measurement of 8.38 metres for Evangelisti *before* the Italian had jumped. The false measurement was locked into the Seiko machine, ready to be produced after the real jump.

Nebiolo's response was astonishing. He ignored the Aiello video tape and ordered a letter to be sent from the London headquarters of the IAAF, challenging CONI's right to make their inquiries. 'Any unauthorised measure or interference could be considered a violation or transgression of the rules of international sport,' he claimed. The use of the London address was deliberate. Nebiolo was trying to deny the Italian CONI the right to probe into the affairs of an international body. CONI ignored this bluster.

Nebiolo tried again to stop the truth coming out. More than a month later he ordered another letter from the IAAF to CONI. 'We have been informed that the Italian legal authorities have closed the case,' it ran. 'As a consequence of this we are sure this will close this argument finally.' Again, CONI ignored him and pressed on with their investigations.

The long-awaited CONI report could have been worse for Nebiolo. The eighty-three page report was damaging to him, but not as devastating as some insiders believed it should have been. When it was published on 25 March 1988 it confirmed most of the disclosures in the Italian press about the way the result of Evangelisti's jump had been falsified.

Nebiolo's assistant Luciano Barra received a rough ride. He was accused of negligence in his investigation for the IAAF. As well as the reports from Seiko and Olivetti he had also obtained statements from all the long jump judges who affirmed the 'regularity' of their actions.

But, as CONI reported, it was known at the time that if one of the judges had been pressed 'he would have been able to provide details helpful in uncovering aspects of a deed which, on the basis of the documentation, lacked adequate explanation'.

And there was more criticism of Barra. 'If instead of limiting the investigation to the acquisition of documents not only irrelevant in ascertaining the facts – but inclined to demonstrate the inexplicability of these – and a more precise investigation had been undertaken the outcome would have had different implications.'

CONI found more evidence of a plot in the way the long jump judges had been selected. They could not understand why almost all the judges had been brought in from Sicily. They were also troubled that the original list of judges had been changed without any reason.

The investigators had obtained that original list. A group had been assembled for the Italian national championships a month earlier and they had worked well together. These judges had been drawn from all over the country. Then the list had been arbitrarily changed and two very experienced judges had been dropped in favour of two Sicilians. CONI concluded that this was irrational.

Then the report moved to its conclusions. It ruled that there had been an attempt to make everything appear above board by a superficial and incomplete inquiry. There was a 'pronounced intervention by the IAAF intended to interfere with the work of the Committee and prevent the ascertaining of the facts'. This was a direct criticism of Nebiolo and, by implication, linked him to the cover-up.

On the jump itself they were clear: Evangelisti had not jumped 8.38 metres. The false measurement was not the fault of the equipment. Thus the error had to be attributed to 'activity initiated by people singled out in our investigation'.

Six FIDAL officials, including Tommaso Aiello who had put the marker in the sand, were banned. Luciano Barra, who was not disciplined, promptly resigned from FIDAL saying, 'To bring calm to athletics and defend myself better, I have put my position as secretary general at the disposal of the FIDAL federal council.'

Belatedly Barra would admit that he should have broken with Nebiolo earlier and he accepted the criticisms of his 'investigation'. He returned from FIDAL to CONI and was put to work planning the 1990 Soccer World Cup. The Italian press was still not satisfied. *Gazzeto dello Sport* expressed surprise that no officials had been punished and added, 'FIDAL's silence evidently means that the leaders are deeply involved and as a result cannot judge this scandal.' A week later Italian coaches in conference in Reggio called on Nebiolo to resign from FIDAL.

Less than a month later the IAAF council met again, this time in London. Sports journalists besieged the Hans Crescent office and Nebiolo must have regretted that he had not chosen a more distant outpost of his empire for this meeting, perhaps the North Marianas Islands. The long jump was right back on the agenda, three months after his council had closed the file.

The astonishing thing was that despite the CONI report ruling Evangelisti's jump invalid and the evidence from the TV tape, Nebiolo had no intention of changing the result. His attitude was so unyielding that the rumour ran around the council that he had even banned members reading the CONI report. That was not too difficult as it was in Italian and nobody was rushing to translate it. As council members arrived in London, Professor Ljunqvist from Sweden was quoted saying, 'If this is true, the athletes can no longer trust us.'

We do not know who swung the council against Nebiolo. When the president finally gave in, he played the Maradonna card again – in the opposite way. Triumphantly he claimed, 'We did what no other international body has done. We changed the result after watching TV. Did FIFA do this when Maradonna handled a goal against England in the World Cup?' It suited Nebiolo to ignore the fact that Myricks and Evangelisti, two members of his 'athletics family', had been victims of a conspiracy by his own officials, not victims of a spontaneous foul.

Few nations know what really happened at Rome in 1987 because the affair has been played down in IAAF magazines and newsletters. There is abundant evidence to prove that the IAAF has continued the cover-up long after they had been found out by CONI and the European media. Many of the IAAF's 170 worldwide members rely on the IAAF *Newsletter* for their athletics news. Only a few dozen of these countries have both a free press and the financial resources to report sports politics. The way the *Newsletter* reported the Evangelisti affair was deplorable.

In its round-up of 1988 it reported the agenda from the London council meeting in April. There was no mention of the long jump scandal. Further on in the lengthy report, sandwiched between a long account of a court case involving a suspended athlete and another section dealing with marketing, was this bleak paragraph.

'After a review of the Men's Long Jump Competition in the IAAF world championships in Athletics, Rome 1987, Council decided unanimously that, notwithstanding the present IAAF rules, the 6th jump of Giovanni Evangelisti should not be counted and the result adjusted accordingly. Therefore Larry Myricks became the Bronze Medal Winner (8.34 metres) and Evangelisti (8.19 metres) dropped one place in the listing.'

There was no mention of the RAI tape or what it had revealed, no mention that six officials from Nebiolo's own Italian athletics federation had been banned from the sport – and no apologies. It was not made clear that Evangelisti himself had been wholly innocent of the conspiracy.

By this time Evangelisti had long ago given his medal away and

Myricks was preparing for Seoul. Most important of all, Nebiolo had avoided the scandal that should have brought him down.

CHAPTER 15

Before Your Very Eyes

Imagine yourself in the banqueting suite of a top-class hotel somewhere in Western Europe. Waiters and waitresses busy themselves serving the hundred or so guests and their wives. The food is good and so is the selection of wines. You've guessed; it is a dinner for the leading officials of one of the most popular Olympic sports. Their president, a member of The Club, is on the top table. It is all part of a weekend of luxury, arranged around a major sporting event.

Everybody is smartly dressed, the men in good suits and the women in evening dresses. We are joined by an internationally famous competitor, a current world champion, whose appearance startles us. The star is the only guest who appears not to have shaved.

It is not the breach of etiquette that surprises us. It is the fact that the champion is a woman – and that she has a heavier growth of beard than most of the men in the room. She was a demonstrable, defiant and successful doper, visibly showing the side-effects of steroid abuse. She was changing sex before our very eyes! The sports officials and their president took no notice. They could see nothing unacceptable. We were the only people in the room who stared.

Many of the officials there that night had made stirring speeches over the years about how they were spearheading the fight against doping. It was only at that banquet that we began to realise how doping has been accepted and accommodated by many of the world's leading sports officials.

A couple of thousand athletes will be selected at the 1992 Olympics to be tested for performance-boosting drugs. The bill will come to several million dollars. If past form is any guide, up to a dozen competitors will be caught, mostly for taking steroids and other drugs that mask the signs of steroids. At his final press conference President Samaranch may well announce that once again, apart from a few unfortunate incidents that have been sensationalised by the media, it was a dope-free Games.

A handful of careless competitors will be shamed, the public deceived and the sponsors relieved that their massive investment has not been tarnished. ISL will look to raise the price again for the exclusive use of this 'communications tool' four years on in Atlanta. That was what happened in Seoul. The public was assured that the steroid-soaked Ben Johnson was a sporting aberration. The dope testing programme for Barcelona will be similar to Seoul.

There is something deeply worrying about the way the world's sports leaders have misled us on dope testing. The brutal fact is that for nearly twenty years it has been known, inside The Club, that testing athletes on the day of competition is a virtual waste of time and money. It is a show, a distraction from the truth. The drug-takers are professionally advised by their doctors and coaches about the length of time it takes for traces of drugs to leave their systems. Only a fool, or a Ben Johnson who took a calculated risk that his last late steroid programme would clear before he competed in Seoul, gets caught.

The only credible deterrent to dopers is random testing; the fear that at any moment during training, the time when cheats do go on their drug programmes, a testing team might materialise in their home town, at their sports club or college and demand an instant sample. Random testing rarely happens although it has been urged for two decades.

The sham of relying only on testing at events was spotted immediately the murky world of sport was investigated by an outsider. After the Ben Johnson scandal the Canadian Government appointed Ontario's Chief Justice Charles Dubin to investigate. His independent and clear legal brain cut through the years of posturing.

'Despite knowing the fallacy of in-competition testing, as they have for many years,' wrote Dubin in his report, 'the medical commissions of sports organisations such as the IAAF and the IOC have taken no steps to make the fallacy more widely known. By failing to do so they have given the impression that their competitions are fair and that the laboratories cannot be fooled.'

The leaders of the IOC and the sports federations have little excuse. Their own leading sports scientists, like Professor Brookes in the UK, Dr Manfred Donike in Germany and Dr Robert Dugal in Canada, called for random testing from the early 1970s. It had not happened by the time of Seoul. If the federations and the IOC had been serious about eliminating doping they could have spent their new wealth from TV and sponsorship to clean up sport. Had they done so, Ben Johnson would never have qualified for his national team.

It may be that even Justice Dubin was denied the whole truth. The evidence over the years is that many national and international federations have ignored prominent dopers, have covered up positive results and on several occasions have been proven to be the dealers supplying steroids to their national team.

A decade has passed since Sebastian Coe addressed the Olympic congress in Baden-Baden and begged the assembled officials to impose life bans on athletes caught doping. Coe, with the backing of many other competitors around the world, has frequently repeated this plea. He has been ignored.

In the autumn of 1991, as we completed this book, the most popular drug in use among British athletes was a veterinary product for which the scientists have not yet devised a satisfactory test. The cheats will have few worries in Barcelona. The athletics federation has now increased its period of suspension from two to more than four years, ensuring that guilty athletes miss the next Olympics. The IOC is expected to follow suit. But this will cause few problems for those who take the many drugs that cannot be detected. One device used by some women dopers is a catheter. On the day of competition they insert it into themselves to infuse drug-free urine – donated by friends – into their bladder. They then offer themselves for testing without any worries.

The IOC and leading sports federations like the IAAF produce stirring documents about the evils of doping. They invest modest sums in symposia for sports scientists to read papers to each other but have been reluctant to invest in research techniques to improve their detection methods, particularly for hormone substances. What they have never done is use their authority to launch investigations into who is doping, who is supplying the dope and whether their own 'policing' of the scourge is effective.

Neither Samaranch at the IOC nor Nebiolo at the IAAF investigated the Ben Johnson scandal. It fell to the Canadian Government to initiate a proper inquiry. In the same year the Australian Government had to set up an inquiry because its own sports leaders would not investigate athletes' doping disclosures. The endless stream of revelations about doping in America has never brought any investigation from their track and field federation or from the United States Olympic Committee, or USOC. It needed action from Senator Joe Biden's judiciary committee to discover America's own doping scandals and extract some of the most compelling and distressing testimony about the side effects of steroids.

They were made clear by American sprinter Diane Williams, who claimed she was coerced by her coach into taking steroids. She told her story to the judiciary committee in 1989. Ms Williams disclosed that when she was recruited by one of America's most successful coaches in the early 1980s he immediately introduced her to steroids. Within a year she noticed changes to her body. Then he put her on 'those little football shaped pills – Dianabol'. It is a well-known brand of steroid.

What she said next reduced the committee to embarrassed silence. 'Masculine features appeared, like a moustache and fuzz on the chin,' said Ms Williams. 'My clitoris began to grow to embarrassing proportions.'

Then she began to cry and the committee allowed her to pause. She continued, 'My vocal cords lengthened to a deeper voice. A muscular pattern of hair growth appeared. Steroids affected my sexual behaviour. In many cases I was a nymphomaniac.'

Steroids also enable men to build up huge muscle bulk but the side effects can be equally distressing. At the same senate hearing coach Pat Croce was asked how he dealt with youngsters who claimed that steroids make them big. He replied 'I tell them to drop their pants and show me how manly they really are. They want to get bigger and manly – but then their testes shrink.'

So why do men and women take these risks? A candid answer was given by Canadian sprinter and colleague of Ben Johnson, Tony Sharpe: 'The glory is too sweet, the dollars are too much.'

The glory and the dollars have been too much for the administrators as well as for the athletes. As 'amateur' sport began to attract new money from TV and sponsorship, it was not only the athletes who benefited.

The federations grew in prestige and wealth. It could all be lost if the public discovered that many of their heroes were pumped up with illicit drugs. These fears created a culture of blindness. Sports officials who should have been rooting out doping looked the other way. Worse still, they then began to protect their stars from exposure.

The scandals peaked at the Pan-American Games in Caracas in August 1983. In the Americas these Games rank second only to the Olympics. More élite competitors than the public would ever have guessed had spent the summer beefing themselves up on steroid programmes.

But there was a surprise awaiting them in Caracas. Dr Manfred Donike from Cologne, who was appointed to run the doping control, had developed new and more precise techniques for testing. This was discovered by accident. A US Olympic committee medical team went to Caracas in advance of the US team to sort out sanitary and food problems. It discovered the new testing equipment. Thoughtlessly, the officials passed word back to the USA of what was in store for the competitors.

A catastrophe was looming and the team most at risk was the weight-lifters. On arrival in Caracas they were urged, secretly, to take screening tests on the new equipment. The results of the tests should have triggered major investigations by America's sports federations. There were eleven weight-lifters on the team. One tested negative and the urine sample from another was too dilute to detect anything – a sign that they were probably using a masking agent. The remaining nine tested positive.

It never seemed to occur to the officials to send their team home immediately and take action to stamp out drug taking. Instead, they opted for a cover-up. It would have been too embarrassing to withdraw ten out of the eleven team members. All the team competed but ten of them turned in abysmal performances. Only medal winners were tested and so they escaped detection.

The one lifter who had passed the test was confident enough to do his best and he won three gold medals. He became the first top doper to discover that it is possible to pass a test one day and fail the next. Traces of the drug remain in body fats and ebb erratically into urine. The graph of body clearance is not a straight downwards line. It becomes jagged in the last days and when the medal winner went to give his urine sample, it showed traces of the drug. He lost all three medals.

His shame had already been overtaken by an even bigger scandal. At least a dozen track and field athletes turned up in Venezuela, assessed the risk and turned right around and went home to the USA. They never set foot in the stadium.

This was not the end of the story. The athletes had pulled out because they were certain to fail the tests and be exposed as cheats. Yet many of them had, two weeks earlier, competed in the first Athletics World Championships in Helsinki when their bodies would have had even larger traces of steroids. No positive tests had been announced in Finland. It was baffling.

Dr Donike had also been in charge of the doping control in Helsinki and had used the same new equipment there. It had been crated up and flown out to Caracas days later. There was only one significant difference between the two events. There were two different sets of officials in charge. The Helsinki championships was the first major event presided over by Primo Nebiolo after taking control of the IAAF. It was his first taste of the millions of dollars beginning to flow into world sport. He announced that there were no positive tests in Helsinki.

There is little doubt that the IAAF event in Helsinki was a drug-ridden championship. Journalist John Rodda wrote in the London *Guardian*, 'There was anxiety and suspicion about how some of these athletes arrived at their supreme peak. The high incidence of injuries led to deep concern and the belief that stress injuries can be caused by the body being put under strain by the use of drugs was never more openly discussed.'

A year after the Helsinki meeting American 400-metres runner Cliff Wiley claimed, 'at least thirty-eight people tested positive, seventeen were Americans. But they were so big the organisers didn't dare name them.'

The story of Caracas and Helsinki was revealed by Dr Robert Voy. He was a sports medicine specialist who became chief medical officer to the USOC in 1984. Dr Voy caused major problems. He would not join their Club. He fought the cover-ups and he campaigned for drug-free sport. He resigned in 1989 when the USOC cut his budget.

'The IAAF must have covered up results in Helsinki,' says Dr Voy.

He reserves his most scathing comments for the president of track and field. 'There is no doubt in my mind that, at least in 1983, Nebiolo would not have pressed for honest, accurate, testing in Helsinki.'

Nebiolo and his IAAF council met three months after Helsinki and announced that they would launch a tough programme of random, unannounced, dope testing. This was widely reported and the public was reassured. The cheats would be frightened out of sport or off the dope. It all sounded very impressive. It did not happen.

The IAAF's deception of the public was bad enough. The US Olympic committee went even further. With only a year to go to the LA Games they set out to teach their team how to beat dope testing. They launched what was euphemistically described as an 'educational, non-punitive drug-testing programme' at the IOC-approved laboratory in California, set up in preparation for the Olympics.

Officially, this scheme was to familiarise athletes with testing procedures prior to the Olympics. It was a transparent joke; few people need an instruction course on how to urinate in a bottle. It was a god send to the dopers. They flocked to use the lab, to discover more precisely how fast their bodies cleared of tell-tale steroid traces. The voluntary donations from individuals and the corporate sector to USOC, to help prepare the US team for the Games, went towards improving the athletes' capacity to cheat. No Americans were caught at the LA Games. Fourteen foreign competitors were.

Not all the American officials were complicit in this scandal. 'When I heard about the USOC's pre-Olympic testing programme that was allowing our athletes to find better ways to keep from being detected by official testing,' said US women's coach Pat Connolly at the senate judiciary committee hearings, 'I felt betrayed, like a child whose parents had deserted her.'

The LA Games yielded more clues about the degree of importance attached by track and field president Nebiolo to exposing the dopers. The high-profile scandal in 1984 was the last minute exit of the Finn Martti Vainio from the start of a 5,000-metres heat. As the runners went to their marks the news reached the trackside that Vainio's dope test after winning the 10,000-metres silver medal days earlier was positive.

One of the technical judges, Britain's Fred Holder, told Vainio that he must withdraw. 'Vainio took it without any argument and left the track,' Holder told us. 'Afterwards, Nebiolo was furious. He insisted that only the IAAF council could take such a decision.'

The council was not due to meet again until after the Games and the suspicion must be that Nebiolo hoped to announce the disqualification of a silver medallist at some stage after the Games when media attention had slackened. Another IAAF official told us, 'This was silly and typical of Nebiolo. It shows his lack of experience – trying to hide a problem.'

Vainio commented later, 'I think there are others. I am the only one who was found guilty. It is right that I am punished, but how many other athletes should be in the same boat?' Later it was disclosed that Vainio had tested positive at the Rotterdam marathon two months earlier. These two offences should have brought a life ban. He was faced only with the offence at the Olympics and suspended for eighteen months.

The scandals ground on, unceasingly. After the LA Games the next major international event was the second Athletics World Championships in Rome. The abiding sour taste from 1987 was the Evangelisti long jump fraud but the toleration of cheating by the dopers was equally depressing.

At the end of those championships IAAF President Nebiolo, with an eye to the rich pickings from sponsorship, claimed that they had been 'drug free'. It was almost unbelievable that a senior sports administrator could so cynically deny what every athlete, official and journalist knew to be true.

One 'triumph' of the championships was Ben Johnson's new 100-metres world record. An IOC member who was at the Championships has told us, privately, 'Some of the Canadian team officials were twitching until it was announced that Ben Johnson had passed his test.' Johnson's doping was an open secret within sport but withheld from the public. In the run-up to Rome he appeared to have got his clearance times right.

Carl Lewis, who ran second to Johnson, went on the record in a TV interview; 'There are gold medallists in this meet who are definitely on drugs. That 100-metres race will be looked at for many years, for more reasons than one. If I were to jump to drugs, I could do a 9.8 right away.'

When reporters challenged Nebiolo about Carl Lewis's accusations the best he could manage was, 'He should make a report to the US federation.' Two weeks after Johnson set the new record he was granted an audience at the Château de Vidy by President Samaranch.

If the public face of Nebiolo's IAAF made observers angry, the private truth about the Italian athletics federation which he also presided over would have rendered them speechless. Ben Johnson and the other cheats at Rome did their doping in secret. In Italy the situation was near unbelievable; top athletics stars had their blood doping and steroid programmes organised and paid for by Nebiolo's FIDAL, the Italian national athletics federation.

From the early 1980s the Italian federation encouraged blood doping. Several months before a major event an athlete would give a pint of blood. The red cells, which carry oxygen, were extracted and infused back into them on the eve of competition. In the meantime the body replaced the missing cells. The result was a lot more red cells and a lot more oxygen going to tired muscles during the race. It was believed that a runner could improve by up to five seconds in the 1,500 metres.

This practice was was not banned by the IOC until later in the 1980s but it was frowned upon as immoral. That did not bother Nebiolo's federation. One of its technical advisers was Dr Francesco Conconi, a professor of bio-chemistry from the University of Ferrara.

There is no question but the leader of Italian athletics was aware of the situation. On 10 June 1983 Conconi wrote to Nebiolo; 'Dear President, The research of the last three years has given us the chance to perfect technologies that are superior to the ones we used in Moscow in 1980, Yugoslavia in 1981 and Athens in 1982.

'The preparatory work for Los Angeles with the athletes that will join the programme will take four months. We will need to start not later than November 1, 1983. The technologies which we intend to use are of long and laborious execution and the programme that will result will be very complex.'

Several Italian athletes who went to LA had been blood doping. The theory did not work out in practice and there were no extra medals.

After the Games the Italian sports press had documents leaked to them and the scandal was exposed.

Blood doping was questionable but still legal; steroids were not. That did not deter FIDAL in its quest to win medals, win the applause of Italy and bring in more sponsorship contracts.

On the eve of the Italian team's departure for the Los Angeles Games national sprint coach Sandro Donati and a colleague went into the office of the FIDAL technical section and stumbled across a cardboard box covered with labels from the USA. It was open and inside they discovered more than a thousand small bottles of steroids. Each bottle contained 100 5mg pills. They came from a New York company and on the box was a label warning 'only on prescription'.

The drugs were being administered under the supervision of a full-time, paid employee of FIDAL. He approached his task cautiously and bureaucratically and insisted that all the athletes he treated signed a waiver form. His first, handwritten draft was found in FIDAL files.

It read, 'I ... [athlete's name] declare that I want to undertake therapy with anabolic steroid ... [name of drug] as an additive to my training. I do this of my own choice and I take the responsibility.'

FIDAL were unhappy with such explicit wording and changed it to a more sanitised version. FIDAL's read, 'I ... [athlete's name] declare that of my own will I want to undertake medical therapy and drugs suggested by the doctors of FIDAL. I will be informed of the dosage and possible side effects, negative reactions and be given information about the possible, eventual toxicity.'

Donati challenged Nebiolo personally and eventually confronted him. 'You must take a broader view of the activity of the federation,' explained the president. 'I put a lot of effort into trying to promote track and field. It used to have a low image in the media and with the public. Ours is a great circus in which if we stretch the tent walls too far the roof will fall in. We have to look at the global thing, not one aspect. We don't want the roof to fall in.'

The roof should have fallen in at the Seoul Olympics. Shortly after congratulating Ben Johnson on his 100-metres world record in Rome Samaranch told the press 'You may rest assured that we shall be very firm where doping is concerned. It is a form of cheating which we cannot tolerate.' The cheats knew better and as the spring of 1988 turned into summer, they were busy popping their pills and injecting drugs.

The first clue came in the May. One of the early season's top class meetings was the Gatorade Classic, in Knoxville, Tennessee. When it was announced that this meeting would have dope testing, many competitors withdrew. Only one out of eight discus throwers showed up and a leading triple jumper pulled out.

It was the same at the Pepsi Classic meeting, held just a week before the US Olympic Trials. Again, there were drug controls. So many athletes failed to turn up that the shot and discus events had to be cancelled.

The Olympic Trials came in July at Indianapolis. Again, there was reason to suspect that the cheats were still on their drug programmes because they needed to qualify for Seoul. The evidence was that eight athletes tested positive for the herbal plant that produces ephedrine, a popular masking agent used to hide steroid abuse. They were excused because ephedrine can also be found in some vitamin products.

A year later Australian marathon runner Lisa Martin claimed that seventeen athletes had tested positive at the US Olympic Trials. Her agent said he had been at a meeting after the trials when athletes were told 'When you get to Seoul, the testing will count.'

The US Olympic Trials produced another sensation: Flo-Jo, the sprinter Florence Griffith-Joyner, whose previous career had been unremarkable. In 1987 *Track & Field News* did not rate her in the world's top ten women and only seventh in the US at the 100 metres. Yet in one year, as Ben Johnson's coach Charlie Francis commented acidly, 'She warped the historical performance curves. Her times were fifty years ahead of schedule.' In Seoul she won three gold medals and set two world records.

Carl Lewis and other leading US athletes have raised the question of whether she dopes or not. A *Times* journalist in London asked, 'Is she a drug-raddled hermaphrodite?' In November 1991 Ms Griffith-Joyner told journalists that whilst she 'did not want to waste time and money sueing', she was going to 'get' Lewis.

After the Seoul Games *Stern* magazine published an allegation by former US 400-metres champion Darrell Robinson that she paid him $2,000 for a 10cc vial of hGH – human growth hormone. On TV she

called him a 'crazy, lying lunatic'. Flo-Jo has passed every dope test she
has ever been confronted with. However there is not yet an acceptable
test for hGH.

Ben Johnson was the best news the IOC and the IAAF had in the 1980s.
At last they had a new 'world's fastest man'. Johnson's world records in
Rome and Seoul excited the public and the sponsors. Samaranch and
Nebiolo tied themselves to his successes.

 Johnson was having problems as he prepared for Seoul. His entourage
discovered late in 1987 that after years of hormone drug doping he had
developed an enlarged left breast. He was turning into a woman! This
was not disclosed and the Canadian public were assured by their
national officials that their sport was clean because random testing had
been announced. It had been announced but it had not happened. Every
excuse had been found to delay. Johnson was on course to bring more
glory and money to the officials in Seoul.

 Johnson's preparations for the Olympics were disrupted by injury but
his drug programme continued unabated. In the late August he began
his final two-week dope programme before Seoul. That allowed thirteen
days to a warm-up meeting in Tokyo, which was not tested, and then it
was on to Seoul where he prayed that his body had cleared all signs of
steroids. He was wrong.

 The IOC have denied suggestions that they would have preferred to
hide the Johnson result, avoid a scandal and not risk scaring off the
sponsors. The fact remains that somebody inside the IOC testing lab
was so worried that the result would be suppressed that it was leaked to
the media.

 If there could be anything more sordid in sport than the 'outing' of
Johnson as a long-term doper then it is the response of the IOC and the
IAAF to the problem of re-awarding the medals. Two years earlier the
Russian athlete Vladislav Tretyak had told Samaranch face to face,
'Where a competitor who wins a medal is disqualified the real winner
should enjoy the honour they deserve – which does not usually happen.'

 It did not happen in Seoul, either. Tretyak's plea was ignored in the
wake of Johnson's disqualification. Damage limitation was the order of
the day. The scandal had been bad enough for the image and financial
value of the Games. The last thing the nervous presidents wanted was to
underline the disaster by holding a second, public medal ceremony.

Samaranch looked the other way whilst Nebiolo confined the 'ceremony' to handing Carl Lewis, Linford Christie and Calvin Smith their new 100-metres medals in the seclusion of his private office at the Seoul Stadium. 'There will be no special ceremony,' IOC spokeswoman Michèle Verdier told the press, 'It's a rule of the IAAF.'

Ben Johnson made three major mistakes in his young life: he took steroids, he got caught and then he foolishly demanded an inquiry to clear his name. The Canadian Government obliged him and appointed senior judge Charles Dubin to head a commission of inquiry. The evidence was given in public on oath in Toronto through 1989. It became the most searching examination that modern sport has ever suffered.

Had the Canadian Government not ordered the inquiry there would have been no investigations after the Johnson affair. The scandal was quickly boxed into a corner. The public were assured that it was nothing more worrying than Ben Johnson's own personal tragedy. Dubin soon showed that these assertions were pernicious nonsense.

It became clear in the hearings that everybody who mattered in Canadian and world athletics knew that coach Charlie Francis' squad of sprinters, including Johnson, were members of 'the brotherhood of the needle'. Yet no official publicly broke ranks and protested as Johnson passed test after test – when it was convenient for him to take them. By structuring his dope cycles, his clearance times and his appearances at meetings with testing, Johnson managed to pass nineteen times in the two years before the Seoul Games.

Dubin examined the pronouncements from the IOC and the IAAF about how their in-competition drug testing was successful in curbing the scourge and turned them on their head. He called witness after witness who admitted that they had either been dopers or involved in supplying drugs to athletes.

The vast scope of doping established, Dubin then destroyed the claim, going back to the 1968 Games, that if only a few out of thousands of tests after an event were positive, it 'proved' that doping was a minor scourge. He established the obvious; that in the words of Britain's Sir Arthur Gold, 'Only the careless or ill-advised get caught.'

Remorselessly the Canadian judge took apart the myths pumped out by the sports presidents over the years. Dubin had spotted where the public had been misled. He tackled head on the statistics produced by the IOC which 'proved' that only a handful of competitors were taking drugs. According to Dubin, these 'have been used misleadingly in various attempts to show that drug abuse affects only a small percentage of athletes. This concern for appearance, not substance, has been a continuing theme in the evidence.'

The Swedish head of the IAAF medical commission, Arne Ljungqvist, came under withering fire. Ljungqvist is an establishment figure in Sweden and in world athletics. Dubin noted that Ljungqvist claimed that, 'The Games in Seoul could not be regarded as the "Doping Olympics". Close to 1,600 athletes were tested and ten of them came out positive. The problem in Seoul was that one of the doped athletes was named Ben Johnson.'

Dubin riposted in his report, 'Dr Ljungqvist and others know that in-competition testing does not catch all athletes. Yet he uses in-competition testing to measure the extent of doping at Seoul. Evidence from this inquiry proves that the athletes caught at Seoul were not the only drug users. They were the only detected ones.'

The lawyer's dissection continued, 'Dr Ljungqvist directs attention at positive tests rather than the real problem of doping in sport. The general public has long been led to assume that if only one athlete tested positive, the others were not also using drugs. We now know, as the IOC and the IAAF have known for many years, that this assumption is false.'

Dubin's critique ground on: in 1985 the IAAF had announced that its member federations would begin out-of-competition testing and that the IAAF would conduct arbitrary tests at national championships. Commented Dubin, 'Little if anything has been done to implement these procedures.'

And there was more: 'The IAAF was also given jurisdiction to conduct testing on its own. However, of the 184 member countries of the IAAF few had an out-of-competition procedure in place in September 1988. Thus, the rule was never enforced.'

At last the public was being told the truth about Dr Nebiolo's federation: 'It is unfortunate that it has not used its influence in a more meaningful way to eradicate the drug problem in track and field. The posture of the IAAF appears to have been to react to the problem only after the fact. The medical commission of the IAAF has known since its inception that in-competition testing alone is not an effective means to detect steroids nor is it an effective deterrent to steroid use.'

Dubin's conclusion was that there was only one way to clean up the Olympics. He urged the IOC to exclude from participation in the Games any national federation that fails to have in place – and actually implement – an effective doping control programme. Dubin set the benchmark for Barcelona.

The Dubin report should have revolutionised world sport. It has been ignored. The word 'Dubin' is seemingly blacklisted by the IOC *Review* and the IAAF *Newsletter*. Only Canada, Australia and the Nordic countries have independent random drug-testing programmes backed by law and run by government-appointed bodies. The sports federations have been stripped of their powers in those countries. It might be thought that the international federations would be pleased because such a policy would build public confidence that, at last, their sports were cleaning up.

This was not Dr Nebiolo's view. In July 1991 the IAAF sent new instructions to all its members around the world.

'A number of national governments have now established National Doping Agencies who have responsibility for doping control within sport. It is noted with some concern that some of these agencies have assumed total control of doping control matters within the appropriate country and the procedures adopted are ones which are contrary to IAAF Rules. The IAAF Doping Commission believe that members should make every effort to regain control.'

There was a further point which seemed to be an another attempt to quietly turn the clock back. There have always been suspicions that track and field officials have been highly selective when picking athletes to be tested, choosing competitors they have known to be 'clean' and ignoring known dopers. Yet the letter went on to urge national officials to try and claw back from the new government agencies the right to choose who was tested.

The wealthy IAAF has at last started its own 'flying squad' testing. In the first year, from May 1990, they managed to test just 113 athletes around the world. None tested positive and no tests were conducted on American citizens. There are civil liberties issues raised in America about random testing. Nebiolo will not tell the sponsor-rich Americans that it is their absolute right not to be tested – and everybody else's right to exclude them from competition. It is fair to say that many leading American athletes welcome these tests.

Despite the sharpness of Dubin's comments, despite the ignominy that the Johnson scandal should have heaped on the heads of Nebiolo and his IAAF council, despite the fact that athletics has signally failed to eradicate doping, they still assert their right to be allowed to control dope testing. It is an ominous sign for Barcelona.

The IOC and the IAAF downplay the disease eating away at sport. Late in 1988 in Lausanne IOC President Samaranch stated baldly, 'The IOC is winning the war against doping.' One of his widely publicised plans was for an IOC 'flying laboratory' to help implement random testing. It was expected to cost $1 million to set up and $500,000 a year to operate. It sounded impressive; the IOC drugs police circling the globe, diving down to catch the bad guys. As usual, it was all appearance and no substance. Eighteen months later the IOC, who are spending $40 million on a new Olympic museum in Lausanne, quietly cancelled the project on grounds of expense.

Even more incredibly, both Samaranch and Nebiolo announced that after Ben Johnson completed his two-year suspension, he would be welcome to compete in Barcelona. It was unbelievably cynical. A competitor who had taken drugs for nearly a decade, had timed his doses so as to avoid detection and lied when he was caught was being encouraged to bring his brand of morality back to the Olympics.

There was little outcry from other sports officials around the world. Many followed the party line and pumped out the message that Johnson had been punished enough and all should be forgotten.

In mid-1989 Nebiolo's Athletics Foundation sponsored a doping symposium in Monte Carlo. The drugs testers and sports officials present had to listen to a jarring contribution from the only non-scientist, former British Olympic coach Ron Pickering, as he rounded on sport's leaders. 'No president can afford to say "We celebrate a drug-free Games" just because there were no positive tests found – or published. No president should be allowed to say we shall "welcome" Ben Johnson back to the next Games. It is sheer hypocrisy to admit him back, let alone make him welcome.' Pickering was a brief rush of fresh air in the otherwise complacent proceedings.

The chief counsel to the Dubin Inquiry was QC Robert Armstrong. In 1991, in a speech at an international anti-doping conference, he reviewed the discoveries they had made in Toronto about the way the world's sport leaders had misled the public on doping. He made the point again that dope tests at events were meaningless in determining the extent of the use of drugs.

He lamented that after the Biden hearings in America, 'It is frankly surprising how little attention that evidence has received from the IAAF and the IOC.' He summed up Nebiolo's whole style of leadership saying that in the past the IAAF 'appeared to satisfy itself with little more than public relations exercises.'

Then he turned to the IOC, 'It has no reason to be smug or self-satisfied about its accomplishments. Its medical commission has known for years that testing for steroids at the time of competition was a virtual waste of time.'

Armstrong concluded, 'There has been a failure of leadership among our sporting organisations at the national and international level. Our sports leaders have let us down.'

CHAPTER 16

A Lawyer from Des Moines

By the end of the 1980s Robert H. Helmick was on his way to becoming the most powerful man in world sport. He was a generation younger than Samaranch, he was American and he knew Horst Dassler. It was all about to happen for him. Helmick had become America's number one man in Olympic sport. Then, in the autumn of 1991, he made the front pages across America. He had been caught out taking money secretly from corporations who wanted to do business with the Olympics.

It was not just a personal tragedy. Helmick's fall from grace went to the heart of the conflict at the modern Olympics: money. For a decade Samaranch's IOC has battled with the powerful United States Olympic committee over the fabulous sums generated by the Games. The biggest single slice comes from the American TV networks and the US corporate sponsors. Without America's dollars, there are no Olympic Games.

Helmick bridged the gap. In Colorado Springs he was president of the USOC, fighting for America's financial interests against the IOC. In Lausanne he was a loyal member of Samaranch's inner cabinet, the IOC executive board, and expected to fight for the wider interests of the Olympic movement.

On the afternoon of Wednesday 18 September 1991 the six-foot-two American with white, close-cropped hair and round steel-frame spectacles emerged from the first-class compartment of a transatlantic jet from Berlin.

'With deep regret I am resigning my position as president of the US Olympic committee, effective immediately,' he announced. For Club member Robert H. Helmick, it was the inevitable end to the worst two weeks in his life.

It began when *USA Today* revealed that in the previous year Helmick had taken $275,000 from clients who wanted to strike deals with the Olympics.

The first embarrassing disclosure was that he had taken $37,5000 from Atlanta-based Turner Broadcasting System, best known for its Cable News Network service. Its boss Ted Turner wanted to break the US TV networks' stranglehold and buy into the Games. Helmick had secretly been on Turner's payroll since 1987, helping him plan his campaign for the 1996 Olympics in Atlanta.

The second revelation was that Helmick had taken $75,000 for advice to sports federations seeking recognition by the IOC. One of the roles that Helmick was trusted with by the IOC was making recommendations about which sports should be allowed to come into the lucrative Olympic fold. He had forgotten to tell his colleagues about his private income from firms representing the World Golf Association and the International Bowling Federation.

Something else that had entirely slipped his mind, until the reporters raised it, was his rewarding relationship with Boris Becker's manager Ion Tiriac. He ran TIVI Amsterdam, a marketing firm which sold the sponsorship and TV rights for the World Swimming Championships. Helmick, until recently the president of FINA, the world swimming federation, received another $150,000.

The last business deal exposed was Helmick's arrangement with the Lifestyle Marketing Group. They are a division of Saatchi and Saatchi and they gave him $14,500 for advice.

The trip to Berlin had been less than pleasant. The newspaper revelations had begun ten days earlier. When Helmick joined his IOC colleagues for their quarterly executive board meeting they had already seen the continental editions of the US press.

Inevitably they had asked him, did his conduct measure up to the promise he had made when he took the Olympic Oath? Helmick was reminded of that day in 1985 when he swore 'I undertake to keep myself free from any commercial influence.' The reports from within their conclave were that they felt he should quit the USOC as soon as possible. For themselves, there was no rush to take a potentially embarrassing decision. The executive board set up yet another commission. Its brief: to investigate the business dealings of one of the most powerful members of The Club.

Resignation was a step that Helmick had resisted to the death. 'These allegations are a vicious attack on not only my sport career but my professional life' said the fifty-five-year-old lawyer when the story first broke. 'There is no reason for me to even consider resigning.'

Two days later and the tall American was not nearly so bullish. After a traumatic weekend meeting in Chicago with his fellow USOC officers, a humbled Helmick emerged to announce that he would be allowed to hang on to the presidency. But a dreadful price had been extracted.

Helmick was forced to acknowledge publicly that he had made 'errors of judgement concerning the appearance of conflicts of interest' and that he would 'terminate and refrain from all current and future representations which could be perceived to be in conflict with his responsibilities'.

The humiliation went on. Helmick had to agree to co-operate with a special investigation into all his suspect business relationships. In spite of this, Helmick continued to maintain that he had done nothing wrong.

As the days passed and more stories appeared, his position deteriorated. Two US congressmen called for an independent investigation into Helmick's business dealings. Then the US Ski Federation dropped another bombshell. They alleged that Harvey Schiller, Helmick's executive director at the USOC, had used his position to gain valuable ski-lift passes. Schiller said it was all a misunderstanding.

In a last ditch attempt to limit the damage, Helmick said he would not seek re-election as the USOC president at the end of his term in 1992. America's other IOC member, Anita DeFrantz, said she thought Helmick's announcement was 'diversionary'.

It was not enough. Two days later the president of the most powerful national Olympic committee in the world left early from his executive board meeting and flew out of Berlin.

'No one has asked me to resign or forced me to resign,' brazened Helmick, back in the USA. 'Anyone who feels I am running from the heat is dead wrong. There hasn't been a single shred of "evidence" since all this media nonsense began.'

The one Olympic victory the Americans always felt was theirs by right was the basketball tournament. The USA had taken the gold since 1936, the year that basketball made its first appearance at the Olympics. But in 1972, the unthinkable happened. The Americans lost. Worse than that, they lost to the USSR.

When the final horn sounded the Americans had won by one point. The Russians protested it had sounded three seconds early. The referee would have none of it. The Americans had won. Enter the general secretary of the international basketball federation who overruled the referee. The final three seconds must still be played.

Tick. Second number one: the Russians hurled the ball from one end of the court to the other. Tick. Second number two: Aleksandr Belov tipped it in for a final basket. Tick. Second number three: the match was over. The Russians had taken the gold. The Americans were so disgusted that they left Munich without waiting for their second place medals.

Watching this defeat and fuming with patriotic outrage was the young Bob Helmick, then manager of the US water polo team. His swimmers had won the bronze medal at Munich despite what he claimed was the blatant bias of the Olympic referees. 'At the water polo in 1972, the cheating of the referees was just awful,' said Helmick twenty years later. 'Then I remember watching the basketball game, the US versus the USSR and the famous last three seconds. I noticed the person who made the change was the secretary of the international federation.

'I realised that the US had no control in international sport. I said to myself "I want to be that secretary of that international federation who decides whether to play the game over in favour of the USSR or the US," not to get an advantage, but so that we could get an equal starting point.'

Wrapping himself in the star-spangled banner, Helmick rose in four years to become the general secretary of the international swimming federation, FINA. Another eight years on, he was president. A year later he took that principled oath and joined The Club. 1985 was Bob Helmick's year. Four months earlier he had collected another trophy; the presidency of the United States Olympic Committee.

Since those angry days in Munich in the early 1970s America has come a long way. The USOC has become the most powerful Olympic committee in the world. Today the fear is that America, whose financial muscle underpins the Olympic movement, stands poised to blow apart Samaranch's carefully constructed house of cards.

'Nobody I know admires Helmick. You never hear any other IOC member speak well of him,' says one Olympic insider. 'He is such a curious figure. If you sit and watch him at IOC meetings where he is on the top table he never sits in his seat for more than five minutes. He is always on the prowl, always moving about, always taking phone calls, he never sits still. It doesn't matter if it's in the middle of a Samaranch speech, he's up and down like a yo-yo.

'I can only assume that he is far more effective than he looks because a small-town lawyer from Des Moines made it to the top. He is clearly very ambitious.'

Helmick's ambitions in the brave new world of business and international sport were nurtured by the man from Adidas, Horst Dassler. 'This Des Moines lawyer has been fostered and feathered all the way through the international scene, right the way up to becoming an IOC member,' says Dassler's former business partner Patrick Nally. 'And by happening to be in the right place at the right time, Bob became head of the most powerful Olympic committee in the world.'

Robert Helmick was born, raised, educated and employed in the city of Des Moines, Iowa. The son of academic parents, the young Helmick first showed an interest in competitive swimming when he started playing water polo at Roosevelt High School. In 1954 he went on to study mathematics at Drake University, where both of his parents taught. He continued with his swimming and was an All American during his time at Drake.

Six years later he'd graduated from Drake Law School, settled in Des Moines and was working with a local law firm. He stayed there thity-one years, rising to become a senior partner. In 1991 he joined the Minneapolis-based law firm of Dorsey and Whitney. It was announced that Helmick would continue practicing international sports law. This surprised many Olympic officials. They had always thought that Helmick was a simple municipal-bond lawyer.

Not so, says Helmick. 'Since 1977 my resumé has always listed international and sports law.' Yet in the most recent edition of the *Olympic Biography* Helmick describes himself as 'Senior partner, Dorsey and Whitney, law firm of New York, Washington DC, Brussels, London, Des Moines, specializing in international and finance law.' It says nothing about sports law.

Throughout the 1960s Helmick continued to swim. He made the Iowa state water polo team but never the US national squad. When it was time to get out of the water Helmick devoted his energies to administration. He did well. He had success with junior teams at national level and following the 1968 Olympics in Mexico, he was appointed chairman of the US water polo team. At the next Olympics in Munich, Helmick as team manager led his players to the bronze medal.

Helmick was already making his way within the world of the international sports federations. In that same Olympic year he was elected chairman of the water polo committee of the international swimming federation, FINA.

It was inevitable that Helmick would come to the attention of Horst Dassler. The puppet-master was widening his business interests. 'Horst had become particularly keen on swimming,' says Nally. 'He had launched a new swim wear company called Arena. The idea was to have a go at the almost exclusive dominance of swimming by the Australian company Speedo.'

Dassler enlisted the all-conquering American swimmer Mark Spitz, who had taken seven gold medals at Munich, to promote his new Arena brand. Spitz was accused of promoting commercial interests during the Olympics, although a subsequent IOC investigation exonerated him.

Promoting Arena was only one of Dassler's concerns. He wanted to make Adidas number one in America, the biggest single market available to him. By the early 1980s America was spending $15 billion a year on sportswear. One in every three Americans owned a pair of running shoes. Dassler wanted all those shoes to be carrying his three-stripe motif. 'Horst talked endlessly about the importance of the USA,' says Nally, 'and how vital it was to us to have the US on side.'

When the partners began their assault on the international federations, swimming was one of the first sports they had marked down. 'I remember that when we were writing the regulations for the swimming world cup I would go out to see Bob Helmick in Des Moines,' says Patrick Nally. 'He had an office in a small regional law firm. He turned up in a red open-top Mercedes 450SL with a girlfriend. I spent quite a bit of time with Bob.

'He always turned up at the international federation meetings in Monte Carlo, usually with an attractive young lady on his arm. He came across as a bit of a playboy. It was funny in a way because Bob was very green, he didn't socialise that well and didn't have a lot to say. But he thought it was great going away for an international trip. He loved the international side of it, becoming involved with the Olympics and then the swimming world championships, which we started to organise for them.

'FINA was no more of a dynamic federation than any of the others. There wasn't a lot of money going into it. But then, like all the international federations in the 1970s, it was becoming more important as they got more money from TV. Bob, who clearly enjoyed the good life, was well placed to observe all this.'

Helmick certainly enjoys the good life today. His penthouse condominium in Iowa houses a collection of contemporary art. It also has a waterfall flowing into the jacuzzi. He owns a farmhouse, an office building and a shopping centre in Des Moines as well as his New York apartment. He prefers fine coffee, classical music and expensive cars. 'He has cars he never drove,' said his friend Bill Reichhardt. 'He didn't want to get them dirty.'

In those early days Helmick was one of the very few Americans active on the international sporting scene. 'It always surprises me when you think that it was an American, Avery Brundage, who was head of the IOC for so long,' says Nally. 'The Americans seemed to be extremely naïve about what was going on in the international federation world.

'It's even more extraordinary when you think that the influx of money that was coming into the Olympics was predominantly from American companies. NBC, ABC and CBS were paying vast sums of money for the US TV rights.

'If you look at the amount of money being poured into the IOC by the US networks, if you look at those early days when the networks were also beginning to pay a lot of money to the international federations to cover their events, there was the US, the financial driver of this whole development, and yet their knowledge and participation within international sport at management and administrative level was very minor.'

'Horst saw Bob Helmick as an interesting potential candidate,' says Nally. 'Horst believed that Bob would be susceptible to the nice times, the dinners, the hospitality, the superb hotel rooms. Horst was going to have a go at seducing this Des Moines lawyer with the lifestyle and the imagery of the international federations and start planning with Bob Helmick what he should and shouldn't do.'

The great leap forward was at Montreal. In 1976 Helmick became general secretary of the swimming federation under the new president, Javier Ostos.

Now swimming developed along the familiar lines of business and sport. New world events were created with Nally supplying the money and the marketing while Dassler supplied his Arena kit. By the time the 1980 Games came round in Moscow, Dassler could boast that Arena had smashed Speedo's domination in the pool. In Moscow, more than half of all the Olympic swimmers were wearing Arena products. Thirty-six medals had been won in Arena swim wear, including a devastating eleven of the thirteen possible men's gold medals.

The one loser in Moscow was president Ostos. Unlike a Havelange or a Nebiolo, the president of swimming can serve only one four-year term. Then he must stand down. The rule does not apply to the general secretary. At the FINA congress in Moscow, Helmick watched and learned as out-going president Javier Ostos attempted to rewrite the FINA constitution so that he could serve another four-year term. Helmick would need to do the same for himself in the years to come.

Standing on the site of an old US Air Force base in Colorado Springs in the foothills of the Rocky Mountains is the headquarters of the United States Olympic Committee. The USOC today is a sprawling sporting bureaucracy dispensing a vast budget of $300 million. It is the most important amateur sports body in America. It has not always been this way. Until the late 1970s the USOC was little more than a glorified travel agency for Olympic athletes. The real control of amateur sport in America was in the hands of two constantly feuding bodies; the Amateur Athletic Union and the National Collegiate Athletic Association.

They were so involved in their own feuding that they neglected the international scene. The American Olympic team came back from the Montreal Games of 1976 with its tail between its legs. It had been humiliated by the Russians and the East Germans, coming third in the medals table. President Ford wanted to know why America was beaten by the communists. He set up an inquiry which recommended a new structure. The USOC came out on top. From now on, they would control amateur sport in America. The country looked forward to new leadership and new successes.

Helmick was president of the AAU, one of the twin targets on which President Ford's commission had trained its sights. Effortlessly, he moved to become a vice president of the revitalised USOC. 'Horst was well aware of the importance of the US Olympic Committee and knew it would be helpful to push Bob within it,' says Nally. Now safe inside the USOC Helmick waited for his time to come. 'I was hopeful that I could lay back and become the USOC President in 1988,' he said. But Helmick's rise to the top came earlier than he expected.

Jack Kelly, the brother of Princess Grace of Monaco and winner of a Bronze rowing medal at Melbourne, took up the presidency of the USOC in 1985. Within three weeks of his election Kelly was dead. 'Here's this fit, healthy man,' recalls Nally, 'out jogging in Philadelphia when he has a heart attack. Bob Helmick had been elected to the number two position, first vice president, and suddenly gets thrust to the top of the USOC at a key time.'

They said it couldn't be done. But the Los Angeles team of businessmen organisers knew differently. For the first time ever the Games made a profit. More than anyone had ever dreamed possible. The mountain of dollars from Los Angeles' 'Enterprise Olympia' soared past any expectations. When all the bills had been paid there was a staggering $215 million in the bank.

In the dark days of the late 1970s, when nobody had expected the Games to break even, the USOC had guaranteed to make up any losses. Now they were entitled to forty per cent of the windfall. Helmick inherited a vast sporting treasure chest.

This financial bonanza became a source of bitter conflict. Around the world the other national Olympic committees argued their case for a share. They reminded the Americans that when the East Bloc pulled out of the Games, they had sent extra competitors to make up the numbers at their own expense. They had a legitimate claim on the profits. They wanted $7 million.

IOC president Samaranch was forced to grovel. 'We are asking. We say please,' he said. 'They can say yes or no. If it's no, it's no.' *The New York Times* sympathised. 'The USOC should pay the $7 million and be glad Samaranch didn't ask for more,' it said. 'They can handle it out of petty cash.'

Indeed they could. But within the USOC feelings were running high. USOC executive director F. Don Miller reminded the Olympic movement that the 1980 Winter Games at America's Lake Placid had lost $11 million. 'No one from the IOC came forward to suggest sharing in reimbursing the costs of those Games.'

He went on to rub Olympic noses in the fact that the Los Angeles profits had 'come from the generosity of American corporations, the American public and our TV industry. Eighty per cent of the financial support for the international Olympic movement comes from the USA, and we are proud, due to our free enterprise system, that we can be of support.' That was the nub of it. The Americans were beginning to wake up to the fact that it was Uncle Sam's greenbacks which underpinned the entire Olympic circus.

The IOC was banking on the new USOC president Robert Helmick to 'find a solution' to the Los Angeles profits row. Helmick visited Samaranch at his official residence, the Château de Vidy in Lausanne. Here the two men discussed the problem, president to president. Helmick left Samaranch 'with new grounds for optimism', said one Olympic observer. The IOC was pleased that with Helmick as president, 'the USOC and the IOC were now closer together than at any time over the last five years.'

The Club announced a vacancy. America's senior IOC member Douglas Roby was retiring. Prospective IOC members are nominated by the IOC president. The IOC members then traditionally endorse his nominee. Roby's replacement was a key appointment at a crucial time for Samaranch. The USOC was beginning to discover its own strength. At the same time Dassler and his ISL team were touring the world persuading national Olympic committees to throw in their lot with his TOP scheme. Dassler and Samaranch were closer than ever. If the TOP scheme succeeded, Samaranch would have a new and alternative source of revenue from the sale of TV rights while Dassler stood to earn more from marketing than shoe making. Their long-term futures depended on picking the right man from America.

There were many well-qualified contenders. Topping the tipsters' list was former US Treasury Secretary Bill Simon. Since leaving government he had made several fortunes in business. He was admirably qualified to make a major contribution to the IOC. That was his downfall. Firstly, he was a professional politician whom Samaranch might find difficult to control. Secondly, he had annoyed Samaranch by declaring at the Los Angeles Games, 'It is about time that some attention be devoted to the long-term future of the Olympic movement. Unfortunately the leadership of the IOC appears to have as much interest in addressing this question as a Third World dictatorship has in free elections.'

Then there was Peter Ueberoth who had led the Los Angeles Games organising team. Another dynamic businessman who had made the Games run smoothly. He was shot down in the crossfire of Olympics politics.

The year had started well for Ueberoth. In January 1985, his Los Angeles committee announced that they were happy to reimburse that $7 million from the profits of the Games to the world's national Olympic committees. It looked as if Samaranch's pleading had worked. The decision had to be approved by the USOC who would not be holding its assembly for another month.

At that February meeting there was bad news for Ueberoth. The backwoodsmen won the day. 'America made this money our own way. Why should we share it. Nobody has ever paid us to go anywhere,' was the mood reported by *Sport Intern*.

If they were going to pay money to the rest of the world, the USOC wanted some political control. The answer they came up with was a 'Friendship Fund'. The Los Angeles organisers objected. Ueberoth's stock fell. It plummetted when they handed over $2 million for a Californian arts festival. 'For seven years it was assumed that any profit would be spent on sport,' protested one IOC member. 'Now, not only is the Olympic movement being denied a modest share, but they are not even giving everything to American sport.'

The USOC had its own official candidate for the IOC. By far the most experienced man for the job, they felt, was the USOC's long-serving executive director F. Don Miller. So concerned was the USOC that Miller should be chosen as the next American at the IOC that they offered Samaranch a remarkable deal. The USOC would drop its opposition to the TOP marketing programme and allow ISL a four-year trial in the USA if Samaranch would nominate their man. This was the breakthrough that Dassler and Samaranch needed. TOP could not succeed without the co-operation of the USOC.

'Don was our official candidate,' says George Miller, who became the USOC executive director in 1985. 'He had the support of the USOC and Samaranch agreed to nominate him. But Helmick went behind our backs to Samaranch and said, "Appoint me! I'm the president of the USOC." Helmick made it very clear to Samaranch that he was in charge and could be very useful to him. I can understand Samaranch's point of view but Helmick was not the man we wanted in Lausanne.' Helmick's request was one which Samaranch was more than happy to grant.

Nine months after joining The Club, Bob Helmick flew to the Olympic president's palace in Lausanne. He had good news. The Olympic family would after all be getting the bitterly disputed $7 million from the Los Angeles profits. 'You are certainly aware how much the IOC, and I personally, have intervened in favour of such a decision which the USOC had no obligation to take,' said Samaranch. Helmick seemed to be living up to expectations. Samaranch had picked the right man.

CHAPTER 17

Alarm Bells

The clues about Bob Helmick, his ambition and where they would lead American and Olympic sport began to appear from the moment Helmick replaced Jack Kelly as president of the American Olympic movement.

The new president's progress at the USOC mirrored Samaranch's takeover of the IOC from 1980. Both men replaced part-time presidents who had been happy to devolve their power to their paid staff. Both men set out to became full-time, hands-on leaders. They both fired their powerful chief executives. Samaranch waited five years before sacking the redoubtable Monique Berlioux. Helmick rid himself of the USOC's executive director George Miller in half the time.

'Helmick came to me when Jack Kelly died and asked me if I would help him get elected,' George Miller told us. 'I thought it important to get a new president in right away and so I backed him. But within months of him taking up the post we began to fall out. He didn't have a good feel for running a business and he had a big misunderstanding about his role. He was a man with great political ambition who used the USOC to further his own position.'

Before taking on the job of executive director at the USOC, Miller had been deputy commander of the United States Strategic Air Command. 'General Miller's problem was that he was almost too good,' said Dr Robert Voy, the former chief medical officer of the USOC. 'He was a dynamic individual. I had the acute sense that, from the very beginning, Helmick regarded General Miller's very presence within the USOC as an indirect threat, and a power struggle seemed to be looming.'

Helmick moved swiftly. He set up an Olympic office for himself in Des Moines. 'It was an unusual move,' recalls George Miller. 'Former presidents like Bill Simon worked from their own offices. All Bill needed was a fax machine. Helmick ran up huge expenses. We'd never paid a president before but we soon began making regular payments to Helmick.'

Helmick's next move was to rule that only he was allowed to sign the major TV and sponsorship contracts. 'Up until he became president all the contracts were signed by the executive director – me,' says Miller. 'Helmick changed all that. He wanted control. That was the style of the man. Because of his position on the IOC I warned him to step back from contract negotiations – he had a potential conflict of interest. But he wouldn't listen.'

By August 1987 the struggle between the general from the Strategic Air Command and the lawyer from Des Moines was over. The general was gone. The final battle came over a plan by the Indianapolis organising committee for the Pan American Games to splash $100,000 on a reception.

After he left the USOC Dr Voy recalled, 'Helmick committed to it. George Miller, although responsible for the budget, had not been consulted. He thought sinking $100,000 into a party was improper, knowing that there wasn't the money in the budget for this type of food, drink and entertainment for non-athletes.' Miller counter-manded Helmick and turned down the full request. Within days Miller was handed an ultimatum. He could either 'resign' or be sacked. He chose the former and negotiated a $700,000 buyout of the remainder of his contract.

No warning bells sounded at the expensive departure of the capable Miller. Helmick was now free to run the USOC his own way. He announced that he intended 'to run a lean, mean ship and get money down to the athletes'. That was what the public wanted to hear.

The treasurer of the USOC during Helmick's first term of office was Howard Miller. His account paints a different picture from Helmick's claim that he was lean – or mean. 'I had no problems with the man until he became president,' Howard Miller told us. 'Like George, I too backed Helmick when Jack Kelly died. Then I discovered that Helmick was flying everywhere first class. Now elected officers like ourselves are supposed to be volunteers who are prepared to work for the good of the organisation. I was annoyed. I told Helmick "Look, you are here to work for the organisation. The organisation isn't here to work for you." '

Under Bob Helmick everything seemed to cost so much more. The costs of the USOC's annual congress, the house of delegates meeting, rose inexorably. In 1986 it cost $98,000, in 1987 it went up to $122,000 and in 1988 Helmick hired a Washington consulting company as organisers. That cost $200,000. His USOC colleagues drew the line at this junketing and the exercise was not repeated.

According to former treasurer Miller, the total budget for the USOC officers between 1980 and 1984 was approximately $170,000. During Helmick's first term as the USOC president during the following four years the figure soared to $575,000. Nearly eighty per cent of this massive amount was accounted for by Helmick's own expenses. 'Helmick spent money like a drunken sailor,' says Miller, 'and used the organisation to enhance his own position at the IOC.' Miller was not re-elected for a further term as scrutineer of Helmick's spending.

More bells should have rung again in 1988. Helmick wanted to be elected to the leadership group at the top of the IOC, Samaranch's executive board. His argument was that America, the nation which made the biggest single financial contribution to the Olympics, was entitled to a seat in the inner cabinet.

Helmick was an attractive candidate to Samaranch. The IOC president needed to bring whoever held the presidency of the USOC under control. America was becoming restless at the endless flow of dollars from the TV networks and the major US sponsors that went offshore to the world Olympic movement. More and more USOC voices were querying the situation where there were insufficient dollars for the country's athletes to prepare themselves for the Games.

To get on to the executive board Helmick would have to win the votes of his fellow Club members. He formally announced his intention to be a candidate at the IOC session at the Seoul Olympics in September 1988. Helmick then started to campaign – using USOC money.

In April 1988, Helmick extended a personal invitation to a number of IOC members to visit him in Washington during the USOC house of delegates meeting in the capital. Money was transferred from the 'Friendship Fund', which the USOC had finally agreed to set up after Los Angeles to help develop sport in impoverished countries, and used to offset the cost of first-class flights for half a dozen IOC members and their entourage. While in Washington these Olympic dignitaries travelled in chauffeur-driven limousines and were taken shopping at Saks on Fifth Avenue.

'The Friendship Fund has been used as a "pork barrel" by a handful of Olympic Officials,' reported the Colorado Springs *Gazette Telegraph*, which broke the story, 'to win prestigious positions in international sports organisations.' A bell was ringing, but no one was listening.

It was only later in 1988 that Helmick woke up to the full implications of the contradictory position he had manoeuvred himself into. To advance at the IOC he needed to retain his powerful position as president of the USOC. He would only be an important player in Lausanne if he remained the key player at home in the growing debate over America's contribution to the Olympics.

But his time at the USOC was running out. He had replaced the late Jack Kelly just three weeks into his period of office and so had served virtually a four-year term. The USOC rules allowed its presidents to serve for one term only. Helmick would have to stand down. Suddenly, he could lose his power base.

Helmick insisted that because he had served a few weeks less than a full term he was entitled to run for the presidency, to compete for a second four years in power. His critics regarded this as a mere technicality but Helmick gathered enough support within the USOC and won the day. He would be eligible for a second term.

His problems did not end there. If he was actually going to win the votes of his USOC colleagues he had to be seen to take a tough stand against the IOC and its endless appetite for US dollars. If he was going to succeed in Lausanne he would have to give *them* his first loyalty.

'The question of the USOC against the IOC was a very delicate one for Helmick,' says former executive director George Miller. 'He always told the USOC what it wanted to hear, that he fully supported our right to negotiate increased TV and sponsorship money from the IOC. But when it came to the negotiations he always fudged on the final percentages and he fudged it for his own benefit with the IOC.

'In 1986 I approached Samaranch and asked for a bigger share of the Olympic TV money. There followed long and drawn-out negotiations between the IOC's Dick Pound and myself. We were asking for about twenty to twenty-five per cent, the IOC came back with ten per cent. We were getting nowhere.

'Helmick suddenly announced that he would chair a meeting between the two sides. The USOC team had decided to settle at fifteen per cent but Helmick told us that Samaranch had asked him to intervene and insisted that we settle for ten per cent. He wanted to do it to further his position in the IOC. I felt he was selling us short.'

It was the same with the TOP-2 negotiations for the sponsorship of the Barcelona Games, which were under way at the time that Helmick was promoting himself as a candidate for the IOC executive board. 'One of his aides came to see me,' says Howard Miller 'and told me that our stance on TOP-2 was not helping Helmick's chances. I said I wasn't going to sell the USOC short just for Helmick's benefit.'

Helmick's response was to hesitate, vacillate and then capitulate at the last moment. He went to the IOC session at the Seoul Games and allowed his fellow American IOC member Anita DeFrantz to submit his official candidacy for election to the executive board. Then Helmick announced he had withdrawn it! At the time he claimed that he had stood down because he had 'confidence in all of the other candidates'. Later he said he had been 'indecisive'. He certainly looked foolish. It posed the question, was Helmick a suitable man to be president of the USOC? No bells rang this time either.

Now Helmick could concentrate on his domestic campaign at the USOC. 'He'd come to see me in 1987 with an increased list of payments that he wanted the USOC to make to various American sports,' recalls George Miller. 'He wanted to increase the budgets by $5 million. I told him that we didn't have that kind of money. Helmick said "Well, go out and raise it." When I told him that even if we did raise the $5 million it would be too late to help the US Olympic teams at Calgary and Seoul he said "I don't care." I have to presume that was his USOC election manifesto.' Helmick was duly elected in February 1989 to serve a second four-year term as USOC President.

His power base secured Helmick returned immediately to his second goal; that precious seat on the IOC executive board. He told reporters

covering his re-election to the USOC that he would be campaigning at
the next IOC session in San Juan, Puerto Rico, in 1989. An
economically important power like the US, Helmick announced, could
not 'exert its influence' within the Olympic family if it was not
represented on the executive board.

Watching from the Château de Vidy was Samaranch. He knew how
important it was to get Helmick and America on to the executive
board. 'It is very important to the IOC that USOC's allegiance is firm,'
Anita DeFrantz told us. 'And it is considered essential that an
American is on the executive board. Had I been senior to Helmick it
might have been me. Perhaps it's just that he also happened to be
president of the USOC.

'Samaranch is keen on allegiance to the IOC. This is also true of
other NOCs, that's why Samaranch is happy to take in a Vitaly
Smirnov, the current USSR NOC president. But the USA is of
particular importance and that is because of the TV money. The
pressures on the USOC are all to do with that TV money.'

At the Puerto Rico session that summer, Helmick was duly elected
to the IOC executive board. He arrived at the top of the movement as
the row erupted about how the Olympic world ate up America's
dollars.

Dassler's first TOP sponsorship scheme was a disaster from the
American point of view. Like other national Olympic committees they
had curtailed their own marketing programme to help the IOC and
ISL. The USOC expected that their share of the payback from the
IOC, when all the revenues were distributed, would be a great deal
more than the $13 million they finally received. Next time round at
Barcelona, the USOC was determined to take a bigger slice.

Just how bitter many Americans had become about the sight of their
dollars flooding out around the world was reflected in the academic
Brookings Review magazine in late 1989. In a waspish piece headlined
'Fools Gold – How America Pays to Lose In the Olympics,' Robert
Lawrence and Jeffery Pellegrom penned some uncomfortable lines for
the IOC. 'We pay, they play,' they complained, 'We bid, they
negotiate'. They laid out a devastating case. The two crucial areas were
the amount the US networks paid for the Games and the colossal sums
flowing out from the large US corporations who joined the TOP club

of sponsors. Not enough of it was seeping back to fund American sport. Especially irksome was the fact that the USOC received only 2.5 per cent of the $609 million that ABC and NBC paid for the Calgary and Seoul Olympics.

'The funding set up for the Games is a travesty,' they complained. 'Americans get bilked three ways. We pay more than our fair share for the Games, we have to put up with an excessive number of commercials to see them and our athletes receive little of the money we do pay.' This was the crux of the criticism. When the IOC shared out the profits too many of Uncle Sam's dollars were going to assist rival countries.

'American money finds its way back to the national committees that organise the efforts of US competitors,' they choked. 'The USSR could be receiving more from this than they pay for TV rights. When it comes to the rest of the world, the IOC extends its hand with a kid glove rather than an iron fist.'

America, they argued, was the victim of her own free enterprise system. Only in America do rival TV networks fight tooth and nail to outbid each other for the privilege of handing over millions to the IOC for the rights to televise the Olympic Games. In most other countries public service broadcasters, pleading poverty, club together before offering a joint bid. The authors had a remedy. The USOC should be allowed to buy the US TV rights from the IOC for a fixed fee. Then they could auction them to the US networks. There would be a considerable profit which could go to fund US athletes.

This was the burden that Helmick carried with him when he joined Samaranch's inner circle. The IOC president could take comfort from the knowledge that Helmick had ambitions to become his successor. Back in 1986, when president of international swimming, Helmick had moved their headquarters to Lausanne to be close to the IOC. The London *Times* had its suspicions about just how determined he was to fight for America's rights. It noted that Helmick 'is careful that his opinion does not surface too forcefully because he sees himself – although not many others do at the moment – as a potential successor to Juan Antonio Samaranch.'

Back in America Helmick also saw himself as a potential successor – to himself. When he began his second term as president of the USOC in 1989 Helmick announced that come 1993, and the end of his term, he intended to walk away and let his successors tackle the challenges. 'I think the past president of the USOC should take a senior citizen status,' he said. 'That's what I intend to do, to be available when asked. Otherwise let the new president run things.'

The public utterances belied the private reality. In February 1991 the USOC board of directors approved legislation to change their constitution. Henceforth the USOC president will be eligible to run for a second term. The first beneficiary of the new rules was to have been Robert H. Helmick.

'I felt what happened to Helmick was inevitable,' George Miller told us. 'I'm just surprised that it took such a long time coming.' Despite the regular alarm bells, few appeared to heed them. The USOC finally reacted only when outsiders publicly pointed out what insiders had privately suspected for years. 'The USOC hates adverse publicity,' says George Miller, the man Bob Helmick fired. 'They have a tendency to corral the wagons when they should throw people out to the Indians. As a result, they allow themselves to be besmirched.'

At least the USOC acted. Swiftly it forced Helmick to admit in public that he had 'made errors of judgement'. Then it set up an independent inquiry into Helmick's secret business deals. By November 1991 the USOC had made public the inquiry's main conclusion.

'Helmick repeatedly violated conflict of interest provisions of the USOC and created a perception that he was trafficking on his Olympic positions for the benefit of private clients,' said Arnold Burns, the former deputy US Attorney General who led the probe. Burns' report flatly contradicted Helmick's continued assertion that he had never done anything wrong. 'Mr Helmick,' Burns told US journalists, 'has underestimated the seriousness of his conduct.'

Samaranch's IOC, by comparison, has failed to take a public stand on Helmick's activities. The self-proclaimed guardians of the Olympic values miserably failed to speak out on one of the most fundamental of ethical issues facing the modern world of sport. True, the IOC assembled a three-man commission of inquiry into the affair. But the commission was composed of the IOC's own members – not independent outsiders. These three IOC wise men, having let the USOC take the lead and force Helmick's resignation, decided to spare themselves the indignity of presenting even a private report on their colleague's secret deals and potential conflicts of interest to their fellow IOC members.

On 3 December 1991, having checked the temperature at an IOC executive board meeting in Switzerland, Helmick decided that his Olympic game was finally up. At one in the morning he pushed a resignation note under the door of Samaranch's suite at the Palace Hotel in Lausanne and five hours later the unethical Olympian departed Switzerland and the IOC for good.

'It's always sad to have an IOC member resign,' said Director General Francois Carrard, as if the dawn departure of one of the most powerful IOC members in such circumstances was a regular occurrence. 'But in as much as it was obvious the Helmick matter was a delicate one for the Olympic movement, he made a wise decision,' Carrard continued. 'And it was a relief.'

Helmick's ambition lies in ruins, a victim of the conflicts inherent in the business of sport, the very conflicts on which the modern Olympic movement is structured, the very thing which Horst Dassler created. It is an irony that the German shoe boss himself would no doubt have appreciated.

Helmick's demise is more than just a personal tragedy. It is a tragedy for American sport. For come 1996, the bespectacled American would have been perfectly positioned to make his bid to replace the retiring Samaranch as president of the International Olympic Committee. After an absence of a quarter of a century an American would once again have headed world sport. For America alas, that is not the way it will be and for that Americans can thank Bob Helmick, the man with the 'great political ambition who used the USOC to further his own position'.

CHAPTER 18

The Benevolent Dictator

A balmy summer evening in the heart of the English countryside. In a marquee on the lawns of Warwick Castle 350 members of the Olympic family and their entourage are sitting down to dine. 'Oh no,' remarks one sports administrator as he studies the menu at his table, 'not salmon again!' It was even worse at the reception in the Castle's Great Hall where footmen in green velvet tail coats had served them champagne.

A Scots piper in full highland regalia leads the host and her special guests of honour to their seats at the top table. In the centre is the Princess Royal, Princess Anne, president of the British Olympic Association. On her left sits the president of the IOC, His Excellency Juan Antonio Samaranch. On the Princess Royal's right is the moustachioed figure of Mexico's Mario Vazquez Raña, president of the Association of National Olympic Committees.

'At the dinner at Warwick Castle,' recalls one of the top table diners, 'it was quite obvious that Raña was being virtually ignored by the Princess Royal. He didn't like it. It was discernible to a lot of the people there.' Raña, who only speaks Spanish, became so annoyed that he eventually dismissed his English interpreter.

The Princess Royal's apparent disdain for Mario Vazquez Raña reflects unease about the Mexican felt by many of her fellow IOC members. This feeling was described to us bluntly by one IOC member as 'fear'. Yet before the week was out, the stocky Latin American to whom Princess Anne could hardly bear to talk would join her in the ranks of the IOC.

One IOC member who confronted president Samaranch with their objections to Raña was told, 'There is no way I can keep him off the IOC.' Another Olympic insider told us a different tale. 'Samaranch,' he said, 'expressed the view that "It's very important for me to get him on the IOC and then I can leave him to get all the national Olympic committees in line." '

Mario Vazquez Raña is one of the wealthiest men in Mexico. He owns more than seventy newspapers as well as a string of radio and television stations. His brothers run other divisions of the family business, including a furniture factory and an aviation company.

Peter Ueberoth, the chairman of the Los Angeles Games of 1984, once described Raña's multi-millionaire lifestyle. 'I remembered a particular feast,' he says, 'a wedding party for his daughter at his estate in Mexico City. We were among 1,600 of his closest friends. While showing us the sumptuous grounds, he'd led us past his own private soccer field and tennis courts toward a large, caged area. Inside we were shocked to see a huge bear.

"A gift from the 1980 Moscow organising committee," Raña had explained nonchalantly. Suddenly my gift of a handcrafted Weatherby rifle to the father of the bride seemed less impressive.'

Raña's Mexico City office complex includes a dining room, a bar, a viewing theatre with seats for sixty, a barber shop, an aerobics room, a relaxation room and swimming pool. His personal fortune is said to be $500 million.

In 1986 Raña paid $40 million for the near bankrupt news agency United Press International. 'Don Mario is a man who has grown too big for Mexico, indeed for Latin America,' an unidentified 'friend' told *Business Week*. Don Mario accumulated his fortune in the family furniture business and rose to prominence as a financial backer of president Luis Echeverria.

Towards the end of Echeverria's administration in the mid-1970s Raña acquired *Organizacion Editorial Mexicana*, owners of the El Sol chain, Mexico's biggest newspaper publisher with fifty-five titles throughout the country. 'Some observers saw the deal as a payoff,' reported *Business Week*. 'Scarcely a year earlier the chain had been taken over by the state development bank, Somex, which wiped out it's former owner's huge debts.' Raña's media empire has made him one of the more powerful political figures in central America.

It is difficult to see how he now makes time for his corporate empire. Raña has been the president of the Association of National Olympic Committees since its creation in 1979. The ANOC now has 165 members. They raise funds to send their country's teams to the Olympics and in wealthier countries they also have the luxury of selecting which of their cities may to go forward with a bid to host future Games and IOC sessions. But the ANOC, dominated as it is by African, Asian and Latin American countries is a poor organisation. President Raña is rumoured to spend around $2 million a year financing it out of his own very deep pocket.

'He always travels with a large entourage and picks up all expenses,' recalled Peter Ueberoth. 'At a Pan-American sports organisation meeting in Los Angeles in 1982, Raña's retinue panicked when the peso plummeted overnight and the hotel management called for immediate payment. Raña took it in his stride and persuaded the hotel to give him a day's grace. The next day one of his assistants presented a suitcase filled with American dollars to the manager of the hotel as collateral. He'd had the money flown in from his bank in Mexico City by his pilot.'

Raña's generosity may not be entirely altruistic. There is power and prestige to be gained from controlling the ANOC. It is the main channel through which the IOC shares out the millions of dollars profit from the Games. It is also the clearing house for more millions in sports aid from the IOC Solidarity fund to poorer countries. Olympic Solidarity was until recently headed up by Anselmo Lopez, for many decades a member of Samaranch's Spanish kitchen cabinet. Lopez is also treasurer of the ANOC. Samaranch now leads Solidarity and Raña is his deputy. This interlinking of individuals and organisations has echoes of the corporatist model that Samaranch served in totalitarian Spain where all sides were welded into one seamless organisation for the greater good of the state and the Leader.

The Adidas boss Horst Dassler quickly spotted Raña's potential. 'Horst spent his life making connections,' says John Boulter, the former Olympic runner who joined Dassler in the early 1970s. 'Some would work out and some would not. Horst thought Raña would be an important figure in the future and knew that he had to get alongside him.'

Dassler supported Rana's ANOC from its very earliest days. He helped fund the fledgling organisation and also donated the use of his Adidas offices and private rooms in Paris for its meetings. 'Raña always needed support because he only speaks Spanish,' says Boulter. 'He and Horst became good friends. I don't know if the friendship helped Horst with his business activities in Mexico, but it's quite possible that Raña opened doors for Horst in Central America.'

In 1990 Raña rewarded his old friend's support with ANOC's posthumous Medal of Merit. It was accepted by Dassler's old political team member for Africa, Colonel Hassine Hamouda, then editing ANOC's magazine the *Tribune*. It still carries full-page advertisements for Adidas, '*La marque au 3 bandes*', emblazoned with the slogan, '*Partenaire de l'ACNO*'.

The national Olympic committees first began meeting together in the late 1960s. They felt the need to stand up to the autocratic leadership of the then IOC president, Avery Brundage. The initiative was driven by the European committees, familiar with the checks and balances at the heart of their own democratic political systems.

Now Samaranch seems bent on swallowing up the independent voice of the world's Olympic committees. The very concept of open discussion and honest disagreement, which lies at the heart of any genuinely democratic organisation, appears anathema to a man whose political education came entirely under the dictatorial regime of General Franco.

In Samaranch's all-embracing structure the leaders of the international sports federations and the national Olympic committees have been sucked into the IOC. Since Samaranch took office in Moscow, thirty-nine out of the fifty-eight IOC members he has nominated have been past or present presidents or general secretaries. This change has distorted the whole nature of the Olympic movement.

'You should have a pyramid organisation with the IOC at the top and the Olympic committees and the federations at each corner,' says one long-serving IOC member. 'It may be that they don't always agree and then you've got an arbiter in the middle, the IOC. But if you keep putting on all the sports presidents and all the Olympic committee presidents then you haven't got the right structure.'

Denis Howell is a professional politician who, unlike the IOC president, has spent his lifetime operating in a democratic system. As Britain's best-known sports minister and as the leader of the Birmingham City bid for the 1992 Olympic Games he has observed Samaranch's political style with a keen professional eye.

'Samaranch doesn't want arguments,' says Howell. 'If he sees trouble looming he buys it off in some way or other. He operates by bringing into the fold anyone he considers troublesome, buying them off in that way by either bringing them into the IOC or onto its various commissions. That's his way of operating and that's what he has done with Raña.'

Both Raña and Samaranch became presidents of their own Olympic organisations at the same time. When the ANOC replaced the much lower profile General Assembly of National Olympic Committees in 1979, Raña became its first and only president. Samaranch won the IOC presidency the following year. Much is made of this dual accession in ANOC's own publications and it is usually expressed in the meaningless jargon of Olympic-speak.

A typical example from ANOC's *Tribune* runs: 'The election of Raña and Samaranch to the head respectively of ANOC and the IOC towards the same period furthered the establishment of friendly personal relations between the two presidents thus allowing joint actions for the universal development of Olympism. In this context, Mario Vazquez Raña never spared his efforts to visit every corner in each continent in order to comprehend problems, attenuate crises, clear up misunderstandings. Juan Antonio Samaranch and Mario Vazquez Raña never doubted in those difficult times that the situation of Olympism and of international sport could be redressed.'

The prose is barren, the content minimal and the concepts banal. The style of the *Tribune* mirrors many of the publications from Lausanne, which are ignored in the more literate countries but are the only sports news available in the remainder of the world.

Raña had to fight one presidential election in 1981 but has never been troubled again by challengers. Every time he has had to renew his presidential mandate it has been organised in the familiar Olympic fashion of acclamation with no opposition.

'Mr Mario Vazquez Raña is the only candidate to the presidency of ANOC,' reported *Tribune* the last time the Mexican was 're-elected' to his post in 1990. 'In agreement with the wishes expressed by the presidents of the five continents and by the NOCs we extend him our best wishes for success.'

Into the ANOC headquarters on the Rue d'Artois in Paris flooded 'addresses of loyalty' from several NOCs. Most of these were from crushingly poor Third World countries with little sporting tradition, grateful for their multi-millionaire president's philanthropic attitude towards travel and accommodation expenses.

Benin praised his 'efficient leadership'; Burkina Faso wrote of his 'remarkable work'; Guinea of the 'services he has rendered'; Morocco of the creation of an 'atmosphere and environment furthering the Olympic Movement'; El Salvador of his 'great vision' and Thailand of his 'force and efficiency'.

Raña's great value has been his unwavering support for Samaranch's vision of an all-encompassing Olympic movement that must remain at the top of the world of international sport. 'It's pretty obvious, the closeness of the two over the years,' says Anita DeFrantz, one of the two Americans on the IOC. 'It's clear that Raña has been what Samaranch would call a great friend of the Olympic movement, he has been very supportive. He has made himself available for tasks which the president wanted carried out. He has also made his plane available to the president when he needed to get somewhere where the commercial airlines don't go regularly.'

Many IOC members have watched nervously as Samaranch has tied Raña ever closer into his IOC. Raña is the vice president of the IOC Olympic Solidarity commission, a member of the IOC commission for the Olympic Movement and sits on the IOC Apartheid and Olympism commission.

But there is now real concern over Raña's elevation to the IOC. Many members are asking what it means for the principles of their organisation, and what it says about the values of their president.

'I was concerned about Raña,' admits Anita DeFrantz. 'I don't think that an IOC member should be elected just because at the time he happens to be the head of an important part of the Olympic structure. He's not president of ANOC for life, it's an elected position, he could loose it in the future. If he does, what use is he then to the IOC? I think you should therefore look at what other things the prospective member might bring in.' When asked what else Mario

Vazquez Raña might bring into the IOC Ms DeFrantz thought for a while before replying, 'I don't know.'

That Raña long supplemented the running of the ANOC from his own pocket is a commonly held belief throughout the Olympic family. At the organisation's general assembly in 1981, delegates discovered in the accounts an amount of $407,318 labelled simply as 'special donation collected thanks to the initiative of the president'. The ANOC treasurer, Spain's Anselmo Lopez, would say only that the money had come from four anonymous companies, three of which were Mexican.

The accounts also revealed that few NOCs had paid their subscriptions. Only Jamaica, Finland, Spain, Bolivia, Norway, China and Mexico had paid the $900 contribution. Without the mystery 'special donation collected thanks to the initiative of the President' and a $200,000 grant from the IOC, there was only $5,900 in the bank. The rest of the Olympic world had not bothered to pay their subscriptions. Their omission was a comment on the importance and value to world sport of both the ANOC and Raña.

The manner in which funds have been distributed by Rana's ANOC has attracted open criticism. 'His treasurer settles down in the hotel lobby,' reported *Continental Sport*, 'and without the slightest discretion displays wads of dollar bills to reimburse his executive committee members' expenses.'

But the real concern is that if Raña is paying the piper, is he also calling the tune? During his 1981 campaign for re-election to the presidency of ANOC Raña helped pay the expenses of many of the NOCs to attend the conference in Milan where the vote would take place. As a result, a record 127 NOCs turned up. Raña beat his British challenger Sir Dennis Follows easily by ninety-five votes to twenty-five with seven abstentions.

It may well be that Raña would have beaten Follows handsomely without the record turn out. Perhaps Raña's funding simply allowed the poorer NOCs to attend an important meeting of their international association. But the funding of voters has offended the principles of those reared in the Western tradition of democratic politics.

Samaranch's predecessor, the Irish peer Lord Michael Killanin, was so concerned that he raised the problem openly at his address to the

the Olympic congress in Baden Baden in 1981. There has been a growing tendency,' said Killanin in the bluntest of speeches, 'towards people trying to obtain posts by currying favour, even, it is alleged, paying the fares of those who may vote.'

The German press jumped on Killanin's remarks. Unfortunately for the *Frankfurter Allegemeine* it also jumped to the wrong conclusion. 'Without any doubt,' reported the German newspaper, it was 'his successor he had in mind.' Alarmed, the IOC press office leapt to Samaranch's defence and rushed out a release insisting that Killanin was not refering 'in any way to the president or members of the IOC'.

'The main objection to Raña,' says yet another Olympic insider who does not wish to be identified, 'is because many of his achievements appear to have been accomplished by the cheque book. It is generational partly. His Mexican colleagues object to him but they are two of the old guard of course. They ran the Mexico Games of 1968 which was still very much pre-Samaranch and part of Avery Brundage's austere and principled era.

'When they spoke to me in Mexico about Raña it was all very cloak-and-dagger stuff. "Of course you know young man," they said to me, "what we are talking about." I didn't know at the time what they were talking about, but it was clear that they did and that they believed their view was the common view.'

The international myth of the much-loved Raña is not universally shared in his homeland. When Raña was re-elected president of his national Olympic committee in 1990, Mexico's President Carlos Salinas observed that, 'eighty-five million people live in Mexico and at least twenty million of them are at an age which they could be elected president of the NOC. Why do we always have to stick to the same old names? Especially at a time when our sport needs new ideas and new energetic organisers.'

Samaranch was so determined to bring Raña into the IOC that he ignored the wishes of the majority of his members. 'Most of us didn't want Raña,' says one IOC member. 'The session wouldn't have him in 1984 when Samaranch proposed Raña and Nebiolo as *ex officio* members. I never knew if Samaranch raised it in the last fifteen minutes of the session to bamboozle people or whether he did it so that he could say to them later that he had tried but failed.

'Until Birmingham I liked to believe that he might have been glad of the opportunity to say to them "Look, I tried". I hoped that he would call for a secret ballot at Birmingham but now I realise that he really did want Raña in.'

The feeling against Raña at Birmingham was so strong that for the first time in living memory, a plot was hatched by members up and down the hierarchy in an attempt to thwart their president.

'In the coffee breaks everyone was talking about Raña,' another IOC member told us. 'One of the vice presidents said "I know what you are all talking about." I told the vice president that if he really was a good friend of the president then he should warn him. Samaranch should make a gesture to the session and say "There has been disagreement and we will have a secret ballot." Let him be the magnanimous person. He didn't do that.'

On the morning of Sunday 16 June 1991 the IOC executive board took breakfast in the drawing room of the Hyatt Hotel before the final meeting of the session.

South Korea's Kim, Canada's Pound, Australia's Gosper, Senegal's Mbaye, Switzerland's Hodler, China's Zhenliang He and the remainder of their colleagues sat round the big oval table. Presiding was Juan Antonio Samaranch. There were eggs, sausages, bacon, mushrooms, tomatoes and potatoes for those still hungry at the end of a week of feasting. Those with more delicate stomachs could nourish themselves on pastries and fresh fruit.

'They were all very important people,' one of the waitresses who served the great men that morning told us. 'By that I mean they all thought they were important. They were all clearly used to being waited on hand and foot. But they weren't polite. A couple of them were forever clicking their fingers in the air, which is something I hate. I'm not a dog.'

'Samaranch was obviously the leader, clearly in charge. I didn't even know who he was to start with, but it was obvious. There were several arguments going on around the table between various people. When Samaranch intervened people would stop and listen to him.'

The final business of the morning was the election of new members to the IOC. By tradition, nominations are put forward for the approval of the IOC membership on the recommendation of the president himself. The IOC members are entitled to vote on the matter but, by tradition, they invariably rubber stamp Samaranch's nominations.

Samaranch had four places to fill on the IOC that morning. The nominations he would put forward were Germany's Thomas Bach, Switzerland's Denis Oswald, the Belgian Jacques Rogge and Mario Vazquez Raña of Mexico.

With their business done, the executive board and the president left their breakfast table in the Hyatt, crossed the connecting bridge to hall four of the International Convention Centre and went into meet the rest of their IOC colleagues who were ready and waiting for the final session.

The opponents of Raña were also ready and waiting. Their plan was to force Samaranch into a secret ballot. If they succeeded, the conspirators believed, Raña would never be elected. The irony was that the conspiracy had been initiated by members of Samaranch's own executive board.

'Some of the most senior people in the IOC thought there should be a secret vote,' explains one IOC member whose opinion was canvassed by the conspirators. 'But the agreement of twenty-five members would be needed to see that done.'

Mary Glen-Haig, one of the two British IOC members, was one of those approached by the opponents of Raña and asked for her help. She told them that while she was not prepared to ask for a secret ballot she was prepared to set the stage for Raña's opponents and to ask Samaranch at the appropriate moment in the proceedings, 'Mr President, will you assure us that your nominees have the support of the present IOC members in that country?'

The first new member to be nominated was the German Thomas Bach. 'In order not to make it personal,' says the IOC member, Mary Glen-Haig asked her question 'then and there'.

Samaranch did not answer. 'He just went on with the business and called out "Vazquez Raña".' Mary Glen-Haig was convinced that, having been ignored, Samaranch thought that would be the end of the matter. So the elderly IOC member pressed her buzzer once more. François Carrard, the director general of the IOC, drew his president's attention to the fact that Mary Glen-Haig wanted to speak again.

Mary Glen-Haig repeated her question: 'Mr President, will you assure us that your nominees have the support of the present IOC members in that country?' According to a report in *The Times*, Samaranch became 'visibly disgruntled' and asked for a show of hands.

Mary Glen-Haig put her hand up along with five other women – the Princess Royal, Pirjo Haggman, Princess Nora of Liechtenstein, Anita DeFrantz and Carol Anne Letheren. Four of the men also put up their hands – Philipp von Schoeller, Prince Albert of Monaco, Pedro Vazquez and Edward 'Tay' Wilson.

At that point in the plan, Anita DeFrantz, one of the two US IOC members, should have asked Samaranch for a secret ballot. But the American didn't speak up.

'I was caught by surprise by the fact that Samaranch called for the vote so quickly,' Anita DeFrantz told us. 'He did it before there was a chance to call for a secret ballot.

'I think a secret ballot would have been desirable, then people could have voted how they wanted without fear. But when you take the oath on becoming an IOC member you swear to uphold the principle that IOC decisions are made without appeal. So now Raña's elected there is a problem with talking about any opposition there might have been.'

'He handled that so cleverly, he was such a brilliant technician,' comments another of those who voted against Raña. 'Samaranch is a benevolent dictator. Thirteen people voted for Raña, ten voted against him and there were sixty abstentions. Can you imagine getting into a London club with sixty abstentions?'

The story of Raña's election brings into stark relief the nature of Samaranch's IOC. The president through his executive board, and not the IOC session, is the real power within the Olympic movement. It is a triumph for Samaranch's apparent belief in corporatism. It also suits many members of Samaranch's inner circle.

'Most of the time the executive board is given a lot of latitude by the IOC members,' says South Korea's Un Yong Kim, who has been a board member since 1988. 'It's partly for practical reasons. The IOC session, which is supposed to be the parliament of the Olympic movement, only meets once a year. With so much work to get through, the executive board is forced to meet many more times than that.' When it does, IOC strategy and decisions are effectively determined there.

'Within the executive board it's Samaranch who makes the final decisions,' says Kim. 'I have never seen a board recommendation turned down by the full IOC session in all my time as an IOC member and I joined in 1986.'

'Kim is technically correct,' says Canada's Dick Pound, Kim's former executive board colleague, 'about the session never rejecting an executive board recommendation. But that is because Samaranch knows what will fly and what will not. Samaranch knows how to organise it all. He's more than a politician, he's a statesman.'

'For Samaranch,' Pound says, 'avoiding a problem is far preferable to trying to solve one which has already occurred.' Many ordinary IOC members would not argue with Pound's assessment. 'The Olympic movement has gained in recognition and that's down to Samaranch's ability,' says one IOC member. 'His great strength is his diplomacy. He does little else. It's his life. He does nothing but eat, breath, think and sleep Olympics.

'But although Samaranch is forever talking about the great unity which we have in the Olympic movement and how we must strive to keep it, I think he's just papering over the cracks.'

The workings of the executive board are cited as an example. 'Even if some of them are against a motion it comes forward to the session as if they are for it. Raña's name came through to the session as if the board were all for it. I know that wasn't right in Raña's case.'

Many IOC members believe that there is something fundamentally wrong with an organisation whose executive board never gives the membership minority reports – even when there is disagreement.

'One of Samaranch's weaknesses,' says another IOC member, reluctant to be identified, 'is that he won't appoint people to the IOC who are too strong. He also runs the executive board meetings like he runs the IOC sessions.'

'Take the IOC accounts. They are presented to the membership in such a way that you can read them and never find out anything you really want to know. You are only given the figures at the meeting. You never get time to really read them. Marc Hodler is an excellent chairman of the Finance commission and he certainly takes you through them, but you'd have to say that because Hodler accepts them we all accept them. It's rubber stamping, like most things at an IOC session. There is never a philosophical discussion about anything.'

Dick Pound dismisses such objections. 'The IOC has never purported to be a democratic organisation with a small "d," ' he told us. 'It has elements of the British club system. It's closed to all but Club members but within the Club, it is run democratically.'

'I think Samaranch is wily and clever and astute,' says another Olympic insider, 'and much more important, energetic in a world which is not particularly energetic. But history may well show that Samaranch is a figure rather like your British Labour Prime Minister Harold Wilson. While he was in charge everyone admired how he manipulated it all. Yet underneath, the very influences he claimed to abhor were just getting stronger and stronger.'

So what does Samaranch's Olympic movement stand for as it approaches the twenty-first century? Ploughing through the morass of Samaranch's public statements over the last ten years offers little insight. 'If you listen to his speeches,' says one Olympic observer, 'and I've heard a good few of them, there's no content in them.'

All Samaranch's oratory follows a depressingly familiar pattern. First comes the evocation of the name of Coubertin, the founder of the modern Olympics. Then follows a shorter or longer list of nebulous Olympic slogans; 'Olympism is essentially an educational movement'; 'sport combined with culture'; 'acting to promote peace'; 'unity is our only strength'; 'bringing people together in peace for the benefit of mankind'. The speaker and his speeches run on auto pilot.

'I don't know what you would say was the ethical base of the Olympic movement these days,' says Denis Howell. 'You would have to trot out what it used to be and have to acknowledge that the foundations are now a bit shaky. Because of the gigantic nature of the enterprise now it is nigh on impossible to find a country that can stage the Games in accordance with the old precepts. I think it has moved away from the principles of amateurism and towards an all-embracing universality covering all sports.

'Samaranch's own personal situation is an important factor in his thinking, especially when he is dealing with television, but he would see the all-embracing nature of the Games and of bringing in everyone that he could, as being a point of principle.

'But in my view, he has taken so many illogical decisions. For example, he talked in Birmingham about the need to reduce the number of competitors in the Olympics, this is having just brought in tennis!'

'Leadership and success.' That is how another Olympic insider sums up the characteristics of Samaranch's IOC. 'He's absolutely determined that the Olympic movement should be the most important body in the world. He sees the Olympic movement in UN terms. That's why it's important to him that every Games is the best ever, everything in his world is bigger and better.'

But what Samaranch claims to hold dear is flawed by inconsistencies. 'It's important to Samaranch, for example, that Stefi Graf plays at the Olympics. But if that's so important, then why not Maradonna? The answer of course is that Havelange and FIFA have no desire to undermine the status of their own World Cup and won't allow it. Yet that situation is not admitted as a failure. The Olympic soccer competition is presented to the public as wonderful because it allows Third World countries to compete on a world stage! There is an answer for everything in Samaranch's Olympic world.'

Older members of the IOC have a more fundamental worry about where their president's polices have led them. They fear that the very spirit of sport is now lacking in Samaranch's IOC.

'There is an aura about the five rings. If Samaranch is not careful it will be self destructing,' believes one Olympic 'traditionalist'. 'It's like the old thing of amateurs and professionals. I had to save money to go to the Games but we had fun. I don't think there's much fun anymore. I think money has ruined it.

'The Olympics will end up like that Wimbledon final with Boris Becker stamping around the court if they are not careful. Would he really have behaved like that if there hadn't been so much money in the sport?'

'My overall judgement would have to be that Samaranch's presidency has been good for the Olympic movement, but that it contains the seeds of its own destruction,' says Howell. 'It now needs someone else to come in – and I don't know who that would be – with their feet firmly on the ground as president who could re-adjust the position and get back to believing in something.'

There is a fundamental problem awaiting the next IOC president. The structures that Horst Dassler set up in the world of sport and the

Olympics to benefit Adidas still dominate, while the man who made it all work is now gone. 'In an odd way,' says Denis Howell, 'one of the reasons why Samaranch wants to keep going may be that if *he* goes too, the succession would create considerable difficulties for the IOC.

'Samaranch has decided to go on on after Barcelona but I think he may have made a grave error of judgement. I don't think he can gain any further kudos. He is almost a monarch. He is treated as such by so many people. The president wants this, they say, the president wants that!'

Samaranch gives no clues about who he thinks should inherit his mantle – although it is unlikely that the man who saw his world fall apart after the death of Franco would allow the same to happen at the IOC. According to one Olympic observer, he appears to keep changing his mind. 'He told me some years ago that Dick Pound was the best man on the IOC. Last year he told me that Kim of Korea was the best man for the job.

'But the best people in the Olympic movement are too modest,' he continued. 'They are so modest that they have failed to get together to fight the growing problems. Some of the best people are now too old. But there are still people who could have great influence, like the Grand Duc Jean of Luxembourg and Prince Merode. The Princess Royal has turned out to be a disappointment.

'Of the up-and-coming people Kevan Gosper thinks he's going all the way and there is Dick Pound but his stock is not high at the moment. If Merode got nowhere then Pound is the man I would wish to see as president. At least he would be independent.'

'I would say that it's very hard to look at the current IOC members and see what contribution they make to the furtherance of international sport,' says a full-time observer of Samaranch's IOC.

'Everybody talks about Pound and Gosper but I can see Raña as the next IOC leader. Especially if Samaranch allows his own name to go forward again after Barcelona which would take him on to Atlanta in 1996. Then clearly he would be elected without opposition. After Barcelona it will be 'Dear president, please stay' and then there's the centenaries coming up which will be very attractive. There will be great pressure on him to stand again because there isn't an obvious heir.

'My guts tell me that in the years to come there will be ample time for Raña to prepare the ground, to get onto the executive board and finally to run for president.'

CHAPTER 19

The Shoe Size of the Second Daughter

The galleried hall of Highbury House in Birmingham's leafy Moor Green suburb is a sumptuous sight. Its walls are decorated with blue-and-white tiles, marquetry panels and gold-and-white plaster motifs. The drawing room boasts a magnificent painted ceiling, inlaid with walnut and satinwood. Its doors are finished with panels of sycamore. The richness of the mansion makes it highly appropriate for the business of bidding for the Olympic Games.

Highbury was the home ninety years ago of one of Birmingham's political leaders. Now it belongs to the city and is used for prestigious civic functions. It is also available for private hire. 'Looking for an extra special venue for a particularly important occasion?' asks the Highbury brochure. 'Do you require facilities set within a building whose architectural magnificence will lend your function a mark of the highest distinction and whose historic associations will make a lasting impression on your guests? Look no further.'

For the whole of the second week of June 1991 Highbury was taken over by men who had spent a king's ransom trying to make a lasting impression on their guests. They were from the Japanese city of Nagano and they wanted to stage the 1998 winter Olympic Games. To defeat their four rivals they needed to win a majority of the votes of the eighty-eight IOC members in Birmingham for their 97th Session. It is always at the IOC's annual sessions that the election of Olympic cities takes place and the Nagano bidding committee left nothing to chance. Nothing that money could buy, that is.

238

They took over Highbury as their secret base for a final round of seductive, corporate hospitality. The house cost £500 a night to rent. That was a drop in the ocean. To make sure that Nagano secured that vital majority of the IOC members' votes, the Japanese had set aside a budget of $10 million.

'When I got up there I was amazed,' says Shirley Hunt, who worked at Highbury that week. 'The Japanese had flown in their own chefs, serving girls, waiters, everything.' As they arrived the IOC guests were greeted by a Japanese tea master. 'They'd travelled out for the evening from the Hyatt Hotel,' says Hunt. 'Around thirty people turned up on the night I was there. They were all wearing little Nagano lapel pins.' After the delights of the traditional tea ceremony the guests were ushered into the dining room where, under the shamrock-and-ivy panelled ceiling, a Japanese banquet was served.

'There were around half a dozen tables which were all beautifully laid out. The Japanese chefs had done an incredible job. They had made a huge display of different kinds of fish. There was salmon and prawns and all kinds of seafood set out in a beautiful ice display. It was wheeled round to each of the guests who made their choice and then watched it fried in batter in front of them. It was a spectacular show.'

Four Japanese chefs laboured in the kitchens of Highbury all that week. Every night, in the elegant surroundings of the historic house, the chefs served up their seafood spectacular to visiting IOC members.

'There was also a full bar,' says Hunt, 'with wine, spirits and saki. The spirits were served by eye. We were told not to bother to use measures.'

As the tired but happy guests departed, they were given a small memento of their Japanese evening. 'There was a Mitsubishi computer system in the hall,' says Hunt. 'Each guest had their photograph taken as if for an ID card. It was fed into the computer and superimposed on a background of the Nagano mountains covered in snow. Then the Nagano mascot was added, a sort of fluffy, fat squirrel and finally the words "Beautiful Nagano". They printed this out like a polaroid photograph. Each IOC member went away with a picture of themselves in Nagano. I had one done too!'

Back at the Hyatt, displaying their Mitsubishi mementos, the guests could pretend they'd spent the evening in Nagano! But not everyone needed to pretend. Many IOC members had spent several happy nights in Japan at the bidding city's expense already.

The entertaining, the junketing and the all-round spiralling costs of mounting a bid to host the Olympic Games has long been an area of discomfort within the Olympic movement. It has also been an area of inaction.

As long ago as 1965 the IOC ruled that cities bidding to stage the Games should be barred from holding receptions or cocktail parties at sessions. They also ordered that no more than six delegates from any bidding city could attend. Most severe of all, no more gifts were to be given to IOC members.

Thirty years later the IOC leadership is still making the same pronouncements while the bidding cities and the IOC membership are still happily ignoring them. In April 1991 the executive board came up with a new set of regulations to crack down on conspicuous indulgence. 'You know the problem of the limitation of expenditure incurred by the cities bidding to host the Olympic Games,' ran Samaranch's coded message to his IOC membership. 'As always, I count on your support.'

These new restrictions came into force on the day after the Birmingham session ended. This meant that Nagano and its rivals could spend whatever they liked and the IOC members could take all that was offered. Both Nagano, the winner, and runner-up Salt Lake City hired private houses for their corporate hospitality, in breach of the spirit of the imminent rule change. There were no reprimands. These two cities alone brought over a thousand supporters to Birmingham. The combined costs of the five cities who went all out to win was $50 million.

Samaranch's 'instructions' have a strong sense of *déjà vu* about them. The latest rules, for cities bidding to host the Games for the year 2000, include: no receptions or cocktail parties; a maximum of six members for each bidding city delegation and a $200 limit on the total value of gifts given to an IOC member.

These new regulations were broken within two months when the IOC executive board had their quarterly meeting in Berlin in September 1991. Members received the following invitation. 'On the occasion of the IOC executive committee meeting in Berlin we should like to cordially invite you to a soirée at the beautiful Witshaus Schildhorn.' The hosts were the Berlin bidding committee for the Olympic Games of 2000. They have not been disqualified from the competition.

There was a time when you could not pay a city to take the Olympic Games. After the huge losses at Montreal few cities wanted to land themselves with two decades of debt. Only Los Angeles had the confidence to bid for the 1984 Games. Inevitably, they did not have to lavish many gifts on IOC members. Theirs was the last of the cheap bidding campaigns. But when the organisers of the Los Angeles Games revealed that they had made a $215 million profit, a whole new world opened up before the exclusive electorate. The next bidding campaign, for the 1992 Games, set the style.

'Nothing like it had been seen before in the history of the Olympic movement,' said Denis Howell, who led Birmingham's bid against the successful Barcelona. 'No limit was set on the number of receptions nor the money which could be spent on them, nor upon visits by IOC members nor the gifts presented to them.'

Birmingham's campaign budget, first estimated at around £1.5 million ended up £1 million higher. The winners, Barcelona, spent £4.5 million. And they were just two of six cities vying for the summer Games. Seven other hopefuls from Sofia to Berchtesgaden were competing for the winter Olympics of the same year. The thirteen candidates spent an official sum of £33 million between them. The unofficial figure is unknown.

All these millions are aimed in one direction; capturing just over forty votes at the IOC. There is no other way to win the Olympics. Any bidding city must target its attentions exclusively on The Club.

'At the end of the day you have to get out and build the relationships with the IOC members,' insists Bob Scott, the buoyant theatrical impresario who headed Manchester's bid against Atlanta and Athens for the Centenary Games of 1996. 'I even know the shoe size of the second daughter of one particular IOC member!'

Scott is settling into the starting blocks again. This time he hopes to lead Manchester to victory for the Games of 2000. One of his rivals will be Beijing. 'It will be interesting to see how the Chinese go about their bid. At Birmingham they had six people, at Sydney for the international federations conference they had fourteen. At the Tokyo Athletics World Championships they had God knows how many. But are they actually wooing the wives of the IOC members? You have to. It's a personal thing in the end.'

Bob Scott's basic law of bidding, to 'get out and build the relationships with the IOC members', was also the foundation of Birmingham's campaign back in 1986. The first thing that Denis Howell's team did was to create a dossier on every IOC member. Every individual's interests and requirements were listed. They made a video extolling the virtues of their bid, built a model of the planned new facilities and went out on the road to find as many IOC members as possible at the worldwide schedule of sporting assemblies.

According to Howell, 'the IOC members expected a reception at each of these meetings. If such receptions were expected then Birmingham must be seen at its best.' On the thorny subject of gifts, Howell took advice. 'It was the invariable practice to give gifts on these occasions to IOC members,' he discovered. 'When they visited us, we decided to follow this practice.'

Howell, a former government minister, was profoundly disturbed by his experience. 'I was acutely aware that the process of competition was getting out of hand,' he says. Despite such concern, Birmingham played its full part in the entertaining process. For their final effort at the IOC session in Lausanne where the vote would be taken, the Birmingham bid team flew over a cathedral choir, hired a steamer and threw a dinner on the waters of Lake Leman. Back on dry land, the West Midlands Police pipe band played in the lobby of the Palais de Beaulieu where the session was held. The former England world cup star Bobby Charlton was on hand to meet and greet IOC members.

Other bidding cities were equally extravagant. Brisbane spent $1 million on its exhibition and presentation to IOC members meeting in Berlin in 1985. On top of that came $200,000 worth of seafood flown into East Germany by Rupert Murdoch for a Brisbane garden party.

Amsterdam projected its claims to the Games by holding daily beer festivals for the world's press. The dark side of Amsterdam's bidding experience was a report that at least one IOC member had asked them for cash to secure his vote.

Direct from the delights of Berlin, thirty-five IOC members flew on to take a closer look at the Swedish winter Games site at Falun. The highlight was a dinner with the King and Queen of Sweden. IOC vice president Ashwini Kumar travelled with his wife and two children. Who picked up the bill for Kumar's family to jet off to Sweden with him is unclear.

When the German audit office examined the accounts of the Berchtesgaden bid it found 'excessive and unplanned expenditure'. Flights for thirty-three visiting IOC members had cost the bid committee DM100,000. The bill for Peruvian IOC member Ivan Dibos alone was DM27,000. He was accompanied by his wife and three children.

Criticism of the campaign spectacle filled the pages of the world's leading newspapers. 'Never in the history of sport has so much attention been paid to so few people who have long passed the bodily shape and age of competition,' cried the London *Observer*. '£33 million has been lavished on securing 43 votes from 85 members of an oligarchy known as the IOC.'

'The long and expensive campaigns have left too many losers in their wake,' reported the *Frankfurter Allegemeine Zeitung*. 'For this reason alone, the IOC must consider reducing the scale of its absurd Olympic theatre back to a more sensible level.'

'The extent to which sporting considerations play a merely subordinate role in this kind of ballot' pointed out Munich's *Süddeutsche Zeitung*, 'is revealed by the poor results of Berchtesgaden (six votes) and Amsterdam (five votes). As far as the athletes themselves are concerned, these two venues offered more or less ideal conditions.'

This picture of IOC members as greedy and over indulged was potentially damaging. President Samaranch thought it necessary to be seen to act. After Barcelona had safely secured its nomination he asked the campaigning cities for their thoughts on how to curtail the excesses of bidding. The result; more new rules from Lausanne.

A ban was slapped on all those exhibitions and receptions organised on every imaginable occasion in the run up to the 1986 vote. In future they would only be authorised 'within the framework of an IOC session.'

Banned too was the flood of outrageously expensive gifts which engulfed the IOC members. Henceforth, Lausanne decreed, all such presents must have a 'relevant character'. What was relevant was not defined.

A stop would also be put to the countless trips to candidate cities made by many IOC members. This was a suggestion which Denis Howell himself had made. Five years on, the former Sports Minister remained sceptical. 'They will never stop all this visiting by IOC members,' he maintains. 'It's clear that the executive board is not going to deprive its members of all this worldwide travel. If they did, they would never get re-elected!'

The latest rules attempt to restrict visits to bidding cities to a single trip for the IOC member and one companion. 'What do you do if someone says I'd like to bring my daughter?' asks one old bidding hand. 'Do you report them to the IOC? Of course not. It's like appealing against your degree level. Nothing will happen. There is nothing in it for bidding cities to either refuse the request or to report it.'

Howell's experience of leading Birmingham's campaign for the 1992 Games drove him to say, 'Nothing like it had been seen before in the history of the Olympic movement.' He added that 'it is hoped that nothing like it will ever be seen again.'

The campaign for 1996 showed no improvement as Atlanta and Athens, Manchester, Melbourne and Toronto lavished their attention on that tiny band of franchisees who held the key to their dreams.

The Athens bid for the 1996 Olympics, the 100th anniversary of the modern Games, began with a ceremonial dinner at the foot of the Acropolis. Greek Prime Minister Andreas Papandreou announced the city's candidature in the presence of President Samaranch and sixteen IOC members from Europe, Africa, Latin America and Oceania. The entertainment continued with a reception given by the Hellenic Olympic committee at the Glyfada Golf Club.

A special flight provided by Olympic Airways took the IOC members to a private airfield near Olympia. Then they cruised back to Piraeus via the the Gulf of Corinth and the temples of Delphi. The following year more IOC members were in Greece. They were treated to the world première of Mikis Theodorakis' symphonic ballet written around the theme of Zorba.

'Throughout this hauntingly melodic work,' reported the London *Times*, 'more than half the IOC members present spent the time talking loudly, drinking and laughing. Had I been Greek I would have felt like jumping to my feet and shouting "Keep your Games and your television millions and your sponsorship deals and your drugged automatons." '

'I'm an independent member of the IOC,' one old timer told us,' and my vote can't be bought.' That may well be true, but many IOC members give the impression that they do enjoy being paid for.

At Birmingham's Hyatt Hotel in 1991 it was gifts galore again as the Olympic bidding circus hit town. In the post room on the hotel's first floor, exotically wrapped windfalls piled up from the five candidate cities.

There was Vennini glass, Gucci handbags, personal computers, watercolours, limited edition prints, silk scarves, ties, books and stetsons. Large Australian gentlemen, who weren't even bidding for the winter Olympics, were walking around with handfuls of free ties to publicise Sydney's bid for the year 2000.

Shirley Hunt, who worked at the Japanese hospitality hide-away at Highbury, also worked at the Hyatt. 'There was so much stuff coming into the post room that the girls there spent the entire week simply delivering gifts to the IOC members' rooms. It was incredible. The gifts started to come in around mid-day and from then on the post room was just heaving with bags and gift-wrapped boxes of all descriptions. I know that Princess Anne returned all her gifts but I think she was the only one.'

At the Hyatt Hotel each bidding city has been allocated an 'official' hospitality suite. 'We've been told to treat them fairly,' says Catriona McFadden, in charge of the Hyatt publicity. 'They each have their hospitality suite and twenty bedrooms. The suites were allocated by Lausanne. We've just given each city a bare room. They've all flown in their own furniture and fittings. Money doesn't seem to be any object.'

Behind each suite are rooms stacked with piles of boxes containing the less expensive giveaways: the track suits, the T-shirts, the pens, the key rings, the beer mugs, the lighters, the pins and the stickers.

Blinds went up across the glass doors as the contenders decked out their rooms in absolute secrecy. The Italian squad from Aosta locked their front door and insisted on bringing everything in through the back.

A Japanese TV crew, with time on their hands and nothing to film, decided to stake out the Italians' front door. When it finally opened, the lights went on and the camera rolled. 'The Italians went demented,' says Catriona McFadden, 'it was like the outbreak of World War Three.'

The team from Jaca has chosen a busy, hi-tech interior, with a continuous multi-screen display of the winter sports attractions of the Spanish Pyrenees.

Aosta has taken a quieter, more classical approach. The centre piece of their display is a mock stone fountain.

Salt Lake City has turned its room into a set for a remake of the 'Trail of the Lonesome Pine'. A cowboy band in plaid shirts is fiddling away against a back-drop of the Rocky Mountains.

'Massive trucks filled with furniture and fittings kept arriving,' says Shirley Hunt. 'Salt Lake City brought in load after load of real pine trees. We had to vacuum up after them. It was a nightmare. It took hours. The whole place looked like a giant green carpet.'

The city of Nagano has plumped for the serenity of a Japanese tea room interior. Its suite, like all the others, offers food, drink, savouries, sweets, and little gifts for all. 'Jaca drove a refrigerated lorry full of food all the way here,' says Shirley Hunt. 'Most of the cities have also brought vast quantities of local drinks with them too; Italian sparkling wines, barrels of Spanish beer, and Japanese saki. We are charging them corkage on it, so it has to be checked!'

We chat with Mr Tasuku Tsukada, the Mayor of Nagano City, at the door to the Japanese tea room set.

'How do you rate Nagano's prospects?'

'We are hopeful,' says the Mayor. Slowly, we begin to open up the more contentious issues. 'What about gifts?' we ask.

Mr Tsukada listens impassively as the young translator interprets our question. He nods wearily, and with a resigned look disappears behind a shelf in the hospitality suite. When he reappears, he is clutching a box of beautifully wrapped sweets.

Mr Tsukada smiles a knowing smile and presses the little gift into our hands. Our question has been interpreted as only a bidding city knows how.

At the far end of the hotel corridor the Swedes have set up shop. Östersund's suite looks like a colour supplement advert for fully fitted kitchens. It's all Swedish-style pine and wall mounted cabinets. The bid team offer glasses of vodka and loganberry juice. There are trays of small pastries stuffed with smoked reindeer meat.

We speak to a Mr Borg. He's in charge of Östersund's relations with the Press. We rattle through the familiar statistics.

'We visited eighty-seven IOC member in their own countries. We brought seventy-two to visit Östersund. We worked through the Swedish foreign office to get to each IOC member around the world. We have a bid team of forty here in Birmingham.'

It turns out that Mr Borg is an old hand at this bidding game. He took part in the campaign of '86. Then he was pushing Falun's claims for the 1992 winter Olympics. We chat about the past.

'Has it changed?'

'Many more of them travel to see the cities than in the Falun days,' says Mr Borg.

That's hard to imagine. Such was the IOC's concern about the frequency of invitations to its members to fly to Falun, that it asked the bid committees 'to refrain from inviting to visit them any persons taking part directly in the election'. Some hope!

'What about gifts?' we ask.

'Too many gifts are now being given,' says Mr Borg. 'I think the value may be down but the quantity is up. We give each IOC member a gift on our personal visits, a gift when they visit our city, a gift when they visit our hospitality suite and a gift every day in the hotel. We give little things like glass and Swedish handicrafts,' he says, and produces a boxed pair of goblets from one of the Swedish pine wall cabinets. They go back on the shelf. We are not IOC members.

'The girls in the hotel who have to deliver the gifts were complaining yesterday,' says Mr Borg. 'Some of the gifts are just too big.' Not to worry. Extra suitcases are on order for the IOC members to carry their harvest away.

Within twenty-four hours of the vote, the victor and the vanquished have cleared out of their rooms at the Hyatt.

'The Spanish didn't even give us a tip which was pretty mean,' says Shirley Hunt. The Swedes gave the girls £10 and a glass paperweight, surplus to requirement by that stage. The Italians gave them a bottle of local liquor. The Japanese gave them a fluffy toy mascot each. They said that they didn't give nice girls money!' says Hunt. 'The Spanish did give me a Jaca tracksuit. Big deal!' The Americans didn't give anyone anything.

'It didn't compare very well with the mountains of gifts they'd given out during the week. It was all so blatant, everyone was trying to outdo each other and it looked just like bribery to me. It wasn't a sincere wish to give someone a present. It was all such blatant sucking up to the IOC members. They were all obviously enjoying the attention and all the flattery they were getting.'

Mr Borg told us that Östersund usually arranged the travel and accommodation needs of the IOC members who visited his city. 'But they can arrange it themselves and charge us,' he confirmed.

This facility, for IOC members to take cash from bidding cities for flights and hotels they claim to have paid for, has proved a murky area.

'The system usually was that if they wanted to come and visit us we arranged the tickets,' confirms Denis Howell of his Birmingham bid of 1986. 'But we got into trouble with one IOC member who wanted to be paid cash. It wouldn't have happened if I'd known about it at the time. It was done and I was furious. It's inconceivable but someone actually went round to the hotel where he was staying and left the cash for him at the reception. But that is what he wanted because he had arranged tickets in some other way.'

Amongst its latest decrees, the IOC has ruled that first-class air tickets for IOC members visiting bid cities are now to be supplied by the IOC itself. They are to be non-refundable to the individual, and reimbursed by the city. 'People will get round it,' predicted one former bid city leader. 'It won't be declared. Who is going to police it? What do you do if someone wants money for tickets? "Oh and by the way, just send the money to my travel agent, he will sort it out." Unless there is enforcement the rules are ridiculous. There's nothing new here unless there are casualties. Disqualification of bid cities is the only thing which will count but how on earth will that happen?'

If this long overdue reform is enforced it will prevent an all-too-familiar trick which was practised by one East Bloc IOC member at Birmingham last year. 'The night before everyone was leaving,' says Denis Howell, 'someone came to me and said that one particular IOC member had a lot of luggage and wanted a car to go to London airport. Our transport man pointed out that given the traffic in London and Birmingham it would be much better to take the Heathrow shuttle from Birmingham airport.

'I spoke to our people and asked if we had any cars, we were totally stretched that departure day. Finally we got two cars. It had been put to me that this IOC member was getting on a bit and didn't want the bother of flying from Birmingham.

'We were absolutely astonished to be told by the drivers afterwards that as soon as the cars left the Hyatt Hotel this member instructed them to go to Birmingham airport. The drivers said "But we thought you were going to Heathrow." "Yes," came the reply, "but I want to go and cash in these tickets." So they went out there to cash in the London to Birmingham section and then drove down to London!'

The aim of every bid team is to visit as many IOC members as possible. Getting them to come and visit your city costs money. Just how much money is open to question. The Salt Lake City bid committee ran a newspaper advertisement to raise funds to entertain visiting IOC members. A section read 'Our goal is to bring 50 to 60 IOC members here to visit. But that is going to cost over a million dollars.'

'Got a calculator handy?' asked Utah's *Park Record*. 'Assuming the full 60 members come, and the figure doesn't surpass a million bucks, the cost per IOC member is $16,666. Let's knock off $1,666 for first class air fare. That leaves us with a nice round sum of $15,000. Subtract another 100 bucks for Salt Lake City '98 sweat-shirts, caps and gym bags, and $700 for a week of first class accommodation and that still leaves $14,200 to spend. Which raises two questions: what do IOC members eat? And how do I join the IOC?'

A large amount of cash goes on wooing the voters before reeling them in to view the delights that the various contestants have on offer. It is rather like a juvenile courtship.

'Give us a kiss,' says the suitor.

'No,' says the object of his desire.

'But I really like you,' says the suitor,' Look, I've brought you a gift!'

'Go on then.'

'The secret of the gift,' says one former bid city leader, 'is not the expense of it but how much the person who receives it really wants it. A clever gift is all. If you give a Seiko watch to say your Princess Anne she sends it back anyway and even if she didn't, the chances are that someone like her has something else on her wrist already. But some other IOC member would be delighted. It's like the best Christmas presents. Some people just buy seventeen of something and give it away. But the best gift givers sit down and work out what X or Y really want.

'One city, for example, gave a gardening book to the wife of Switzerland's Raymond Gafner. It must have cost practically nothing, but she adores gardening. She was so thrilled. Not so much at the gift but with the fact that someone had taken the trouble to find out what she wanted. Now that's gift-giving talent.'

Atlanta had gift-giving talent. One member of their bidding team was dedicated to the job of working out the gifts. 'One inspiration was to fly three golf-loving IOC members out for a round of golf at Augusta, the home of the US Masters. If you are into golf, as those three are,' says the former bid city leader, 'then nothing equals that.'

Even more cash is gobbled up subsidising the many IOC members who decide they need to visit bidding cities more than once. 'There was one particular IOC member who came to see Birmingham more than anyone else,' remembers Denis Howell. 'I found out by accident that my office was fixing up for a caravan tour around the country at this member's request. My office thought they had to do what they were asked until I told them otherwise.'

Birmingham also had several visits from one long-serving African IOC member. 'What a piece of work he is!' recalls a former bid team member. 'He tells everyone that he will definitely be voting for them!' The same African member turned up in Toronto during their bidding campaign demanding business deals with their commercial sponsors. He was unsuccessful.

Bob Scott takes a relaxed view of the need to accommodate Manchester's potential voters. 'Are there votes in sending them a third-class ticket and saying "You've got to hitch-hike from Heathrow to get here?" Of course you put your best stall out. Of course you give them first-class treatment. Of course you look after them in that sort of way. And if one of them says "I'm very keen for my son to come to England and learn English" you arrange it. Not at great expense. It's partly good manners. It's how arms contracts are achieved, it's how any contract is achieved. If abusing them and being rude to them and not inviting them to your home wins you votes then that's what we would all do.

'I don't feel particularly jealous of a person who gives a $5,000 mink coat to an IOC member's wife. On the other hand Manchester didn't do it and we didn't do very well! But I don't think that's why. I got thanked by endless people for the presents I'd given them, when I hadn't, because they assumed I'd given presents because everybody does.

'We did give presents in the sense that for example Francisco Elizalde, the Philippines IOC member, joined us on to a private jet to Sardinia to watch a World Cup match when he came to England. Now it actually didn't cost us anything because a friend of the bid laid on their plane and paid for it. I don't know where that ranks. If he hadn't been an IOC member, would we have done it?'

Scott has a point, for in the world of Olympic bidding, he who pays the piper doesn't necessarily get to call the tune. 'When I was in Tokyo in 1990,' says Denis Howell, 'Manchester gave a party. Princess Anne was there. When I got there I saw some sixteen IOC members. I had spoken a few moments earlier with two of them who had told me categorically that they would be voting for Atlanta!'

These days Bob Scott is sanguine. 'What gets people down is that they believe what they are told. It's rubbish. I know that most people hate to offend. My overwhelming memory of decision day, and I have been at the last four big ones, is the long looks on the faces of the IOC members. They hate it. They have to choose amongst their friends. They don't like it.'

President Samaranch says that it is the best bid that wins. 'The IOC goes to a lot of trouble to make the right decision,' says the President. 'What is of decisive importance, as always, is the presentation.' And maybe he's right. But a host of losers from Sofia to Salt Lake City will tell you otherwise.

'Barcelona's was a very good bid, so was Paris, but Barcelona was always going to win,' says Denis Howell. 'It was quite obvious from the beginning of the campaign that members were being reminded about to whom their loyalties lay and that was to President Samaranch'.

The real catalyst came at the final vote in Lausanne with Jacques Chirac's presentation of the Paris case. He did it in such grand oratorical terms that he swept many of the IOC members off their feet.

'It had such a devastating effect,' Howell believes, 'that the decision was made by the Barcelona strategists to split the sympathy for France by supporting the French winter bid for Albertville. The tactic was to give that to France so leaving Barcelona in the strongest position to win the summer Games. Members were rung up all night and told to vote for Albertville.'

Samaranch stayed neutral and declined to be associated with the bid from his home town of Barcelona. 'He could afford to,' says Howell. 'The longer he is in charge, the more IOC members he appoints and many of them feel a sense of obligation to him. This in itself is unhealthy. In my view, the way in which members are appointed to the IOC lends itself to a distortion. Individual judgements should be sacred and based only on merit.'

Other politicians agree with Howell. Former Australian Prime Minister Bob Hawke, lamenting Melbourne's poor showing in her bid for the 1996 Games, remarked pointedly that 'half of today's voting power have been IOC members for a maximum of nine years and came in on the new wave of commercialism. They have never had to pay their own fares or hotel bills.'

The campaign for the centennial Olympic Games of 1996 was disfigured by even greater bitterness between the leading competitors. The struggle for the Games saw a four-year-long battle between the old world and the new, Olympic tradition versus Olympic finances, Athens against Atlanta.

The moral imperative for the centenary Olympic Games to be celebrated in Greece, the country of their origin and revival, was overwhelming. But bigger cash contracts could be anticipated if the Games went to America. Athens lost out to Atlanta. What had been the President's wish? As is his style, Samaranch maintained a studied public neutrality.

'What I long to know,' says Bob Scott who led Manchester's bid in that campaign, 'is how does Samaranch communicate his view on these matters? People hang on his every word and look into his eyes and they say "What about Toronto?" and Samaranch just gives a look which could mean either "Maybe" or "You can't be serious". People say he has spies out, testing which way the wind is blowing. Everybody claims an inside track to Samaranch. I just don't believe them. I'm not saying that people don't talk to him but the notion that he calls them in and says "Now lads, this is what we are going to do" is absolute nonsense. I know he doesn't do that.'

Nonetheless, there were press reports that Samaranch hinted 'strongly' that he did not want the Games to go to Greece. In an attempt to neutralise Athens' historic claims to stage the 100th anniversary of the modern Games, Samaranch said that he wanted 1994, and not 1996, to be the centenary year. It had been in 1894 at the Sorbonne in Paris, that Pierre de Coubertin called for a revival of the Olympics. Now that Atlanta has won that particular campaign, President Samaranch is planning lavish celebrations for both dates!

But Samaranch also gave hints supporting the Athenian bid. 'I think he got perturbed at the abuse directed at Athens,' says Bob Scott. 'He spoke up for them in certain quarters, which some people got fussed about, like Atlanta's Billy Payne, who made a very effective protest.

'I'm impressed by Samaranch. He always seems to be in a position where he cannot lose. Everybody loves him. They really do. Everybody seeks his smile and his blessing. Samaranch is a great espouser of lost causes. My hunch is that he played the same role over Athens.

'Most IOC members approach the final vote thinking that most of the candidates could stage the Games,' says Scott. 'It therefore comes down to other factors. Where do I want to go? What is best for the movement? But also, what does my president want? Samaranch is a force because everybody thinks of him, not because he goes around saying what he wants.'

Athens was not just up against America. It was up against Atlanta, the home of Coca-Cola. For over sixty years Coke has been a consistent investor in the Olympic Games and since the mid 1980s the company has become the most important of the TOP sponsors.

Such is Coke's influence in the Olympic movement that the fizzy drinks giant felt forced to follow Samaranch's example and declared itself neutral. 'Coke will deny it,' said Gerald Bartels, president of the Atlanta chamber of commerce, 'but the close observer would have to say that Coke was a factor. I don't think they had to campaign openly for it.

All I think they had to do was sit there.'

Coke's self-denying ordinance, made during one of President Sama-ranch's personal visits to the company's headquarters in Atlanta, did not stop them giving $350,000 towards Atlanta's $7 million war chest. Coke claims it acted fairly. It also gave money to rival campaigns. Toronto received $125,000 and Melbourne got $80,000 from the local bottlers and distributors. Coke remains highly sensitive to any suggestion that it influenced the selection of the centenary Games. 'It would be arrogant even to suggest it would be possible for us to be able to influence the vote,' said Coca-Cola boss Don Keough.

Nonetheless, the IOC owes Coke a massive debt. When Dassler launched the first TOP scheme to fund the Seoul Games it was Coke who were the first to sign up. The world's lesser multi-nationals followed and the Olympics prospered.

When the Japanese city of Nagano won the vote for the 1998 Winter Olympics, their bidding committee president Goro Yoshimura said, 'We made many promises and we would like to carry them out.' This was a clue to why there was so much anger in the camp of the runners up, Salt Lake City. They had not made promises – they had virtually completed building the facilities.

Ready for inspection were the Salt Palace, a vast convention and press centre; a 50,000-seat Olympic stadium; an Olympic village for 4,000 athletes; all the ski venues and 50,000 hotel rooms providing all the necessary accommodation. The skating and ice hockey sites were under construction and due for completion in less than six months.

In contrast, when Nagano got the vote it did not even own the sites destined to stage the speed-skating, figure-skating, ice-hockey, opening and closing ceremonies or the press centre. The Japanese admitted as much in their press statement after the vote. 'If the IOC has considered our documentation carefully, they will have been aware that we have to produce the land.'

What was President Samaranch's wish at Birmingham? The one man who knows for sure isn't saying. 'In accordance with the decision taken by the IOC executive board,' read the usual announcement at Birmingham, 'The president of the IOC will not participate in the vote.' The emperor remained neutral in public once again. We are forced back onto private clues.

'I said to Samaranch on the day before the vote in Birmingham,' one long-serving IOC member told us, 'that the best technical bid is clearly Salt Lake City. They have everything in place. I asked him can you still give it to America after Atlanta? Do you vote on ability to deliver the Games or politically on this? He said gruffly, "We can't give it to the Americans again." Then he changed the subject.'

Samaranch certainly appeared satisfied with the result. He told a reporter, 'What do you think your press colleagues would have said and written about the degree of dependency of sport and particularly the IOC on the US dollar and the North American television companies if, following on the 1994 World Cup and the 1996 Olympic Games, the 1998 Winter Games would also have taken place in the USA?'

The IOC has its own evaluation committee whose job it is to assess the technical competence of the contenders. Even that assessment has been neutered in the past. It was never allowed to tell the IOC session in Tokyo in 1990 how it ranked the contending cities. Samaranch's executive board stopped them.

The committee, headed by Sweden's Gunnar Ericsson, wrote a draft report for the board. It divided the six candidates into two groups. Group One was ranked 'excellent' and included Atlanta, Toronto and Melbourne. Group Two was ranked 'good' and included Manchester, Belgrade and Athens.

The executive board were not happy with the idea of rankings and asked the committee to alter its report before it was presented to the members. 'How is an evaluation committee supposed to fulfil its duties correctly if it cannot actually make an evaluation?' asked one disgruntled committee member.

The Association of National Olympic Committees, headed by Mario Vazquez Raña, also made an evaluation of the 1996 bids. Their report came up with a system of plus and minus points. These were allotted in such a simplistic way that they could hardly be of use to anyone.

'Athens plus: Moral contribution to Olympic tradition.

Athens minus: Probably high temperature and scarcely any precipitation.

Atlanta plus: Games will generate considerable financial profit to the benefit of the Olympic movement.

Atlanta minus: Fairly high temperature with probably low precipitation.

Melbourne minus: Long journey for most participating countries.

Toronto plus: Special hospitality programme for athletes.'

This last bonus point clearly did not cut much ice when the IOC members came to vote.

Samaranch and his IOC executive board publicly abhor excess. The flow of new 'instructions' in 1991 apparently restricting the junketing are just the latest in a long list of prohibitions from Lausanne. To date, Lausanne has done nothing about enforcement. By contrast, the president himself is often found out and about, visiting contenders, spurring them on to greater endeavour and the inevitable increase in costs.

In Salt Lake City Samaranch learnt that forty-eight IOC members had visited the Utah capital. The president appeared impressed but reminded his hosts that 'forty-eight is not ninety-one'.

At a press conference before departing he told them, 'Members who came here were very much impressed. Many of them reported to me that Salt Lake City is a very strong candidate.'

Rising to the bait the local supporters demanded to know 'Are we number one?' Samaranch said 'Maybe. I will only add one word: it's a very, *very* strong candidate.'

With that the Emperor of Encouragement left to visit his Japanese suitors in the rival city of Nagano.

Presidential encouragement is a way of life. When former Prime Minister Yasuhiro Nakasone asked Samaranch for his help to bring the Games back to his country, the reply was that 'Nagano is a strong candidate.'

'I was speaking to a British businessman in China recently who was getting involved in Beijing's bid for 2000,' says Denis Howell. 'He told me that Samaranch had made some very flattering remarks after his visit to China. I said "Join the queue." He does that everywhere he goes. That's his stock in trade. He wants a number of bids because its all part of the collective ego of the organisation, which is why I say we should stop that method of selection. It's quite wrong and a terrible waste of public money.

'I think that Samaranch and his colleagues now find the bidding process so essential and important to the future of the IOC that they never will restrict it. What's really happening is that the six bidding cities are providing millions of pounds of publicity for the IOC which doesn't cost the IOC a penny. If you look at it in those terms then it's very rewarding for the IOC and that's why in my view they will try and keep it within bounds but they will never really stop it.'

In the public areas of the International Convention Centre outside the conference hall in which the IOC members were gathered to vote, Nagano's child violinists fiddled in furious competition with Salt Lake City's cowboy band while Jaca's wandering minstrels attempted to drown out Östersund's mixed-voice choir.

In the rain outside, hundreds of Nagano supporters with fixed grins and Japanese kites waved with maniacal sincerity at bemused passing Brummies. For the previous three days the Japanese supporters had been practicing their chanting and singing under several Busby Berkeley-style umbrella routines.

Inside the inner sanctum the TV cameras were rolling, clogging up the ether with a bi-lingual television spectacular fronted by off-duty BBC sports anchorman Desmond Lynam and a French-speaking counterpart. Like a pair of talking birds the two presenters parroted each other's lines. 'Well, and now for a look at Salt Lake City,' enthused Des. 'Eh bien,' piped up his colleague, 'et maintenant, Salt Lake City.'

Endless video tapes of various snowy parts of the world were played into the show to fill time as the TV juggernaut lumbered on to its ultimate destination: the announcement of the winner by Juan Antonio Samaranch.

The IOC members trooped on stage followed by the IOC president himself. The band struck up the Olympic anthem. You half expected the stage to start revolving. With the entire cast assembled and remaining static the spotlight finally fell on Samaranch.

A single sheet of paper was produced from an envelope. 'The winner is – Nagano'. Inside and outside the hall grown men wept. Some with joy, others in sorrow.

Salt Lake City had narrowly avoided elimination in the very first round. The American's had managed only fifteen votes, the same as Italy's Aosta. In spite of the difference in the quality of their bid, the Americans were forced to go through an insulting sudden death ballot against the Italians. One less vote in the opening round and the one of the strongest bids would have fallen at the first hurdle.

'There would have been one hell of a row,' says Bob Scott. 'There were a lot of people voting for Jaca in the first round without intending to stay with it.' The Americans were furious. Mrs Smirnov, the wife of the Russian IOC member Vitaly Smirnov, was due to go on from Birmingham to Salt Lake City. The Russians had been supporting the American bid. After the vote, her passport and visa were pushed back under her bedroom door. Her trip was now cancelled.

At the final press conference in Birmingham the IOC president was asked if that first-round vote had discredited the IOC. 'It's the last round that counts,' snapped back Samaranch.

Outside the hall, IOC vice president, Australia's Kevan Gosper, appeared more disturbed by the proceedings. 'We must reconsider the system,' he confided to a journalist but added, 'and not declare the voting figures.'

Marc Hodler, in charge of the commission which drew up the latest rules on bidding, appeared resigned.

'Any plans to revise the bidding and gifts situation?' asked one reporter.

'We do our best,' he said. 'Our policy is to limit the value of gifts, to avoid heavy expenses like big receptions – these are prohibited.'

Hodler went on to remind the journalists that the entertaining of IOC members could only be done in the Hyatt hospitality suites. He seemed unaware of Nagano's Japanese nights at Highbury. So did the journalists.

'Are the bid delegations too big?'

'We do our best,' said Hodler repeating the mantra. 'We wanted to limit them to six each but we couldn't get agreement. It's a free world you know.'

'What figures are given for the ceiling on gifts?'

'We are looking at various items which have caused expense in the past, like exhibitions. We try to avoid gifts of substantial value.' And that was the end of the discussion.

Samaranch says that he is tightening up on the excesses of the bidding process. But his new rules are aimed only at bidding cities, not at his IOC members. For the first time he has threatened to disqualify any city that offers too many inducements. Yet his new rules contain no sanctions against IOC members, the very people who accept them. In the 1980s angry bidding cities complained to Samaranch about the unacceptable demands of certain IOC members. No member has been asked to resign – as they would in any other area of public or commercial life.

The reality is the world of Birmingham, Highbury and the Hyatt Hotel where a teenaged student on a vacation job was first exposed to the guardians of the Olympic ideal.

'I didn't know what to expect when I started,' says Shirley Hunt, 'and we did get caught up in the atmosphere of who would win the nomination. But I became very cynical about the whole thing. By the end of the week I wondered about how much all this had to do with sport. It was just a great big show. It just seemed so blatant, they all seemed to be determined to spend as much money as possible.

'It didn't seem to me to be connected with anything that I had thought the Olympics was about – you know, human excellence, achievement and all that. The Olympics is not as nice and innocent as you think or are led to believe. The moral side is not obvious. It's just the money that's important, it's just another business deal. By the end of the week though,' she added, 'I'd decided what I wanted to be. An IOC member.'

CHAPTER 20

Destroy the Olympics

The Olympics still hold out a special opportunity: the prospect of a better world as all our young people compete together freely and honestly every four years. That it is as important to take part as it is to win is more than a sporting cliché, it is an ideal; this is the very bedrock of a democratic way of life.

It is surely unacceptable that the right to take the critical decisions about the future of the Olympics has been usurped by just two old men whose main concern appears to be to pit their egos, their ambitions and their rivalries against each other in their battle to dominate world sport.

Juan Antonio Samaranch and Primo Nebiolo bear the major responsibility for transforming our Games from a festival for amateurs into a professional, show-business spectacle. Amateur sport is only about the intrinsic value of healthy participation; the professional variant is all about making money, winning at all costs and being manipulated by impresarios. Fun it may be, profitable it has to be but ethical – and democratic – it ain't. The indictment against the two of them is devastating. They have led the way in the auction of sport and the once-pure five rings to the highest commercial bidders. They have made speeches about the menace of drugs in sport and then soft-pedalled on taking stringent action. Yet all that time they have known that the cheats were escaping their tests. They have now been at the summit for a total of twenty-three years. Our sport cannot afford them any more.

Even as they have been locked in the battle for supremacy both Juan Antonio Samaranch and Primo Nebiolo have followed similar paths.

There seems to be little philosophical difference in their approach to stage-managing our world of sport. They have both hoisted themselves above their fellow officials to levels of absolute power previously unknown in the democratic world of sport. All that divides them is who should wield absolute control.

They come together in this Olympic year in Barcelona at what may be the turning point for the Olympic movement and for world sport. Many people outside the complacent membership of The Club feel that too much has been conceded to the demands of the media and the multi-nationals. The spectators and the participants have never been consulted about 'communication tools' and 'exclusive categories' of product merchandising. The TV viewers around the world increasingly believe that many of the stars are junkies, puffed up into chemical champions. In the scramble for more money, more perks, more self-indulgence, more TV viewing hours and more dubious world records the fundamental rights and concerns of the worldwide, silent majority outside The Club are ignored.

A decade ago when Samaranch addressed the Olympic Congress in Baden-Baden the new president proclaimed, 'In a world in which sport daily gains in size and importance the IOC president must remain its head.' That was the corporatist job description he set himself in his first year in office. The legacy is the presence of synchronised swimming and millionaire professional tennis and basketball stars at the Games.

As he stands on the Olympic rostrum Samaranch may congratulate himself on his considerable achievement in the last decade. Not only has he re-invented himself; he has also re-invented the Olympic movement and our Games. What is remarkable is that Samaranch appears to have sculpted the Olympic movement on a similar model to that of Franco's Spain. Not unlike the general who ruled from the Pardo Palace, the IOC leader has virtually unchallenged power and sits on top of a structure where practices considered corrupt in any other sphere of life appear to be accepted as the norm.

The General Franco to whom Samaranch pledged fealty dealt ruthlessly with opponents. They were murdered, tortured and jailed. Those who were too strong were bought off with membership of Franco's club and benefitted from tax evasion, business fraud and commercial favours.

Samaranch of course cannot punish his dissidents even if on some occasions he might wish he was running the Generalissimo's *Movimiento* rather than the Olympic movement. But he does have the power to exclude potential trouble-makers from decision making at the pinnacle of his Club. Ambitious IOC members who hope to succeed him would be unwise to confront him privately or publicly; they risk exclusion from key committees where they can achieve the prestige that will win them votes in the future. The less ambitious enjoy their Club membership and take the privileges. This may well explain the remarkable situation of a ninety-four member organisation with no public dissension. There are no minority reports at the IOC. No member calls press conferences to argue publicly with decisions. Even behind closed doors there is no debate unless the leader allows it. Nobody complains – on the record – about the vice-like grip of Lausanne.

But this is sport we are talking about, not the security of the state or the private lives of individuals. How have we allowed the Olympic Games, the epitome of openness, democracy and free debate, to be turned on their moral head? The ideologues of Lausanne tell us that sport is ours and is of value to us all. Simultaneously, they deny us any role in their deliberations. They produce endless press releases, speeches and declarations of intent about the Games being for the world but all the time they twist reality. We are allowed no input. The majority of IOC members have little more. They mostly take their gifts, their prestige and hold their tongues. The leader of world sport is utterly unaccountable and, taken in by a mix of flannelled fools and the smooth talkers from the world of sponsorship, we have fallen for his sleight of hand.

Because we are not sports reporters and are not part of the Olympic circus we can step back and assess the reality. The spirit of the Europe of the Dictators that most of us believed had been destroyed appears to us to be alive and prospering in Samaranch's 'bunker' overlooking Lake Leman. A rogue survivor of that era has in our view managed to hi-jack one of our most precious and idealistic institutions.

To us it is not a case of one old fascist getting under the wire and fleeing to live anonymously in a far-away continent. Samaranch has fled the new democratic order in his own country and appears to have found a safe haven in the IOC in which to continue living in the same authoritarian way he did under the system that collapsed shortly after his fifty-fifth birthday. It is unlikely that he could have done anything else. His early life experience was forged in dictatorship, repression and the denial of the basic freedom to dissent.

It seems to us that Samaranch has attempted to impose something resembling the structures of Franco's Spain upon our Olympic movement. A decade ago the institution based at the Château de Vidy was only one third of the Olympic family. It was complemented by the international sports federations and the national Olympic committees. By bringing more federation leaders and national committee members on to his IOC Samaranch has attempted to create something approaching the old syndicalist model where workers and their employers were dragooned into one organisation, supposedly in the best interest of the state. Sucking in potential opposition has virtually stifled healthy public debate.

Samaranch's IOC breaks many of the accepted rules of behaviour in public life. The practices it condones during the bidding process are discreditable and the very opposite of the ideals of sport.

No business seeking a contract with another company could get away with the level of gifts that pass from bidding cities to individual IOC members, the people who award the contract. No company seeking contracts with local or national government could indulge in such conduct. The donor and the recipient in either case would face dismissal and the possibility of criminal charges. The endless round of presents and the lavish hospitality is immoral and indefensible. The citizens of Birmingham and Manchester and any other community which has used public funds to buy gifts for IOC members should ask themselves if this is a proper use of taxpayers' money.

The leader could end this scandal with just one edict. He could write to each of his ninety-three fellow members and order them to refuse any further gifts. He could warn them that any breach of this instruction would lead to instant, humiliating ejection from the Olympic movement. Why has Samaranch not issued such an edict? Why has he, instead, asked bidding cities to cease this cascade of bribes? There can be few other public bodies in the world that seek to legislate for those outside its jurisdiction, whilst leaving its own members free to misbehave as they choose.

There is little doubt that some of his members would be outraged if the goodies tap was turned off. But are these the kind of people we want in charge of world sport? The names of that handful of disreputable IOC members who seek out presents and try to gouge under-the-table payments and other dubious deals are well known to cities that have organised bids. The same names go round the circuit and were surely reported to the IOC in both 1986 and 1990 after the scandals which led to the victories of Barcelona and Atlanta. Perhaps Samaranch has warned them privately.

World sport, *our* sport, is entitled to better treatment; these so-called Olympians should be named and then evicted from the IOC. It seems that Samaranch's policy is to keep the lid on the depravity in his precious movement. It could trouble the sponsors.

Millions of trite phrases about the 'Olympic Ideal' will pour from the world's media before and during the Games. One contribution certain to be missing is the truth about the IOC as the IOC members see it themselves. What they really think about the undemocratic way in which their leader runs the movement is hidden from the rest of us. There are more leaks from the world's intelligence services than there are from Samaranch's tight ship. Why this reticence? One answer was given by the doper Tony Sharpe who told the Dubin inquiry, in a parallel context, 'The glory is too sweet, the dollars are too much.'

During the research for this book one IOC member granted us an interview. We produced a tape recorder and were given a lengthy critique of Samaranch's undemocratic style of management. Occasionally we were asked that a comment be 'off the record' and this was agreed. Later the member panicked and, without warning, instructed a prestigious law firm to stop us publishing these honest opinions. The interview was only about Olympic sport and the way its leader runs the IOC, hardly a subject for suppression and litigation. When it came to making a choice, that member preferred to hide the truth and reinforce the great Samaranch deception – whilst enjoying the honour and prestige of an Olympian position at home and on the world stage.

Also enjoying a privileged lifestyle in Barcelona will be that third of the IOC membership who come from countries with little or no traditions of political democracy. They are mostly men, for Samaranch's thoroughly modern IOC has only seven female members.

In this he echoes many of the international sports federations which, like Nebiolo's athletics council, have no room for women.

More than half of the current IOC members have been appointed by Samaranch, a professional politician who never fought a democratic election and whose world view was forged in a repressive and discredited ideology. There must be concern that the leaders of world sport, as we enter the next century, may turn out to be the nominees of a survivor of a discredited movement.

For eager IOC members their lifetime positions can be near paradise on earth. Consider what is on offer. In a four-year 'Olympiad' there will be four annual sessions. In Olympics year the session is held with the Games so the festival of self-indulgence stretches from one to three weeks. In the new two-year cycle of winter and summer Games will come many heavily indulged trips to upwards of ten candidate cities who will fawn on them for their vote. On top of that they will belong to a number of the IOC's grandly named commissions. These provide yet another round of first-class travel and accommodation in exotic parts of the world.

There is a commission for the eligibility of athletes; its task is to find ways of pleasing the TV companies by admitting more and more professionals to the 'amateur' Games. Then there is the athletes' commission and those for the press and also for TV. There are commissions for cultural, medical and apartheid affairs, for finance, new sources of financing and sport for all. The list continues: there is one for the Olympic programme and two more commissions for the preparation of the twelfth Olympic congress and for the co-ordination of the Games.

Alternatively, members may sit on the commission for the preparation of the 1998 Games or perhaps the two councils. One is for the Olympic movement and another for the Olympic order. Samaranch chairs this last one. He must look further afield for worthy recipients now there are no more more East Bloc tyrants to reward.

The least credible of all the commissions is the one for the International Olympic Academy. This bizarre institution meets at Olympia in Greece and members and their guests engage in serious debate about their philosophy of 'Olympism'. One of the stalwarts on this commission, who helps develop theories about the purity of the

Olympic ideal, is Abdul Muttaleb Ahmad, the late Sheik Fahd of Kuwait's personal assistant, who was active in securing the 'election' of Fahd's son Ahmad to the presidency of the Olympic Council for Asia.

The most politically important is the Solidarity commission, which distributes the Games' profits to provide sports facilities and coaching around the world. This is presided over by Samaranch himself. He has chosen Mario Vazquez Raña as his deputy, who is joined by his ANOC general secretary, the former Polish diplomat Marian Renke, who also sits on the Olympic co-ordinating commission. Other members of Solidarity are Raña's brother Olegario and Samaranch's long-time Spanish associate Anselmo Lopez. Another Samaranch associate from the old Francoist days in Spain, Barcelona journalist Andre Merce Varela, sits on the press commission.

After the games the IOC will enshrine their version of the Olympic ideal in a cascade of expensive, beautifully produced commemorative books, pamphlets and magazines. Leading journalists from around the world will contribute supportive essays about Olympian values and hagiography of the leader. Much of it is banal and none of it will be read outside the tiny 'Olympic family' but it serves to buttress their system and distract attention from the reality.

Samaranch's image of the modern Games will be perpetuated in his greatest folly, the Olympic museum, which will soon open its doors in Lausanne. It will cost nearly $40 million. Much of this money has come in $1 million contributions from many of the TOP sponsors. In 1989 Samaranch asked Prime Minister Kaifu to give tax concessions to Japanese companies which made donations to his museum.

Dictators have always sought to be commemorated in grandiose architecture and Samaranch is no exception. He will donate his Olympic archives to the museum. We will offer our contribution: a copy of the letter he wrote in 1956 which ended with the words 'Always at your command, I salute you with my arm raised.'

Samaranch can no longer salute his revered Generalissimo Franco but he has new idols. In the lobby of the Hotel Princesa Sofia in Barcelona will be the men in suits; those equally unelected controllers of the destiny of our sport, the TV executives and the marketing men. In public they will respond to Samaranch's embrace but privately they will be pondering what future value to place on the Olympics.

The price TV pays for the Games may have peaked. As the grip of the American networks on their audience is weakened by the spread of cable stations and the losses they have made on domestic sports coverage they must re-assess how much they can afford to pay. The sponsors face a similar dilemma as TV coverage of sport proliferates, creating new venues for their advertising boards.

Also in the lobby of the Princesa Sofia, cementing his relationship with the sponsors, is Primo Nebiolo, the man to whom the IOC said no. His revenge, revealed in the autumn of 1991, may lift him above his rival Samaranch, make him the most important man in world sport, wreak a terrible revenge on his fellow Club members and could well destroy the Olympics as we know them.

It would have all been so different if the IOC had opened the door to Nebiolo. From the time he took control of the IAAF in 1981, without the inconvenience of an election, he had lusted to join the Lausanne élite. As president of the prime Olympic sport he felt entitled to an IOC seat; being Primo Nebiolo he was forever driven to be *primo* and that would mean having to supplant Samaranch.

When Nebiolo succeeded Adriaan Paulen he was fifty-eight years of age and had seventeen years to go before reaching the IOC retirement age. His first opportunity came in 1982 when a vacancy occurred for a new Italian member of the IOC. Despite having been the leader of the premier Olympic sports federation for a year he was overlooked and Franco Carraro was sworn in. Nebiolo kept up the pressure on Samaranch and in 1984 the president recommended that both he and Raña be made *ex officio* members. Nebiolo hungered for the compromise, confident that once he had a formal presence on the IOC no other candidate from Italy could overtake him when a vacancy for a full member came up.

But the IOC membership rejected the idea. Nebiolo was livid – and responded as only a bully can. For the first time, and with the success of the first Athletics World Championship in Helsinki behind him, he suggested that holding his own championships every two years would be no bad thing. This was the first sign of his insurance policy, his fall-back plan against the possibility that he would never achieve Olympian power.

The continuing obstacles to him joining the Club of Lausanne have been Italy's two IOC members. Franco Carraro appears in good health and at the age of fifty-one has many years ahead of him at the IOC. The other member, the distinguished former tennis player Giorgio di Stefani, now aged eighty-eight, is an honorary IOC member who walks with the aid of a stick but seems determined to stay in place just to keep Nebiolo out. It would not be impossible for Samaranch to create a third Italian member but it would be difficult.

Less than eighteen months after the scandal of the Evangelisti long jump Nebiolo was forced from the presidency of Italian athletics by further scandals. He lost his presidential seat on CONI – the Italian Olympic committee – and is unlikely to receive their backing when a vacancy does occur at the IOC. Nebiolo also parted from his long-term aide Luciano Barra. Despite the alleged acrimony of their separation Barra refuses to discuss their years together at FIDAL and the IAAF.

The rejection in 1984 spurred Nebiolo to try and create a vacancy at the IOC. In 1989 in Rome we asked Giorgio di Stefani about a rumour that Nebiolo offered him a huge bribe to step down from the IOC and so create a vacancy. Di Stefani confirmed it to us. 'Nebiolo promised me fifty million lire four years ago to retire from the IOC,' he said. 'Samaranch asked me not to make a scandal of this. Nebiolo denies this. But everybody knows the story.'

Nebiolo kept up the pressure through the 1980s to gain admission to the Château de Vidy by the back door. He repeatedly suggested that senior federation presidents – like himself – should be involved in evaluating candidate cities. At the IOC session in Lausanne in 1985 he proposed that presidents like himself 'should be consulted about the choice of location for the Games, bearing in mind the international and political implications and not solely from the technical point of view'. This was tantamount to giving himself a vote on the IOC.

As Giorgio di Stefani continued to show no signs of retiring Nebiolo pushed again. When the IOC met in Tokyo in 1990 to award the Games for 1996 Nebiolo and his fellow senior presidents drafted a letter to Samaranch demanding a right to vote on candidate cities, to be allowed to become *ex officio* members of the IOC and also be given a share of the TOP sponsorship revenues.

Nebiolo, personally, put even more pressure on Samaranch and as ambition overcame him, he made a series of diplomatic blunders. The media were briefed that Nebiolo was determined to initiate a two-year

world athletics championships. As ever, the row continued behind
closed doors but it was so well known that communiqués dampening
down the dispute had to be published. Nebiolo stated that
relationships between the IAAF and the IOC were 'better than ever'
and Samaranch responded that they were 'as always, very positive and
friendly'. The failure in Tokyo spurred Nebiolo to move against the
IOC. He embarked on a path which may destroy the Club he cannot
join.

As Nebiolo sits in the VIP box at the Montjuic stadium and watches
Samaranch open the Games he will know that, at the age of sixty-nine,
it is now too late for him to lead the Olympic movement. Even if a
vacancy came up in this Olympic year and Nebiolo was rushed aboard
the IOC he would only enjoy six years' membership before he reached
the age limit for full membership of seventy-five – leaving scant time to
take the leadership.

But there are no such constraints at his IAAF. Nebiolo's model is
João Havelange, seven years his senior and still very much in control of
world soccer and his own prestigious world cup tournament. What
works well for Havelange may yield the same benefits for Nebiolo. His
third world championships, staged in Tokyo in September 1991,
were a huge success. The week-long world TV coverage was massive
and he profited from a crop of new world records, especially in the 100
metres and the long jump. At last he has a spectacle to rival the
Olympics.

Now Nebiolo cannot advance himself any further in the Olympic
movement he is moving to undermine the Games and establish his
world athletics championship as the world's premier TV sporting
event. During the Tokyo championship his press officers were rushing
out releases claiming that the viewing figures around the world were
between four and five billion. Few noticed that this is around the
globe's total population. What mattered was the signal he was sending
to TV executives and sponsors; his championship, not the Olympics,
was the one to watch.

And so in Tokyo Nebiolo made his move. In future, he announced,
the athletics world championships would be held every two years
instead of every four years. His marketing agents, ISL, have assured
him that overall, more TV and sponsor money will flow into the IAAF

coffers. ISL vice president Paul Smith told us, 'In future we only expect to raise seventy-five per cent of the revenue we secured when holding the championships every four years. But doubling the number of championships means that we end up with 150 per cent of what we used to bring in.' That would mean an increase of more than $37 million which would have to come from the increasingly finite budgets of the world's sponsors.

World athletics championships are now in the planning stage for Stuttgart in 1993 and again in Gothenberg in 1995. This means that the Olympics, whose most popular sport is athletics, will be sandwiched each time by an athletics world championship in the preceding and succeeding years.

Nebiolo's next step has also been signalled. He is actively threatening to follow Havelange's example and ban competitors over twenty-three from competing in the Olympics. For Havelange, this protects his soccer World Cup. If Nebiolo can force the same rule through the IAAF he will at one stroke devalue the Olympics and corral most of the star athletes in his own event.

The majority of world records would be set at the athletics championships and not at the Olympics. TV coverage would shrivel away, followed instantly by the sponsors. If the lid can be kept on the drug scandals the championships will provide riveting TV coverage, as they did in Tokyo. The collapse would continue down the business chain that has become the Olympics. Cities planning to bid for the Games would ponder the alternative of bidding for the athletics championships. Much of the cost of staging these events comes from the fees paid by the TV companies. If they could not televise world records at the Games they would cut the price dramatically. As cities lost interest, the flood of gifts and perks to IOC members would dry up. The only benefit for sport would be that The Club of Lausanne would find its true place: on the margins.

It is long overdue for us to ask what is the relevance of Samaranch's corporatist Olympic movement and Nebiolo's power-mad leadership of the IAAF to ordinary, decent sport. Do they really provide role models for our children? If the response is a no, then let us ask another question: if we, our sport and our children do not benefit, who does?

The answer must be this new breed of professional sports

presidents, the gift-grabbing members of the IOC, the TV companies and the sponsors who have purchased our sport and driven our competitors to drugs to provide more spectacle than the human body should safely deliver.

We are told that the Olympics are for all of us – but does this great festival of sport need the IOC? Since the Games of 1984 when the Olympics first became a vehicle for profit, the private and remote Club of Lausanne has remorselessly pursued its own well-being at the expense of sport. The appalling TV ceremonies where one city is rewarded with the Games and up to half a dozen rivals are humiliated has been created as a media event to project the image and importance of the IOC. If the Club could bring itself to give up its five-star hotels and first-class travel then the millions spent staging each session could be devoted to improving sports facilities around the world. It would be a good test; many members of the IOC would resign overnight if these perks were removed. Then we might bring sport back down from this wasteful Mount Olympus and into the hands of ordinary people.

The lofty view from Lausanne is that the problems of sport are always someone else's, always created by people and organisations outside The Club's magic circle. But they are the problem. There was no need to turn the amateur Games into just another arm of show business, just another entertainment staged by professionals. If the guardians of sporting morality at the Château de Vidy had thought of us, rather than themselves, the commercial interests might have been kept under control.

Consider this: Samaranch said recently of yachting, a splendid activity that inevitably takes place far away from the land-based TV cameras, 'Any sport that does not get TV interested has no future.' Who is Samaranch to dictate thus? Does all discussion have to cease because the quisling of Catalonia has made up his mind? Is this the new rule – that if TV is not interested then a sport is worthless? How does this square with Samaranch's alleged concern for Sport for All?

Consider this also: at the Seoul Games Samaranch instructed the organisers of events at which there would not be large audiences to ensure that spectators were bunched up at key points so that the TV cameras did not show empty seats. The criteria that we thought applied to sport, that all that matters is to take part, is now redundant.

We must all blame ourselves for allowing our sport to be hi-jacked and then raped by commercial interests. But there is still time to rescue its beauty and purity. If we care enough it can be wrested back. The great boil of the IOC on our sporting body could be lanced in weeks if we signalled to the TOP sponsors in Barcelona that we do not approve of their dollars propping up an Olympic movement that now bears comparison with elements of Franco's *Movimiento*.

Perhaps Coca-Cola, Kodak, Ricoh, National Panasonic, Philips, Mars, Visa, Bausch & Lomb, Brother, the EMS parcel delivery group and 3M products are unaware of the history of the Olympic leader and what he has done to sport, that most democratic of pursuits. Perhaps the journalists of Olympic sponsors *Time* magazine are unaware of Samaranch's background. It will be interesting to read in Olympic year how they report his long career as a professional fascist politician or how they square the universal Olympic ideals with the activities of the fascist Olympic Council of Asia and its Israeli-hating leadership.

Perhaps the journalists will ask Mr Ed Meyer of Grey Public Relations if he is happy taking Samaranch's money to create a new image for the IOC. A dozen years ago, before Samaranch came to power, the Olympics had a marvellous image. Maybe Mr Meyer will discover what has gone wrong before he tries to put it right. Indeed if Mr Meyer cares as much as he says for the Olympics he might feel that his fee would be better diverted to investment in running tracks and soccer pitches and the Olympians left to drown in their own dollars.

It was not a pretty sight to watch the Olympians in Birmingham with their snouts in the overflowing trough. Much of what we saw was offensive. If we want to reclaim our sport from them, if we want to bring morality back into sport, then we need to recall our IOC members and ask them to explain what, if anything, they do for our sport.

We must wonder whether it is in the best interests of sport to contribute to Olympic appeals and to buy products with the five-ring logo. In countries where taxpayers' money goes towards Olympic sport we must ask if we get any value back? What is the worth of funding an unquantifiable number of junkies to perform for the TV cameras?

Perhaps it is time to turn our backs on the Olympics as we know them.

Sport will not suffer. Children will always kick a ball in the park and race against each other. But our children may be at risk if the only role models we can offer them are the brotherhood of the needle, the leadership of the Falange and the choice of only those sports which can be manipulated as TV marketing tools.

It is too late now to change much before this year's Games. But in 1994 the Olympic movement meets in Paris to celebrate its centenary. That could be the time for renewal. If the world sent its national Olympic committee delegations to Paris with strict instructions to insist on a wide-ranging debate about how to return to amateur sport organised by a more broadly based democratic body then the ideals could be resuscitated.

So far, the omens are bad. The Olympic Charter lays down clear rules for the way that Paris Congress will be conducted. It states 'The President of the IOC shall preside and determine the procedure. The Olympic Congress has a consultative character.'

That is not good enough. If the leader presides then we are guaranteed a celebration of him and the status quo. It is time to bypass the IOC and work out a new structure for organising world sports festivals.

As with all other Olympic Games, sessions and congresses the Paris meeting will be sponsored by commerce. Any company thinking of funding Samaranch's attempts to maintain his hegemony should be told bluntly that their products are as unsavoury as the IOC itself.

We wrote in our introduction to this book of our difficulties in finding officials and administrators who were prepared to go on the record and tell the truth in public about all the things wrong with modern sport. One of the few who did not lack the courage to speak out was the eminent former British Olympic coach, teacher and broadcaster Ron Pickering, who died suddenly in 1991.

'I think there's the gravest danger that sport is on a slippery slope from which there may not be any return,' Ron told us shortly before his death. 'A lot of us feel that in the last decade or so it's been violated by greed, by drugs, by hypocrisy, by cant and by political intrusion. And by bad leadership.

'Sport is the only human institution that is based on idealism. It's survived thirty-three centuries because of that. If it was simply competition it wouldn't have lasted thirty-three weeks. Anything which is not based on ethics cannot be called sport. If it's a corrupt environment, we can't invite our children into it.

'We must be the jealous guardians of that ideal if we're going to bring them into it and every time we see anyone breaking that ethic we've got to jump on them. Otherwise we lose the precious jewel that we hand to the next generation. And I don't think that my generation has been particularly good at looking after it.'

APPENDIX A

Calendar of the Modern Olympics

	Summer Games	Winter Games
1960	Rome	Squaw Valley
1964	Tokyo	Innsbruck
1968	Mexico City	Grenoble
1972	Munich	Sapporo
1976	Montreal	Innsbruck
1980	Moscow	Lake Placid
1984	Los Angeles	Sarajevo
1988	Seoul	Calgary
1992	Barcelona	Albertville
1994		Lillehammer
1996	Atlanta	
1998		Nagano

APPENDIX B

Members of the International Olympic Committee

IOC members take their protocol very seriously and so there is an Order of Precedence weighted towards the longest-serving members.

The first fourteen members are life members. The rules have now changed, compelling members reaching the age of seventy-five to retire. They become honorary members without a vote.

The ninety-three members have an average age of more than sixty-two years. There are just seven women members.

As we go to press there is a vacancy for the USA to replace Robert Helmick who resigned abruptly in December 1991. The status of the two members from the now defunct USSR has not been clarified.

Name in Order of Precedence	Nationality	Date of joining IOC	Date of birth	Date of Retirement
1. Grand-Duc Jean de Luxembourg		1946	1921	LM
2. Raja Bhalendra Singh	India	1947	1919	LM
3. Giorgio di Stefani	Italy	1951	1904	LM
4. Alexandru Siperco	Romania	1955	1920	LM
5. Syed Wajid Ali	Pakistan	1959	1911	LM
6. Ahmed Touny	Egypt	1960	1907	LM
7. Wlodzimierz Reczek	Poland	1961	1911	LM
8. Hadj Mohammed Benjelloun	Morocco	1961	1912	LM
9. João Havelange	Brazil	1963	1916	LM
10. Marc Hodler	Switzerland	1963	1918	LM
11. Prince Alexandre de Merode	Belgium	1964	1934	LM
12. Major Sylvio de Magalhaes Padilha	Brazil	1964	1909	LM
13. Gunnar Ericsson	Sweden	1965	1919	LM
14. Mohamed Mzali	Tunisia	1965	1925	LM
15. Juan Antonio Samaranch	Spain	1966	1920	1995
16. Jan Staubo	Norway	1966	1920	1995
17. Agustin Carlos Arroyo	Ecuador	1968	1923	1998
18. Louis Guirandou-N'Diaye	Ivory Coast	1969	1923	1998
19. Virgilio de Leon	Panama	1969	1919	1994
20. Maurice Herzog	France	1970	1919	1994
21. Vitaly Smirnov	USSR	1971	1935	2010
22. Pedro Ramirez Vazquez	Mexico	1972	1919	1994
23. Roy Anthony Bridge	Jamaica	1973	1921	1996
24. Manuel Gonzalez Guerra	Cuba	1973	1917	1992
25. Ashwini Kumar	India	1973	1920	1995
26. Kéba Mbaye	Senegal	1973	1924	1999
27. Mohamed Zerguini	Algeria	1974	1922	1997
28. Matts Carlgren	Sweden	1976	1917	1992
29. Kevin O'Flanagan	Ireland	1976	1919	1994

Name in Order of Precedence	Nationality	Date of joining IOC	Date of birth	Date of Retirement
30. Peter Tallberg	Finland	1976	1937	2012
31. José Vallarino Veracierto	Uruguay	1976	1920	1995
32. Bashir Mohamed Attarabulsi	Libya	1977	1937	2012
33. Kevan Gosper	Australia	1977	1933	2008
34. General Niels Holst-Sorensen	Denmark	1977	1922	1997
35. Lamine Keita	Mali	1977	1933	2008
36. Shagdarjav Magvan	Mongolia	1977	1927	2002
37. Philipp von Schoeller	Austria	1977	1921	1996
38. René Essomba	Cameroon	1978	1932	2007
39. Hamzah Bin Haji Abu Samah	Malaysia	1978	1924	1999
40. Yu Sun Kim	North Korea	1978	1932	2007
42. Vladimir Cernusak	Czechoslovakia	1981	1921	1996
43. Nikos Filaretos	Greece	1981	1925	2000
44. Pirjo Haggman	Finland	1981	1951	2026
45. Zhenliang He	China	1981	1929	2004
46. Flor Isava-Fonseca	Venezuela	1981	1921	1996
47. Franco Carraro	Italy	1982	1939	2014
48. Phillip Coles	Australia	1982	1931	2006
49. Ivan Dibos	Peru	1982	1939	2014
50. Mary Glen-Haig	United Kingdom	1982	1918	1993
51. Chiharu Igaya	Japan	1982	1931	2006
52. Prince Faisal Fahd Abdul Aziz	Saudi Arabia	1983	1946	2021
53. Anani Matthia	Togo	1983	1927	2002
54. Roque Napoleon Muñoz Pena	Dominican Republic	1983	1928	2003
55. Pal Schmitt	Hungary	1983	1942	2017
56. Princess Nora von Liechtenstein		1984	1950	2025
57. David Sibandze	Swaziland	1984	1932	2007
58. Major General Henry Olufemi Adefope	Nigeria	1985	1926	2001
59. Franciso Elizalde	Philippines	1985	1932	2007
60. Carlos Ferrer	Spain	1985	1931	2006
61. Prince Albert de Monaco		1985	1958	2033

Name in Order of Precedence	Nationality	Date of joining IOC	Date of birth	Date of Retirement
62. Dr Un Yong Kim	South Korea	1986	1931	2006
63. Lambis Nikolaou	Greece	1986	1935	2010
64. Anita DeFrantz	USA	1986	1952	2027
65. Jean-Claude Ganga	Congo	1986	1934	2009
66. Anton Geesink	Holland	1987	1934	2009
67. Slobodan Filipovic	Yugoslavia	1987	1939	2014
68. Ivan Slavkov	Bulgaria	1987	1940	2015
69. Paul Wallwork	Western Samoa	1987	1942	2017
70. Princess Anne	United Kingdom	1988	1950	2025
71. Fidel Mendoza Carrasquilla	Colombia	1988	1925	2000
72. Edward Wilson	New Zealand	1988	1925	2000
73. Ching Kuo-Wu	Taiwan	1988	1946	2021
74. Rampaul Ruhee	Mauritius	1988	1927	2002
75. Marat Gramov	USSR	1988	1927	2002
76. Sinan Erdem	Turkey	1988	1927	2002
77. Willi Kaltschmitt Lujan	Guatemala	1988	1939	2014
78. Major General Francis Nyangweso	Uganda	1988	1929	2004
79. Borislav Stankovic	Yugoslavia	1988	1925	2000
80. Fernando Ferreira Lima Bello	Portugal	1989	1931	2006
81. Walther Tröger	Germany	1989	1929	2004
82. Philippe Chatrier	France	1990	1928	2003
83. Carol Anne Letheren	Canada	1990	1942	2017
84. Shun-Ichiro Okano	Japan	1990	1931	2006
85. Richard Carrion	Puerto Rico	1990	1952	2027
86. General Zein El Abdin Gadir	Sudan	1990	1940	2015
87. Nat Indrapana	Thailand	1990	1939	2014
88. Charles Mukora	Kenya	1990	1943	2009
89. Colonel Antonio Rodriguez	Argentina	1990	1926	2001
90. Thomas Bach	Germany	1991	1953	2028
91. Mario Vazquez Raña	Mexico	1991	1932	2007
92. Denis Oswald	Switzerland	1991	1947	2022
93. Jacques Rogge	Belgium	1991	1942	2017

APPENDIX C

Abbreviations used in the text

ANOC Association of National Olympic Committees
BOA British Olympic Association
CONI Italian National Olympic Committee
FIDAL Italian National Athletics Federation
FIFA International Federation of Football Associations
GAISF General Assembly of International Sports Federations
IAAF International Amateur Athletics Federation
IAF International Athletics Foundation
IF International (sports) Federation
IOC International Olympic Committee
NOC National Olympic Committee
OCA Olympic Council for Asia
SLOOC Seoul Olympic Organising Committee
TOP The Olympic (marketing) Programme
USOC United States Olympic Committee

INDEX

Passim indicates frequent but separate mentions within the given pages.
OG = Olympic Games

AAU (Amateur Athletic Union) 208-9
ABC television 54, 56, 143-4, 207, 219
Abdul Muttaleb Ahmad 133, 266
Adams, Ken 151
Adidas company
  and gifts/bribes 19, 95
  and FIFA 36, 40-42, 47
  and Montreal Games 48-52
  and ISL 101, 106-7, 108-9
  and East bloc 112-13
  and Korea 142, 149
  and IAF 163
  and USA 206
  and ANOC 225
Advertising Age 157
advertising *see* sponsorship
Afek, Uri 136-7
Africa 32-3, 50
Afro-Asian Games 127
Agabani, Hassan 170, 177
Agnelli family 85
Ahmad, Sheik (son of Fahd) 15, 132-6, 266
Ahmed Al-Saadoon 129
Aiello, Tommaso 172, 179
Al-Sabah family 119-21, 128, 129
Albert, Prince, of Monaco 158-9, 161-2, 232
Albertville OG 11, 252
Alexander, Reggie 9
American Express company 105
Amsterdam 2, 242, 243
  OG (1928) 87
Anne, Princess 16, 222, 236, 245, 251
ANOC (Association of National Olympic Committees)/NOCs 7-8, 103, 224-7, 255-6
Aosta 245-6, 258
Apartheid and Olympism conference 131

Arena company 206, 208
Armstrong, Robert 200
Arreu 79
Asian Athletics Championships 127-8
Asian Football Confederation 126, 131
Asian Games Federation 121-4, 149
  see also OCA
Asics company 11
Athens 159, 241, 244-5, 252-3, 255-6
athletics 33, 85-91, 95-8, 165-6
  see also IAAF
Athletics World Championships 91, 95, 189, 191, 242, 269-70
  Rome (1987) 106, 159, 164-83
Athletics World Cup 90, 96
Athletics World Gala 162, 177, 178
Atlanta 241, 250, 252-4, 255-6
Auletta, Mino 95, 161
Australia 103, 187, 198

Bach, Thomas 231
Baden-Baden, Olympic Congress in 186
Ballet-Latour, Comte Henri de 2
Bangkok 122
Bangladesh 123
Barcelona
  city 59, 62, 72-3, 74, 77, 79
  Mediterranean Games 67-8, 69
  OG (1992) 1-12, 20, 43, 54, 241, 252, 261
  Popular Olympics (1936) 3
Barra, Luciano 165, 173, 174-81, 268
Bartels, Gerald 254
basketball 107, 118
Bausch and Lomb company 107
Beckenbauer, Franz 37
Becker, Boris 235
Beijing 256-7
Belgrade 2, 13, 255

Belov, Aleksandr 204
Benin 227
Berchtesgaden 243
Berlin 240-41
  OG 3, 25, 32, 38
Berlioux, Monique 56, 213
Biagini, Mario 171-2
Biden, Joe 187
Birkle, Heinz 151
Birmingham
  hosts IOC session 12-20, 133, 153,
    160, 230, 238-59, 263, 272
  Olympic bid 2, 226
Blanco, Admiral Carrero 77
Blatter, Joseph 46
BOA (British Olympic Association)
    16-17, 222
Bolivia 228
Borg, Mr (Ostersund) 247-8
Boulter, John 25, 29-30, 32, 224-5
boxing 33, 129, 149-53
Brazil 38-9
Brezhnev, Leonid 93, 96
bribery 52, 67-8, 125, 128, 150, 152
  see also gifts
Brightwell, Robbie 25
Brisbane 2
Brookes, Professor 186
Brookings Review 218
Brother company 19, 104, 105-6, 107
Brundage, Avery 26, 53, 100, 207, 225,
    229
Brundage, Mrs Avery 70
Bruns, Howard 142
Bubka, Sergei 173
Bucharest 92, 94
Budapest 13
Bulgaria 112, 117
Burkina Faso 227
Burma 121
Burns, Arnold 220
Business Week 223
Byun, Jong-Il 150

Cable News Network 202
Cadbury company 15
Calgary OG 105, 143, 144
Campbell's Soup company 105
Canada 185-7, 196, 198

Canberra 156
Canon company 57
Carr, Raymond 66
Carrard, Francois 221, 232
Carraro, Franco 174, 175, 267-8
Carter, President Jimmy 83, 96
Casablanca 123
Castell, Jaime 70
Cavan, Harry 36
CBS television 56, 143-4, 207
Ceaucescu, Nicolae 92, 114-15
Cernusak, Vladimir 9, 117
Ceylon 121
Champion d'Afrique 32-3, 164
Charlton, Bobby 242
cheating 151-2, 164-83
  see also drugs
China 8, 94, 123, 124, 134, 135, 136,
    228, 241-2, 256-7
Chirac, Jacques 6, 252
Chowdhry, Anwar 32, 149, 151, 152-3
Choy, Man Lip 134-6
Christie, Linford 196
Chun, President 146
Chung, Jin-chul 151
Clegironnet, Huguette 153
Coca-Cola company 11, 19, 43-7, 51,
    57, 101-2, 104, 107, 253-4
Coe, Sebastian 186
Cologne Sports Institute 176-7
Commission for New Sources of Finan-
    cing 100
Commission for the Protection of the
    Olympic Emblems 100
Conconi, Dr Francesco 192
CONI (Italian National Olympics
    Committee)175, 179-82, 268
Connolly, Pat 190
Continental Sports 126, 130, 228
Corriere dello Sport 176
Coubertin, Baron Pierre de 2, 17, 23,
    234, 253
counterfeiting 142
Craxi, Bettino 174
Croce, Pat 187
Cross, Lance 84
cycling 57
Czechoslovakia 112, 117, 126

Dali, Salvador 69
Danone company 11
Dassler family 24, 26, 108
Dassler, Adi (son of Horst) 108, 109,
    153
Dassler, Adolph (father of Horst) 24
Dassler, Horst
    and Adidas 21-35
    death and heritage 22, 153-4, 236
    and East Bloc 112-13
    and football 36-7, 40-47
    and Helmick 205, 208, 210-11
    and IAAF 89, 95-8
    and ISL 99-110
    and Monte Carlo 55-8
    and Montreal Games 48-54
    and Raña 224-5
    and Samaranch 76, 81, 82-4
    and Seoul Games 139, 141-2, 147,
        149
    and TOP 218, 254
Dassler, Rudolph 24, 26
Daume, Willi 84
Davies, Mervyn 27
DeBus, Chuck 169
DeFrantz, Anita 203, 217, 218, 227-8,
    232
Delhi 123, 124, 127, 135
Dentsu company 103-4, 108
Dhillon, Sathiavan 122-3, 125, 133-4
Dibos, Ivan 243
Donati, Sandro 167, 179, 193
Donike, Dr Manfred 186, 188, 189
Dorsey and Whitney law firm 205-6
Drapeau, Jean 49-50
drugs 114, 167, 169, 184-200
Dubin, Charles 185, 196-200
Dugal, Dr Robert 186
Duran (boxing judge) 152

East Asian Games 136
East Bloc countries 33-4, 92, 93-4,
    111-18, 147
Echeverria, Luis 223
El Salvador 227
El Sol publishers 223
Elizabeth II, Queen 16, 17
Elizalde, Francisco 251
Emmiyan, Robert 169-70, 170-71

EMS group 108
Ericsson, Gunnar 255
European Broadcasting Union 11
Evangelisti, Giovanni 166-83
Ewald, Manfred 114
Exeter, Lord 26, 90, 95

Fahd Al-Sabah, Sheik 15, 119-37
Fairfax Group 148
Falun 242-3, 247
Faulkner, David 148, 150
Federal Express company 104
federations see IFs
FIAT company 85
FIDAL (Italian National Athletics
    Federation) 94, 165, 167, 175-83,
    192, 193
FIFA (International Federation of
    Football Associations) 6, 31,
    36-47, 82, 101, 106, 131, 235
Filipovic, Slobodan 117
FINA (swimming federation) 204, 206,
    207, 208
Finance commission 234
finances 9-12, 13-14, 49, 54, 238-59
    ANOC 224, 228-9
    Barcelona Games 1-2, 11, 54, 241
    FIFA 46-7
    IAAF 86
    and Olympic ideals 266-7, 272
    Seoul Games 140-41, 143-6, 153,
        155-63
    USOC 209-12, 214-15, 217-19
Finland 228
Follows, Sir Dennis 228-9
football 33, 36-47, 82, 125-6, 129
Ford company 29
Ford, President 209
Foster, Todd 151
France 103, 126, 252
Francis, Charlie 169, 194, 196
Franco, Francisco/Franco regime 3, 59,
    61-70 passim, 72-5, 77-9, 261,
    263
Franco, Carmen 70
Frankfurter Allgemeine Zeitung 229,
    243
Friendship Fund 216
Fuji Film 104, 107

Gadir, General 177
Gafner, Raymond 61, 250
GAISF (General Assembly of International Sports Federations) 53-4, 56-8, 141, 146
    see also IFs
Gattai, Arrigo 175
Gazette Telegraph 216
Gazzeto dello Sport 177, 181
Germany 87, 103
    GDR 112, 114, 118, 147
Ghandi, Indira 124
Giannone, Paolo 173
gifts 52, 223, 238-51 passim, 258-9
    see also bribery
Glen-Haig, Mary 13, 231, 232,
Goizueta, Roberto C. 107
Gold, Sir Arthur 196
Golden Series 90-91
Gorbachev, Mikhail 147
Gosper, Kevan 18, 230, 236, 258
Graf, Stefi 235
Gramov, Marat 9, 116-17
Great Britain 16-17, 103, 222
    see also Birmingham; London; Manchester
Greece 244-5, 252-3
Green Shield company 29
Grey Advertising Agency 10, 272
Griffith-Joyner, Florence 194-5
Guardian 189
Guinea 227
Gutendorf, Rudi 126-7
Gymnastics World Cup 57

Hamouda, Colonel Hassine 32-3, 152, 164, 225
handball 129
Havelange, Jean (João) 5-6, 37-47, 82-3, 102, 164, 269, 270
Havrovic (boxer) 151
Hawke, Bob 252
Heineken company 57
Heinze, Gunther 9, 118
Helmick, Robert H. 8-9, 108, 119, 201-12, 213-21
Helsinki OG 38, 112
Hempel, Klaus 108-9
Hendry, Frank 151

Hodler, Marc 84, 230, 234, 258
Holder, Fred 88, 89, 95, 96, 97-8, 191
Holland 87
Honecker, Erich 114
Hong Kong 136
Horizons (OCA magazine) 132-3
Howell, Denis 48, 226, 234-5, 236, 241-57 passim
Hristov, Alexandr 150
Hukuhodo agency 104
Hungary 118, 123
Hunt, Shirley 239, 245, 246, 247-8, 259
Hussein, Saddam 131
Hyatt Regency hotel (Birmingham) 12-20, 230, 245-7, 258

IAAF (International Amateur Athletics Federation) 7, 26, 31, 86, 91, 130, 270
    and drugs 184-200 passim
    and Evangelisti scandal 164-83
    and IAF 160-63
    and marketing 95, 106-7
    and anti Semitism 122-3
    and Seoul Games 156-8, 159
    see also Nebiolo
IAAF Newsletter 161-2, 182, 198
IAF (International Athletics Foundation) 160-63, 199
IBM company 11
IFs (International Federations) 6, 31-3
    see also GAISF
Igaya, Chiharu 130
India 121, 123, 124
Indianapolis 165-6, 194
Indonesia 121
International Amateur Boxing Association 32
International Association of the Sporting Press 32
International Basketball Federation 118
International Equestrian Federation 16
International Federation of University Sport 92
International Management Group 102
International Olympic Academy 265-6
IOC (International Olympic Committee) 2, 4-6
    and Asian Games 121, 124, 136-7

Birmingham session 12-20, 133, 153, 160
commissions 10-11
and Dassler 21, 26-7
and drugs 184-200 *passim*
and East Bloc 111-18, 159
finances of *see* finances
and GAISF 53-4, 56
and media 10-11, 18-20
and Olympic bids 238-59
and Olympic ideals 260-74
and Raña 222-37
and Sheik Fahd 119, 123
and Seoul 141-6 *passim*
and television *see* television
and USOC 201-12, 213-21
IOC *Review* 33, 68, 75, 83, 120, 124, 129, 131, 136, 157, 159, 198
ISL Marketing 36, 99-110, 210, 212, 269-70
Islamic Sports Conference 131
Israel 4, 68, 120-25, 127, 130, 131, 136-7, 272
Italy 94, 164-83

Jaca 246, 257, 258
Jakarta 121
Jamaica 228
Jannette, Christian 33-4, 76, 81, 112, 113
Japan 44, 103, 104, 123, 127, 134, 135, 141
 see also Nagano
Jean, Grand Duc, of Luxembourg 236
Jefferson (Cuban athlete) 170
Johnson, Ben 5, 166, 169, 185, 186, 187, 191-2, 193-4, 195-6, 199
Jones, Roy 151, 152
Juan Carlos, King 73
Juantorena, Alberto 50
JVC company 104

Kaifu, Prime Minister 266
Kalfin, Don 140-41
Kasule (boxing judge) 152
Keller, Tommy 52-4, 56, 57
Kelly, Jack 209, 213
Kelly, (Princess) Grace 55
Keough, Don 254

Kidane, Fekrou 126, 131
Killanin, Lord Michael 80, 229
Kim Il Sung 147
Kim, Seung-Youn 149-50, 151, 153
Kim, Un Yong 8, 18, 139-54, 160, 230, 233, 236
Kirsch, August 176-7, 178
Kodak company 104, 107, 272
Korea
 North 124, 136, 147-8
 South 126, 133, 136, 138-63
 see also Seoul OG
Kraft company 29
Kumar, Ashwini 243
Kuwait 13, 15, 119-37
Käser, Dr 38, 46

La Republica 175
Lake Placid OG 210
Larbi (boxing judge) 152
Lawrence, Robert 218
Lens, Jürgen 108-9
L'Espresso 176, 179
Levi's company 113
Lewis, Carl 166, 168-71, 191-2, 196
Liddell, Eric 87
Liechty, Philip 139-40, 154
Lifestyle Marketing Group 202
Lineker, Gary 42
Ljungqvist, Arne 182, 197
Llarch, Juan 63
London OG 38
Observer 243
Lopez, Anselmo 224, 228, 266
Los Angeles OG 23, 43, 105, 114, 143, 147, 190-91, 192-3, 209-12, 241
Lynam, Desmond 257

McCormack, Mark 29, 102
McFadden, Catriona 14, 245-6
McManaway, Clayton 148
Madrid 3
Maggiari, Sergio 171
Magvan, Shagdarjav 9, 116
Mahrlig, George 105
Malaysia 126, 134
Malms, Christopher 108-9
Malouf, Albert 50
Manchester 241, 251, 255, 263

Mannisi, Marco 172
Maradonna, Diego 36, 178, 192, 235
Maragall, Monica 72
Maragall, Pasqual 1, 2, 72
Marino, Renato 167, 173
Mars company 11, 15, 19, 107
Martin, Lisa 194
Matthaus, Lothar 41
Mbaye, Judge 20, 230
M'Bow, Mahtar 119, 164
Mediterranean Games 67-9
Mehta, C.L. 135
Melbourne 252, 254, 255, 256
    OG 26-7, 38
Mercedes company 116
Merode, Prince 236
Metaxa company 57
Mexico 223, 228, 229
Mexico City OG 26, 43, 54, 75, 88, 95
Meyer, Ed 10, 272
Micheletti, Anna 167
Milla, Roger 41
Miller, David 133
Miller, F. Don 210, 212
Miller, George 212, 213-14, 216, 217, 220
Miller, Howard 214-15, 217
Monaco see Monte Carlo
Mongolia 116, 124, 134
Monte Carlo 8, 13, 55-8, 158-9, 160-62, 177-8, 199
Montjuic stadium (Barcelona) 2-4, 59, 63, 72
Montreal OG 33, 43, 49-54, 94, 209, 241
Morocco 227
Moscardó, General 65
Moscow 13, 93
    OG 33, 43, 80-81, 83-4, 96, 113, 147
Movimiento see Franco regime
Mukora, Charles 15
Munich OG 4, 33, 43, 54, 88, 94
Murdoch, Rupert 242
Myricks, Larry 166, 170-71, 172, 182-3

Nagano 238-40, 246, 254, 256-8
Nagoya 141-2
Naidoo, Bobby 32
Nairobi 13

Nakasone, Yasuhiro 256
Nally, Patrick 23, 28-30, 45-7, 57, 89, 92, 113 (also quoted throughout the book)
Nardiello, Vincenzo 151
National Collegiate Athletic Association 208
National Pansonic company 104, 107
NBC television 11, 56, 105, 143-6, 148, 150-53, 155-60, 207, 219

Nebiolo, Giovanna 86
Nebiolo, Primo 6-7, 15, 17, 85-6, 90-98, 106, 130
    and drugs 189-92 passim, 196, 198-200
    and Evangelisti scandal 164-83
    and Olympic ideals 260, 267-70
    and Seoul Games 156-63
Nepal 123, 126-7
New York Times 102, 210
New Zealand 126
NHK television 11
Nieuwenhuys-Paulen, Iet 87, 88, 90, 98
NOCs see ANOC/NOCs
Nordic countries 198
Norway 228

OCA (Olympic Council for Asia) 124-5, 127, 132-7, 272
    see also Asian Games Federation
Oerter, Al 88
Olivetti company 178, 180
Olympic Charter 7, 119, 137, 273
Olympic Congress (Baden-Baden) 186
Olympic Games
    two/four-year cycle 108
    ideals/loss of 260-74
    symbol of 2, 100, 102-3, 104-5
    year 1996: 241, 252-4
    year 2000: 241
    see also venue cities
Olympic museum 10, 17, 266
Organizacion Editorial Mexicana 223
Ostersund 247, 248, 257
Ostos, Javier 208
Oswald, Denis 231
Ovett, Steve 91
Owens, Jesse 25

Pakistan 121, 123
Palestine 123
Pan-American Games 103, 188, 214
Papandreou, Andreas 244
Paris 2, 252, 273
    OG 87
Park, Chong Kyu 146, 154
Park Chung Hee, President 139
Park Record (Utah) 249
Park Si Hun 151, 152
Paulen, Adriaan 86-91, 94, 95-8
Payne, Billy 253
Peace and Friendship Games 131
Pellegrino, Paulo 171-2
Pellegrom, Jeffery 218
Pepsi Cola company 46, 110
Philip, Prince 16, 17
Philippines 121
Philips company 11, 104, 107
Pickering, Ron 199, 273
Poland 34, 117
Pound, Dick 8, 18, 61, 103, 144, 145,
    217, 230, 233, 234, 236
Press, Tamara 88
Price Waterhouse company 9
Princesa Sofia hotel (Barcelona) 4-5
Puente, Victor 36
Pujol, Jordi 76-7
Puma company 24, 26, 27, 95

RAI television 171, 174, 176, 179, 182
Rainier, Prince 55, 56
Rank Xerox company 11
Raña, Mario Vazquez 7, 103, 222-37,
    255, 266, 267
Raña, Olegario 266
Reczek, Wlodzimierz 9, 117
Reichhardt, Bill 207
Renke, Marian 266
Ricoh company 19, 107
Riyadh 13
Robertson, Rod 151
Robinson, Darrell 194-5
Roby, Douglas 210
Rodda, John 189
Rogge, Jacques 231
Roh Tae Woo 146, 147, 153
roller hockey 65-6
Romania 92, 94, 112, 114-15, 117

Rome 164-83, 191, 193
    OG 9, 11, 43
Rono, Henry 91
Rous, Sir Stanley 38, 39, 40
rowing 57
Rugby Football Union 27
Russia/USSR 33-4, 80-81, 112-14, 116,
    123, 147, 167, 204

Saad, Crown Prince, of Kuwait 120
Saatchi and Saatchi company 202
Salinas, Carlos 229
Salt Lake City 240, 246, 248, 249,
    254-8 *passim*
Samaranch, Juan Antonio 5-20 *passim*
    background and politics 59-71, 72-84
    and drugs 193-4, 196, 199
    and Dassler 103
    and East Bloc 111-18
    and gifts/bribery 240, 243, 244,
        251-9 *passim*
    and Havelange 37, 39, 102
    and Helmick 213, 217-21
    and Nebiolo 178
    and OCA 123, 124, 127-8, 131-7
        passim
    and Olympic ideals 260-72
    and Raña 222-37
    and Seoul Games 144-7, 153-9
        passim
    and USOC 201, 210-12
Samaranch, María Teresa ('Bibis') 69,
    70, 73, 81
Sanchez, Hugo 42
Sanshoe company 140-41
Sapporo OG 75
Saravejo OG 105
Schillaci, Salvatore 42
Schiller, Harvey 203
Schmitt, Pal 118
Schoeller, Philipp Von 232
Scott, Bob, 241-2, 250-51, 253, 258
Scott, Steve 91
SEAT company 11
Seiko company 11
    measuring device 170-72, 178, 179,
        180
Seoul OG 2, 5, 8, 43, 103, 104, 105, 130,
    138-63, 193, 197, 215, 217, 271

Sharpe, Tony 187, 264
Shaw, Glyn 27
Sheffield, Student Games 1991 93
Simon, Bill 211, 214
Singh, President, of India 124
Siperco, Alexandru 9, 117
Slavkov, Ivan 9, 117
SLOOC (Seoul Olympic Organising
    Committee) 143
Smirnov, Vitaly 9, 116-17, 218
Smirnov, Mrs Vitaly 258
Smith, Calvin 196
Smith, Paul 101, 107, 108, 110, 270
SMPI (Société Monegasque de Pro-
    motion International) 55
soccer *see* football
Sofia 117
Solidarity fund 224, 266
Spain 1-3, 59-71 *passim*, 72, 77-81
    passim, 126
Spanish Olympic Committee 70, 228
Speedo company 208
Spitz, Mark 206
sponsorship 11-12, 15, 19, 29-30, 35,
    113, 158, 272
    see also Coca-Cola; ISL
Sporis AG 108
Sport Intern 160, 211
Sports Illustrated 105
Stankovic, Boris 117-18
Stefani, Giorgio di 175, 268
Stern 194
steroids *see* drugs
Stockholm OG 112
Stoichkov, Christo 42
Student Games 91-4, 178
Sudan 177
Sweden 247
swimming 38, 39, 204-8 *passim*
Süddeutsche Zeitung 243

taekwondo 139-40
Taiwan 134, 136
Takac, Artur 52, 170, 177-8
Tapie, Bernard 108
Tarragona, Eduardo 73, 74
Tele-Exprés (Barcelona) 70
television 11, 31, 54, 56, 88-9, 105,
    108, 202, 207, 215-19 *passim*, 257
    and Olympic ideals 261, 265, 269-71
    and Evangelisti 170-82 *passim*
    and Seoul Games 143-6, 150-53,
        155-9
terrorism 4, 77, 147, 148
Thailand 121, 122, 126, 227
Theodorakis, Mikis 244
3M company 104, 108
Time magazine 105, 107, 272
Time-Life company 104
Times 133, 194, 219, 244-5
Tiriac, Ion 202
TIVI Amsterdam 202
Tokyo 92, 121
TOP (The Olympic Programme) 103-6,
    210-12, 217, 218-19, 254
Toronto 254, 255-6
Toyota company 44, 141
Track and Field News 171, 194
Tretyak, Vladislav 195
Tribune (ANOC magazine) 225, 226-7
Tsukada, Tasuku 246
Tunisian Boxing Federation 32
Turner Broadcasting System 202
Turner, Ted 202

Ueberoth, Peter 211, 223
United Press International 223
US Ski Federation 203
USA 90, 103
    and drugs 187-90, 194-5
    see also Indianapolis; Los Angeles;
        USOC
USA Today 202
USOC (United States Olympic Com-
    mittee) 8, 108, 187, 190
    and Helmick 201-12, 213-21
USSR *see* Russia/USSR

Vainio, Martti 190-1
Varela, Andre Merce 266
Vazquez, Pedro 232
Verdier, Michèle 18, 19, 160, 196
Viren, Lassie 30, 50
Visa company 11, 104, 108, 158, 272
Voy, Dr Robert 189, 213-14

Walker, Keith 150

water polo 38, 39, 205-6
Welt am Sonntag 126
West Nally Ltd 29, 113
West, Peter 28-9
Wieczisk, Georg 170, 177, 178
Wiley, Cliff 189
Wilkins, Alf 172
Williams, Diane 187
Willing, Klaus 45
Wilson, Harold 234
Wilson, Edward 'Tay' 232
women 94-5, 264-5
World Basketball Championships 107

World Cycling Championships
    57
World Games (California) 140
World Taekwondo Federation 8, 139
Worrall, James 84

Yoshimura, Goro 254
Young, Arthur 27
Yugoslavia 117

Zambardino, Vittorio 175
Zhenliang He 18, 118, 136, 230
Zhivkov, Todor 115, 117